'Well-balanced, detailed and very readable, providing undergraduates and others with a clear and sound analysis of the war.'

—**Charles Tripp**, *School of Oriental and African Studies, University of London*

The Iran–Iraq War was personified by the determination and ambition of the key leaders, Saddam Hussein and Ayatollah Khomeini, and characterised by mass casualties, the repression of the civilian populations and chemical warfare. Fought with lucrative oil money, it left the belligerents with crippling debts.

In this important reappraisal, Rob Johnson explores the major issues surrounding the war, offers a fresh analysis of the military aspects and assesses the far-reaching consequences for the wider world. It is essential reading for anyone who wishes to understand the ensuing conflicts in the region, including the invasion of Iraq in 2003.

Rob Johnson is Deputy Director of the Oxford Changing Character of War research programme and Lecturer in the History of War at Oxford University. A former Army Officer, his previous publications include *British Imperialism* (2003) which is also published by Palgrave Macmillan.

THE IRAN–IRAQ WAR

Rob Johnson

First published 2011 by
PALGRAVE MACMILLAN

Palgrave Macmillan in the UK is an imprint of Macmillan Publishers Limited, registered in England, company number 785998, of Houndmills, Basingstoke, Hampshire RG21 6XS.

Palgrave Macmillan in the US is a division of St Martin's Press LLC, 175 Fifth Avenue, New York, NY 10010.

Palgrave Macmillan is the global academic imprint of the above companies and has companies and representatives throughout the world.

Palgrave® and Macmillan® are registered trademarks in the United States, the United Kingdom, Europe and other countries.

ISBN-13: 978-0-230-57773-2 hardback
ISBN-13: 978-0-230-57774-9 paperback

This book is printed on paper suitable for recycling and made from fully managed and sustained forest sources. Logging, pulping and manufacturing processes are expected to conform to the environmental regulations of the country of origin.

A catalogue record for this book is available from the British Library.

A catalog record for this book is available from the Library of Congress.

10   9   8   7   6   5   4   3   2   1
20   19   18   17   16   15   14   13   12   11

Printed in China

Contents

Part V   Consequences and Conclusions

Maps and Figures

Maps

Figures

Preface

A number of people have assisted me in my research over the last few years and it would seem invidious to mention a few and miss out the many. Nevertheless, I am in debt particularly to some outstanding individuals whose dedication and original thinking have been for me an inspiration. Oxford has a particularly rich seam of scholarship and endeavour. The Department of Politics and International Relations, the Faculty of History, the Middle East Studies Centre and the Islamic Studies Centre have been especially helpful, and the library staff of the Middle East Centre Library of St Antony's College and the Social Sciences Library are excellent. I have been fortunate to work within the Oxford Changing Character of War (CCW) Programme over the last two years and the sheer quality of seminar speakers, of whom there are so many, has been profoundly helpful in the preparation of this work. Professor Hew Strachan provides outstanding leadership of the programme, and his insights on strategy always provoke serious thought. I have benefited from all my conversations with Professor Adam Roberts, Professor Henry Shue and Professor Anne Deighton, all of whom bring their own disciplinary expertise to bear on the programme. Professor Avi Shlaim has also inspired me and given me original insights into the Middle East with a depth of experience I think unmatched even in this prestigious institution. But I have profited from working with other experts on the *mentalités* of the Islamic world, including Gil-li Vardi and Alia Brahimi, two Research Fellows of the CCW, and the many officers of the British and American armed forces who have had recent operational experience in Iraq. They acted as conduits for so many enquiries and questions, and their opinions were valued deeply. As always, my students never fail to impress me with their creative ideas and critical questions. I am fortunate in that I enjoy teaching so much and the rewards from listening to my students, who are always sharp and discerning, are very great.

I must also mention thanks to Professor Roger Stern, at Princeton, with whom I spent a few intense days in Annapolis and learned so much, and who continues to collaborate with me. Commander Jeff Macris, USN, and Professor Saul Kelly of Kings College, who made possible the Gulf and the Globe Conference of 2009, and who introduced me to so many useful contacts for this book, deserve not just thanks but also medals. Commander Tim Ash and the team at The Defence Academy of the United Kingdom have been extremely helpful and I am grateful for the opportunity to present work on naval operations in the Gulf at the Staff College. Shohei Sato, who works on the Gulf, has been a very stimulating scholar to work with at Oxford. Above all, I must thank Professor Jeremy Black, who not only inspires and challenges me, but who has remained a most warm and generous friend indeed. I have chosen not to list many of the contacts and interviewees from Iran and Iraq for a variety of reasons, but Mohammadjaved Ardalan deserves thanks for helping me in my first steps in learning Farsi although illness and work prevented me from completing my studies with him.

It is in the nature of academic study to be subjected to peer review and I must point out that any errors which appear in this book are entirely my own. I can only plead *mea culpa* for oversight or honest error. I am also conscious, however, that wars evoke strong emotions and often entrenched partisan judgements. I have tried to approach this conflict with an open mind and without any favour or prejudice. Yet, where I feel there was error, courage, cowardice, injustice or cruelty, I have pointed it out. Nevertheless, I acknowledge it is the historian's craft to attempt to reconstruct the past from imperfect fragments when we ourselves are flawed, and therefore I submit this book to you conscious of my own failings and with humility.

Maps

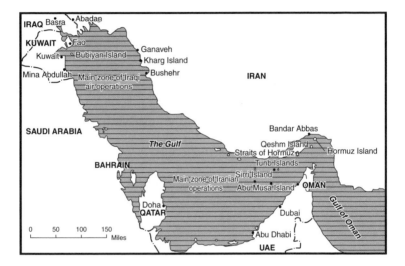

Map 1   *The Gulf*

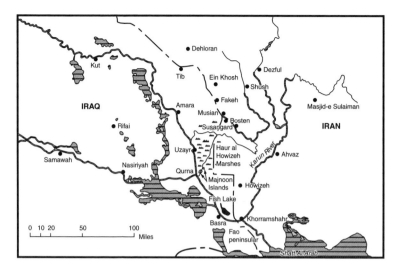

Map 2   *The Southern Fronts*

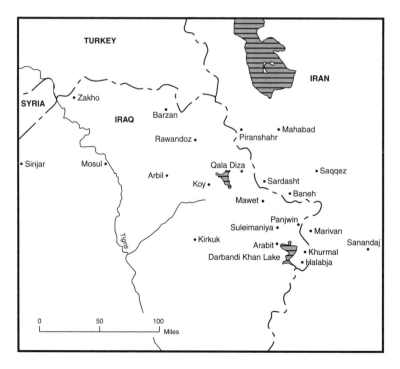

Map 3   *The Northern Fronts*

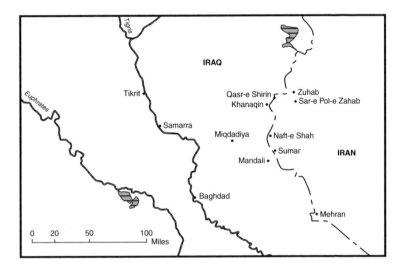

Map 4   *Central Fronts*

Part I

The Causes and Context of the Conflict

1
Introduction

The invasion of Iraq in 2003, led by the United States, was an illustration of the overwhelming conventional military power of the Western world. In just three weeks, Iraqi forces had been swept aside and the Coalition had occupied Baghdad. Saddam Hussein al-Tikriti, the Iraqi President, was a fugitive in his own country and there were scenes of celebration at his demise. Yet soon after the invasion, the Americans announced that Iraq was to be de-Ba'athised, ordering that all members of the Ba'ath Party, who were implicated in the crimes committed by Saddam, were to be removed from positions of power. In addition, it was declared that the Iraqi armed forces were to be dismantled, temporarily depriving thousands of their income. These announcements, coupled with a fear that the Americans might re-engineer the entire country contrary to the will of the Iraqi people, had the effect of generating resistance from Basra to Baghdad. Ba'ath Party loyalists believed they could never be reconciled to the occupation forces and chose to fight on.[1] Some Iraqis fought in the hope of forcing the Americans out of their country, while others hoped for material gain.[2] Fears that the Shia majority might take power and persecute the Sunnis led to sectarian violence. The fighting, by groups with different if sometimes overlapping agendas, escalated into an insurgency. There was a steady rise in the number of security incidents from sniping to suicide bombings against both Coalition forces and Iraqi civilians. Journalists spoke of an imminent civil war as death squads from Shia or Sunni communities sought out and killed their sectarian rivals. Kurds battled with Sunni Iraqis in the north. Iran, hoping to influence the outcome, sought to sponsor and arm Iraqi Shia militiamen, the Jaish-al-Mahdi, in the south. Amid the fighting, with the infrastructure in ruins, and despite the fact that mass graves were exhumed from the old regime's reign of terror, some Iraqis began to speak nostalgically about the stability and sense of national unity under Saddam.

3

It was surprising that, at the time and indeed afterwards, little reference was made to the conflict which had been so formative for Saddam Hussein, for the Iraqi people and for the region, namely the Iran–Iraq War of 1980–88. It was perhaps understandable that Westerners thought back to the Gulf War of 1990–91 and the liberation of Kuwait, but many appeared to overlook the significance of the war of the 1980s. Yet, there were some unexpected and striking parallels between the invasion of 2003 and the Iran–Iraq War. At a time when even Ba'athists in the Iraqi regime were contemplating ousting Saddam in 1982, Ayatollah Khomeini had stated that his aim was to purge Iraq of the Ba'ath Party and reorganise the country. This had the unexpected effect of binding the Iraqis closer to the regime, and galvanised resistance. When the Americans announced in 2003 that they too intended to dismantle the Ba'ath and to reform the country, resistance broke out in many quarters. Similarly, irregular warfare, by Kurds and by Iranian-sponsored groups like Al Daawa, had flourished during the Iran–Iraq War as deep-seated lines of division in the country came to the surface. In 2004, the deposing of Saddam permitted these forms of resistance to reappear as rival groups tried to assert themselves.

In the light of subsequent conflicts, the purpose of the book is to re-examine the Iran–Iraq War of the 1980s. Although overshadowed in Western minds by the conflict of 1990–91 and the occupation of 2003, it was the Iran–Iraq War that shaped the political landscape in the region. Far from neutralising the revolutionary rhetoric of Iran, the theocratic regime in Tehran used that war to consolidate its grip on power internally and exported its revolution by proxy methods. Saddam, far from showing signs of exhaustion, looked to escape Iraq's financial problems and ensure his own political survival with a war against Kuwait, his former ally. Much of the existing literature, while comprehensive, was written before the events of 2003. Some official or semi-official items emanating from the United States tended to portray the revolutionary Iranians, and then, after 1990, the aggressive Iraqi regime, in ways that reflected their immediate concerns about Gulf security. Neutral analyses were rare. The chief exception, which still stands today as the most definitive work, was Anthony Cordesman and Abraham Wagner's *Lessons of Modern War, II, The Iran-Iraq War*.[3] Cordesman and Wagner believed, back in 1987 that projections of how the war would end were unclear and the course of the Iranian revolution was unknown.[4] They noted that most revolutions took twenty to thirty years to run their course. Such a projection would make an appraisal of the war today a timely one. Saddam's regime has now gone and Iraqis are able to contemplate the Iran–Iraq War without fear of official censure. Iranians, too, have begun to reconsider the war. In many ways we now have the advantage of the distance of time to reflect on the war more deeply, while the West, after the struggle to stabilise Iraq in the first decade of the twenty-first century, has also begun to reassess the period before the war of 2003.

This book attempts to give a history of the war, its strategies and its character. It is not a study of Iranian and Iraqi politics, which would require a volume of its own, nor is it a thesis of international relations. Readers familiar with international relations as an academic discipline will, I hope, find familiar patterns and issues, but space does not permit a full exposition of the theoretical and practical approaches. However, the book does attempt to give a brief explanation of decision-making in the region by international actors in order to contextualise the conflict and, specifically, how it was eventually brought to an end. The book also tries to offer some explanation of how the war shaped the region and set in motion the events that followed. For example, Iraq became more militarised as a result of the war, possessed the largest army of the region and was in significant debt. The relative military success in the war in 1987–88 and tacit American backing convinced Saddam that he could continue to act unilaterally, leading to the invasion of Kuwait. The war also explains some anomalies of the Middle East. Although Iran was the strongest regional power on the Gulf coast, it was not a member of the Gulf Co-operation Council (GCC: Bahrain, Kuwait, Oman, Qatar, Saudi Arabia and the United Arab Emirates). This was because the GCC was formed as a counterpoise to Iran during the war of the 1980s, and the Gulf States even created a joint rapid deployment force to confront the Iranian threat.

The Iran–Iraq War was one of the longest conventional wars of the twentieth century, and it was a classic example of 'limited war' escalating into a 'total' war. Not surprisingly, perhaps, it has been likened to the First World War, with battles over trench lines, the use of poison gas, and the mass mobilisation of the belligerents' populations.[5] While there are some parallels here, there were, of course, fundamental differences that made the war unique to the region and to the late twentieth century. Iraq was tacitly supported by the superpowers and by the powers of Western Europe, despite their official neutrality, but Iran attracted fewer foreign backers, its support being limited to Syria, Libya and South Yemen, and to some extent from China and North Korea. These sponsors offered funds, munitions or intelligence assistance. Nevertheless, Iran was ideologically isolated, with Gulf monarchies fearful of its revolutionary agenda and most of the Muslim world suspicious of

Shi'ite claims to doctrinal leadership. The conflict was therefore between 'developing countries', but with considerable support from outside.

International interference has, over the last few decades, been much criticised and has sometimes been blamed for prolonging the Iran–Iraq War. The United States supplied intelligence to Iraq, but was also involved in the damaging 'Irangate' or Iran–Contras scandal, supplying arms to Iran in order to conceal clandestine CIA activities in Central America. However, the aim of the United States, the USSR, the Europeans and the GCC states was to contain the conflict. The reason for foreign interests was understandable: 54 per cent of OPEC oil reserves, a quarter of the world's total, were located in the region, giving it distinct strategic value.[6] There was one major concern: the war could cause a sudden rise in global oil prices through a restriction of actual production or an interruption to the supply across the sea lanes. The combination of foreign interests confined the war successfully to the territories of Iran and Iraq, with limited air operations spilling over into the upper Gulf. The United Nations, which was also criticised for apparently favouring Iraq, nevertheless provided the framework to allow both countries to withdraw from the war. The fact is that neither belligerent was prepared to contemplate a peaceful resolution to the war while it still believed it possessed a strategic advantage. Although Iran was being steadily weakened by 1987, there was every prospect that the fighting would go on for several more years. For both sides, it was the intervention of the United States in 1988 that was decisive in bringing the war to an end.

This was a 'broken-back' war with alternating periods of stalemate and intensity. It was also distinctly asymmetrical. Iraq made use of advantages in its technology wherever possible, but Iran, lacking any tactical advantage, was compelled to make use of its manpower and use fighting spirit as a substitute. This war therefore resulted in very heavy casualties. About 1 million are thought to have perished. It was also a war of enormous financial cost, with a bill of about $1,190 billion.[7]

Iraq's initial military objectives were apparently limited – it sought modest territorial acquisitions – while Iran was weak following the so-called Islamic Revolution. But Iraq's strategic aims were ambitious. What alarmed Baghdad was the possibility that the Iranian revolution might spread westwards, and the only way to neutralise that threat was to destroy the Iranian government while it was still struggling to gain control of the country. Saddam planned to seize Khuzestan province in south-west Iran and annex the largely Arab population. The capture of this oil-rich region would give Iraq more coastline to develop its oil industry, earn credit with the Arab League and, in turn, probably give

Iraq the chance to replace Egypt as the leading power of the region. The defeat of the Iranian regime even in such a limited territorial space would, it was reasoned, encourage the rest of the Iranian population to overthrow the government, and therefore neutralise Iran as a threat on Iraq's eastern border.[8]

Iran's initial objectives also seemed limited, namely to expel the invaders, but it too had a more ambitious agenda for the long term. It hoped to galvanise the Muslim world against secular leaders like Saddam and spread the Islamic Revolution. It reasoned that unrest in other Muslim states in the region would weaken it, giving Iran regional power and influence, and protect the revolution. Similar ideas that the defence of the revolution meant exporting the ideology by force have been expressed by previous revolutionary regimes like France in 1792 and Russia in 1917. Iran had harboured these wider plans *before* the war began. Under the Shah, Iran had supported subversion and insurgency inside Iraq. The Iraqi invasion, while genuinely threatening, offered an enormous opportunity for both belligerents. The war was therefore the culmination of long-harboured objectives *and* the opportunity to fulfil greater ambitions.

This was, to borrow Fritz Fischer's expression, a 'war of illusions', for the war both sides actually got was one of misconceptions and miscalculations.[9] Saddam had assumed that Iran was fragile because of the reports of Iranian émigrés in Iraq, a similar problem to that which affected the Americans in 2003, but Iran, while weakened, exploited the outbreak of the war to deepen the commitment of Iranians to the regime, and make the revolution synonymous with the survival of Iran, their way of life, their territorial integrity and the Iranian identity. Yet the view from Tehran was equally flawed. About 55 per cent of the Iraqi population consisted of Shias and the Iranian regime wrongly assumed there would be such sympathy with the Islamic Revolution that sufficient pressure and revolutionary rhetoric would turn the tide of the war. Their ideological interpretation of the world sometimes clouded their strategic judgement.

For many contemporary observers, the war seemed to be between secular Arab nationalism and Iranian universalist religious ideology, but Iranian motives for fighting were also nationalistic.[10] Even the defence of the revolution was, underneath, a desire to protect the nation state and was not such a sharp division with the Shah's regime as is sometimes assumed. The rhetoric of universal Islam was just one facet (an important one, nonetheless), of other objectives; while demanding sacrifice on the battlefield, the regime was actually cautious in how it conducted the war economically and strategically. It did not escalate the war after the counter-attack into Iraq in 1982 (which was supposed to bring down the regime of Saddam Hussein). The universalist agenda was designed to appeal to Shia, Sunni and Kurds against Saddam, and although the world was divided into 'oppressors' and 'oppressed', they attempted to make direct conflict with Saudi Arabia and the GCC, and they cooperated readily with the dictatorial regimes in Libya, Syria and South Yemen. There is a teleology often at work here because commentators in the West tend to interpret the past through the lens of their present-day concerns with religious extremism, particularly after high-profile attacks by Jihadists in the early twenty-first century. In Iran, the reasons for going to war and for fighting were just as often expressed in terms of national identity. The idea of smashing Arab nationalism was only partly a theological argument, for it was also about defeating a coalition of Arab leaders against Iran. National loyalty was especially important in Iraq, where Shia Muslims did not rise up in favour of the Iranian revolution as the Iranian regime had assumed and, similarly, the Sunni population of south-west Iran did not desert Tehran, despite Saddam's hopes that they would. However, we must acknowledge that the oppressive nature of the regimes often prevented widespread dissent and revolt. Opponents of the governments in both countries suffered arrests, purges and repression, before, during and after the war. There were episodes of violent resistance, including by the Kurds in northern Iran, and a fully fledged insurgency in Kurdish areas of Iraq.

The nationalist divisions of Iran and Iraq reflected a historical difference between the two peoples dating back at least to the Ottoman and Safavid dynasties and it is tempting to suggest that these deep-seated differences added to the store of antagonisms that made the conflict of the 1980s 'inevitable'. Yet such a view would give insufficient weight to the short-term factors that actually led to war. Saddam played on a number of sentiments, including the long history of disputes, in order to portray the war as one of national defence, and used the fear of the 'mad mullah' or the anarchy of revolution to mobilise the public. To sustain the war effort, he used both persuasion and coercion against a backdrop of black propaganda.

Saddam was able to use the Pan-Arabist message to acquire funds from Gulf states and Saudi Arabia, and when Iraq failed to get direct intervention by Arab allies, or the USSR and the United States, it was Kuwait's call to protect its tanker fleet in 1987 that gave Iraq more substantial if indirect support. However, Saddam also frequently misread the situation. The United States had been deterred from a full backing of Baghdad by the Iraqi use of chemical weapons and the threat that Iraq might use them against Iranian cities. Saddam was fortunate that the Americans perceived Iran to be the greater threat to Gulf security. Saddam was also disappointed on a number of occasions when the Arab League, while making supportive statements and offering some significant financial packages, did not offer military backing. Moreover, Iraqi attacks on Iranian cities with air strikes and missiles were another of Saddam's miscalculations about Iran itself. The bombing of cities did not persuade the Iranians to end the war or to relent in their crippling offensives; every time they were hit, the Iranians intensified the ground war and put the Iraqis under further strain.

Each of the Iranian ground offensives was horrendously costly. At best they gave Iran some territorial gain with which to bolster morale, but their most important benefit was to consolidate the regime. For the sake of the war effort, the opposition was eliminated. Saddam, too, made use of the war and its crises to strengthen his grip on power. Both countries carried out far-reaching internal reorganisation, but, in Iraq, the army was able to reassert some of its authority after years of rivalry with the Ba'ath. It did so not in opposition to Saddam's party but alongside it, and became a fully integrated part of the loyal political apparatus.

Saddam aimed to defend his position in power and Iraq's integrity as a state by getting foreign powers involved. Iraq's attacks on Iranian oil installations were strategic and there was a calculation that, since Iraq had no tankers and it was reliant on foreign vessels, Iraqi oilfields would be hit as well and this would be detrimental to Western interests. Moreover, the Iranians might be tempted to close the Strait of Hormuz to all foreign shipping and this would almost certainly bring in the United States. The US Navy did indeed increase the number of warships patrolling the Gulf from six to thirty-two as the war in the Gulf intensified, and engaged the Iranian navy in combat in 1988. Saddam was therefore accurate in his forecast that there were limits to the West's tolerance of a threat to its own interests in the Gulf. The war was regarded as a major risk, but it was also an opportunity that encouraged some Westerners to pursue their own commercial interests with the sale of arms to both sides.[11] Russia and France, which had no wish to see their investments jeopardised by the defeat of Iraq, armed Baghdad overtly, while other states tended to make use of intermediaries. Several European arms manufacturers sold explosives and weapons to Iran as a cartel, including those in France, Italy, Sweden, Belgium and Austria. The purchase of foreign weapons and munitions was a substantial proportion of the cost of the war for Iraq, which spent 57 per cent of its gross domestic product on the conflict.[12] Iraq also increased the size of its army and brought in foreign labour to fill the gap in the economy, until the 1.5 million migrant workers made up 40 per cent of the workforce. One-tenth of the Iraqi male population was mobilised, with almost one million under arms and another 600,000 in the Popular Army militia, out of a population of 16 million. The equivalent for the United Kingdom would have been 2.5 million, or for the United States, 5 million. During the war, Iran mobilised 1.6 million out of a population of about 48 million.

Iraq fought the war on borrowed money as well as its own domestic revenue, consuming an average of $1 billion for each month of the war. It is interesting to note that foreign loans and grants constituted $85–90 billion of that total, but also that Iraq wiped out the $35 billion it held in foreign currencies at the start of the war. Iran spent just marginally less than Iraq at $85 billion. These figures not only indicate the costs of waging a conventional war in the late twentieth century, they also indicate the price that both regimes were willing to pay. Winning the war was regarded as vital to both sides not just to fulfil their strategic ambitions but for the political survival of the governing regimes. In Tehran, without the foreign backing that Iraq enjoyed, the Iranian economy could endure less pressure and the regime's leaders were aware that there were limits on how far they could make demands on the Iranian public and what the economy could support. Considerable efforts were made to portray the war as one being fought on behalf of the poor. Yet the rhetoric of total sacrifice they propagated contrasted with the regime's cautiousness about the economy. Once foreign powers started to get involved, and with the economy in steep decline because of the unbearable costs, then Iran had to end the war. There was also an awareness that the Iranian people were wearying of the war and, by early 1988, they no longer had positive battlefield results to show for the efforts. The shooting down of an Iranian civil airliner by a US warship became the pretext the regime needed to sue for peace.

Saddam used the return of peace as a chance to punish the Kurds in the north and to end the insurgency there. He had acquired more military power and commanded a vast conventional force that had enjoyed some battlefield successes at the end of the conflict, but Iraq was crippled financially and Saddam could not demobilise immediately without flooding the labour market, thereby damaging the economy and, potentially, the regime too. Iraq's debts and Saddam's unquenched ambitions led ultimately to the conflict with Kuwait in 1990. Saddam's desire was to recover losses, acquire Kuwait's oil and refining capacity, and then complete his operations against Iran at a later date. Remarkably, Saddam survived defeat in the Gulf War of 1991. His military power, while curtailed in terms of missile capability and chemical munitions by UN weapons inspectors, remained sufficiently intact to crush internal opposition. His defiance of the West in the period 1991–2003 can be attributed to his experience of surviving previous catastrophes and his resolute ambition to remain in power, regardless of the cost to others. Iran, too, learned to deal with the United Nations and the West through its experience of the war in 1980–88. It learned in particular to look inwards and rely on its own resources. Iran's leaders took pride in the fact that, against foreign influences and the onslaught of Iraq, they had remained in power, preserved the revolution and maintained their territorial integrity. These principles resurface time and again, and have been manifest in the negotiations over Iran's nuclear programme.

Chapter 2 examines the causes of the war, the historical context, and the situation in the late 1970s that shaped the decisions for war. For the purposes of clarity and analysis, this book then divides the war into themes and phases. The themes are the causes and context of the conflict; the early military operations, their escalation and the involvement of foreign powers in the war; the search for a decisive result either on the battlefield or using other strategic methods, and the impact of these on the economies and home fronts of the belligerents. The final broad theme is the attempts to break the impasse, through operations in the Gulf, in the most intense land battles of the war, or through the engagement of foreign states. The first phase of the war lasted from the invasion by Iraq in 1980 to the end of the first period of large-scale Iranian offensives in mid-1982, and this book analyses the actual invasion, the Iranian counter-offensives and the first interventions by foreign states in that period. The second phase includes Iran's land offensives up to early 1984, including the capture of the Majnoon Islands, the first use of chemical weapons and Iraq's defensive strategy. Phase three saw the broadening of the 'Gulf front', with the 'Tanker War' in spring 1984, and Iranian land operations in 1984–85. The fourth phase consisted of Iran's Fao and Basra Offensives in 1986, the period of economic and military crisis for Iraq, the intensification of the air war and Gulf operations, and the gradual internationalising of the conflict. The final phase of the war saw Iraqi counter-offensives, the destruction of a portion of the Iranian fleet by the US Navy, a growing economic crisis in Iran, and the loss of the Iranian Airbus in 1988, which led to negotiations and the end of the war. The book ends with a retrospective look at the conflict and some of its legacies.

2
Iran's Revolution and Iraq's Ambitions

> At school there were always mullahs coming to speak to us and interrupting our lessons. The teacher didn't like them coming, but he was too afraid to say anything in case he lost his job. They talked about the glorious Islamic revolution and the Ayatollah who had rescued us from the hands of the Americans. Then we would chant, 'Death to America; Death to Israel; Death to Saddam' for a long time. The mullahs said it was an honour to go and fight for Islam and to be martyred for Islam, just like Imam Hussein.[1]

Samir was a fourteen-year-old Basiji fighter for the Iranian republic who later explained how he had been swept along by the panoply of patriotism and propaganda. He had taken part in mass demonstrations that supported the war effort and he wore his red headband that announced his status as a warrior with pride. Around his neck he sported a yellow key, the standard issue to all fighters of his age to denote automatic entry to paradise if they were martyred on the battlefield, and a piece of white cloth to represent his shroud. He admitted he had no idea what patriotism and martyrdom really meant, but he and his fellow boy soldiers enjoyed the attention and the sense of excitement their status bestowed on them. On the battlefield, his instructions were to run at the enemy, regardless of minefields or enemy fire. Shouting '*Allah'u akbar*' at the top of their voices, they swarmed towards Iraqi positions and they were cut down in swathes. Many were killed or maimed as they detonated mines, but fresh waves stepped over their comrades and pushed on. With only an elementary training in military skills and unaware of the broader tactical situation, those who managed to cross the battlefield simply sought out Iraqis in close-quarter battle and, when positions were overrun, they tended to remain where they were, exhausted and without any sense of what subsequent actions were required of them. Samir was captured in an Iraqi counter-attack, but he was fortunate that, despite being a mere cog in this human battering ram, he survived the war. Perhaps more than any other aspect of the war, the motivations that lay behind these practically suicidal charges remain an enigma.

It is rare for wars to break out between states without some longer-term antagonisms, but equally the final escalation to a major conflict is dependent on just a few trigger factors. In this sense, the causes of the Iran–Iraq War were to be found both in long-term antipathy and in crises that occurred just before the outbreak itself. However, it is too convenient and simplistic to suggest that the causes of conflict began essentially in the sixteenth century and reappeared periodically until they reached their culmination in the1980s. This linear narrative would take insufficient account of the long periods of peace and cooperation that exceeded the duration of wars. Before the 1820s, for example, during a long peace, there had been frequent migration across the boundaries of the Safavid and Ottoman empires. Definitive borders had not been demarcated, a factor which accounts for the presence of so many Iranians of Arab descent in Khuzestan and the Shia population of Iraq. Nevertheless, the more enduring causes of enmity were: sectarianism (complicated by the location of Shia shrines and a significant number of Shi'ites living inside Iraq); border disputes, particularly over the Shatt al Arab (which was strategically important if either country wanted to ensure the passage of its own goods, including oil); conflict with the Kurds in the north (located astride both borders and inside neighbouring Turkey); rivalry over which state could offer leadership of the region; concern to protect their own interests (including oil resources, military power and influence); and, most damaging of all, interference in each other's internal affairs.

Yet another feature of the foreign policy of both states was the importance of maintaining freedom of action in a post-colonial era. Both nations had been dominated by Turkey, Britain and, to some extent, Russia. After 1945, both came to regard the United States as a potential 'colonial' power, too. The United States sought to influence the Middle East to prevent it falling into the Soviet sphere, but the Americans' efforts merely reinforced the Iraqis' desire to remain free of foreign influence, and this coloured their policies and alignments. Iran took a different path, and when the Shah embraced the United States in the 1960s, Iraq turned to the Soviet Union for backing because it was afraid of a strong US–Iranian combination. Many of these older lines of division between the Iraqis and Iranians resurfaced during the war of the 1980s or were exploited to reinforce the war effort. In short, the war deepened old antagonisms and created legacies of distrust and bitterness that lasted throughout the 1990s and early 2000s.

A history of conflict

The origin of sectarian disputes between Shia and Sunni can be traced to the decision of Shah Ismail of Persia to make Shia Islam the official religion of the empire in 1501, converting the Shia, or 'partisan' theology and jurisprudence into elements of the state.[2] The Ottomans, adherents of the Sunnah, or 'trodden path', regarded Shi'ism as heretical, but the power of the Persian empire meant they grew to fear the growth of Shi'ism within their own domains. Fear bred atrocities: it is alleged that 40,000 Shia were killed in 1512 in one of many crackdowns against internal enemies. There were similar repressive campaigns against rebellious Christians in Bulgaria and the Balkans in 1876.[3] The situation between Shia and Sunni was complicated by the existence of shrines sacred to Shi'ites in Ottoman Najaf and Karbala. Six of the famous twelve imams were buried in what became Iraq, while the twelfth went into 'occultation' in Samarra, destined to return at some period of crisis for the Shia. The Safavids demanded free access to these shrines consistently through history and relations between the two empires reached a nadir in the seventeenth century. The Safavids invaded and occupied Mesopotamia between 1623 and 1638, but the region was retaken by the Ottomans and the war ended with the Treaty of Zuhab in 1639.[4] The terms of the treaty settled a borderline that included Kurdish areas, and permitted an annual pilgrimage by Shias to the shrines of Najaf and Karbala.

Persia was wracked by internal unrest in the early eighteenth century because of the overthrow of the Safavids by the Ghilzai Afghans (1722–30). Subsequently, Nadir Shah reasserted centralised Persian power against the tribal groups in the 1740s, and set on a course of expansion eastwards, overrunning Afghanistan, asserting influence over central Asia and defeating the Indian Mughals. The Zand rulers, who succeeded Nadir Shah in 1747, were eventually defeated in 1790 whereupon Shah Aga Muhammed restored Shia Islam amid atrocities against the Sunnis, until his assassination in 1797.[5] However, cross-border problems between the Ottomans and the dynasty of Qajar Persians was further complicated by Kurdish tribes who did not recognise the borderline which cut across their lands, and they owed little true allegiance to either regime. Moreover, in the south of Mesopotamia, Arabic-speaking tribes gave only nominal allegiance to the Persian rulers. In 1812, the Muhaisin tribe declared its principality of Muhammarah (known since as Iran's Khorramshahr, but at that time inside the borders of the Ottoman Empire) to be autonomous. The declaration escalated to a war over the fate of Muhammarah between the Persians and Ottomans in 1821. The Europeans were eager to intervene in the Middle East to safeguard their own interests. Britain had been anxious to influence Persia because of French expansionism during the Napoleonic Wars, but subsequently it was concerned about the aggression of Russia when the Tsar appeared to threaten the approaches to India.[6] Britain therefore mediated between the Ottoman Empire and Persia, leading to the Treaty of Erzerum in 1823. The new treaty stated there should be no asylum for dissidents in either empire and that the borders should be restored. However, the mutual sponsorship of intrigues continued, and Persia encouraged the Kurds to rebel against the Ottomans.

During Persian operations against Afghanistan in 1837, the Ottomans seized the opportunity to attack the population of Muhammarah. The attack signalled a general crackdown on the Shias in Mesopotamia. To preserve the status quo, Britain and Russia intervened and a joint commission was appointed in 1843, its results being confirmed by a treaty concluded in 1847. By the terms of this second Treaty of Erzerum, Persia ceded Suleimaniya (in what became Iraqi Kurdistan), and the area of Zuhab to the Persian Kirmanshah province, and got Muhammarah and the island of Khizr (Abadan). Persia was also awarded the strip of land between the Shatt al Arab (known in Persian as the Arvand Rud) and the Bahmanshir River. In addition, the fluvial 'border' was moved from the western bank of the Bahmanshir to the eastern bank of the Shatt Al Arab for the last third of its 120-mile (193 km) length in order to give both states adequate access to the Gulf.

As Persia under Nasrudin Shah (1847–96) tried to maintain its mouldering authority in western Afghanistan and its peripheral provinces, it was weakened by a rebellion in Khorrassan in the north-east, by another in the far south, and then by the military intervention of Britain. In the Anglo–Persian War of 1856, British forces landed on the southern coast to compel the Shah to abandon his siege of Afghan Herat, a city which the British regarded as strategically imperative to their defence of India.[7] The Persian defeat in that war marked the end of a long retreat. By the mid-nineteenth century, Persia had lost its jurisdiction of the tribes of Central Asia to the Russian Empire. It had also lost its Caucasus provinces to the tsar in 1820s. Without a navy, the Shah lost influence over the Persian Gulf to Britain and the Gulf states became part of a British sphere of influence. Kuwait signed an alliance with Britain in 1899, while the other sheikhdoms, although nominally still owing their suzerainty to the Ottomans, increasingly looked to the British to guarantee their security. The call by Kuwait for British military assistance against the military threat posed by the Iraqi dictator Qassim in 1961 illustrated that the Gulf states were still dependent on support from outsiders. Arab states had failed to heed Kuwait's call for assistance and the British maintained their 'watch and ward' until their departure in 1971.

Despite foreign interest in maintaining peace, the delimitation by a Border Commission in 1848 and the production of a detailed map in 1869, the frontier issue between the Ottomans and the Persians was not closed by the beginning of the twentieth century. Part of the problem was that Muhammarah continued to act autonomously and Arabs continued to move freely across the Shatt al Arab in one direction while Shia pilgrims flowed in the other. These factors meant that the south-east of Persia remained strongly 'Arabian' in culture, while Shias continued to dominate southern Mesopotamia. The lack of recognition for a single authority plagued both empires and faction fighting among southern 'Arab' Persian tribesmen was common. To this instability was added the complication of relative economic decline. As the industrial powers of the West extended their economic lead, both the Persian and Ottoman empires struggled to compete with Western commercial power.[8]

The gradual economic penetration of Persia led to intrigues between Britain and Russia, and the carving out of spheres of influence in 1907, practically rendering the country a colony of the two European powers. Although oil was discovered in 1908 in Masjid-i-Suleiman in Khuzestan (known to the Iraqis as Arabistan), the Persians lacked the technical expertise to extract it or to convert it into state revenue without European assistance. As a result, foreigners established control of the Imperial Bank of Persia and obtained the lion's share of the Anglo–Persian Oil Company. By 1914 Britain controlled all the oilfields in the south. Economic decline fuelled the steady decay of Persia's political system, and the rot was accelerated by the assassination of Nasruddin Shah and by a revolution in 1905–06.[9] The Young Turk revolt in the Ottoman Empire in 1908 marked a similar decline in the old order.

The extent of foreign domination was evident in the foreign relations of both Persia and the Ottoman Empire. In 1911, a new border agreement, the Protocol of Teheran, arranged the establishment of a border commission that could settle outstanding disputes, but the commission, convened in November 1913, was effectively directed by the representatives of Britain and Russia. Their aim was to delimit the border from Mount Ararat to the Gulf and to realign the border along the Shatt al Arab waterway from Muhammarah to the sea. Since Britain was keen to develop the Persian oil industry, Tehran got possession of six islands in the waterway south of Muhammarah. The border was thus confirmed in 1914 on the eve of the First World War.

Ottoman Turkey had looked to Germany for support in maintaining the empire in the early twentieth century. German military advice reinvigorated the Turkish army and the triumvirate of dictators in Constantinople considered the conquest of Persia among their strategic objectives. When Turkey joined the Central Powers (comprising Germany, Austria-Hungary and Bulgaria) in the First World War, Britain landed an expeditionary force in Basra in 1914 and advanced through Mesopotamia the following spring. While the British were checked at Kut al Amara until 1917, Persia was thrown into turmoil by competing tribes and factions as well as the warring powers. The Swedish-trained Government Gendarmerie tended to work alongside the Germans and Turks, but southern Persian tribesmen enlisted in a British militia.[10] The British, nevertheless, drove the Turkish army back through Mesopotamia and forced it to relinquish the occupied parts of Persia by 1918. Although the Turkish revived and reasserted its control of Asia Minor, it made no attempt to resurrect the moribund Ottoman Empire and it was dismembered.[11] British attentions turned to Bolshevik revolutionary unrest and its potentially destabilising effects on Afghanistan and India, and they were keen, along with France, to create national homelands that would prove resilient to communism and factionalism.

Iraq was created as an independent state based on the populated Mesopotamian plain, but there was uncertainty at first as to what to include in the territory and who should govern. Much has been written about this crucial period of state-building in Iraqi history and the fact that the Kurds of the north were added to create a *cordon sanitaire* around Turkey in 1921.[12] In the south, Basra Port Authority (which had been under direct British administration) went to the new Iraqi government in the hope that Iraq would be able to develop its commerce, but Persia refused to recognise the Iraqi ownership of the Shatt al Arab, and sent its vessels with its own pilots down the waterway. Persia believed the protocol of 1911 had awarded it the thalweg as a boundary and therefore both countries had the right to free navigation. It was not until 1929 that Iran recognised Iraq, which did little to improve relations between them.

Politics in both states remained unsettled. Dissatisfaction with the partition of the Kurdish provinces led to serious unrest in northern Iraq, in Khanaqin, and Qasr-e Shirin in Persia. In Tehran in 1926 Reza Pahlavi Shah seized power in a coup d'état having proved his military value by defeating Sheikh Khazal of Muhammarah.[13] Worse, both states felt that unrest within their borders was being encouraged by the other. Disorder in Khuzestan was blamed on Iraqis; Kurdish rebellion in northern Iraq was blamed on Iran. Iranian repression forced some Kurds to flee to Iraq and seek protection, but this only served to reinforce Iran's prejudices.

The chances of improved relations were undermined by lingering dissatisfaction over the status of the Shatt al Arab. Iraq, which did not have a long coast along the Gulf like Iran and which was dependent on this principal waterway, felt it should have full sovereignty. Iran, nevertheless, believed that Iraq should not have exclusive control of such an important economic artery on which so much Iranian commerce depended. Iraq referred the matter to the League of Nations, but in 1936 both sides agreed to settle through bilateral talks. Just at this point, in October 1936, the army staged a coup d'état in Iraq, and during the period of instability that followed, the new government agreed to the thalweg principle for 4 miles (6 km) opposite the Abadan island in the hope of avoiding Iranian or British intervention. The subsequent Iran–Iraq Frontier Treaty, concluded on 4 July 1937, opened the Shatt al Arab to all countries of the world and confirmed the land boundaries as agreed in 1913–14. Iraq later claimed it had signed this agreement under duress and argued that this made the agreement void. The British had pushed for a free waterway as a way to benefit both countries commercially, and they had no reason to offer support only to Iran. The discovery of oil in the Kurdish north in 1927 offered new business opportunities for mutual gain. Anglo–Persian Oil was dominant in the Iranian economy, but the wealth derived from oil was already assisting with modernisation there. Britain envisaged a profitable future for both states and hoped to avoid any further antagonisms over the border issue.

It has often been argued that both Iran and Iraq were made to serve British interests because of the presence of oil, and the independence of the two countries was illusory, not least because of Britain's armed intervention during the Second World War.[14] However, Britain had withdrawn its garrison of Iraq during the 1930s and when the war broke out there was no automatic military intervention. No forces were sent into either country until 1941 when the Iraqi military regime and the Iranian government not only favoured the Nazis, but looked as if they might join the Axis and support Hitler against the Soviet Union and

Britain. Consequently, even though its resources were already stretched, the British government intervened to overthrow the nationalist government of Rashid Ali Gailani in Baghdad, while Iran was invaded by both British and Soviet forces.[15] The Allies believed Iran provided a useful staging area and logistics route to get war materiel to the Soviets, and this led to the building of a bridge across the Shatt al Arab, as well as improved road and rail networks. The West did not regard Iran and Iraq as colonised countries on the basis of Britain's extreme wartime measures, but to contemporary Iraqis and Iranians, the British and Soviet moves amounted to precisely that. National pride had been injured by the Allies' action, and both countries were determined, in the post-war era, to achieve total freedom of action in foreign affairs. More importantly, the notion of anti-colonialism was to take deep root in the political rhetoric of both nations.

In the immediate post-war era, relations with the Western powers were good. Iran and Iraq signed the Treaty of Good Neighbourly Relations in June 1949, and in February 1951 both countries became members of the Middle East Treaty Organisation (METO), known subsequently as the Baghdad Pact. The latter agreement was the West's attempt to maintain influence over the region against the Soviet Union, but both Iran and Iraq hoped to gain by their association with the United States and Britain.[16] However, relations between Iraq and Iran were ruined by the Iraqi military coup of July 1958. The pro-Western monarchy was overthrown by nationalists, Iraq distanced itself from the Western alliance in preference of the Non-Aligned Movement, and it formalised its withdrawal from the Baghdad Pact in March 1959. Yet Iran, under the leadership of Muhammad Reza Pahlavi Shah, moved closer to the United States. In March 1959, the Shah signed a Military Cooperation Agreement that provided for the American defence of Iran in event of aggression by the USSR. Confident of American backing, the Shah then demanded from Iraq the acceptance that the thalweg principle be applied to *all* of the Shatt al Arab. The prime minister of Iraq, Abdul Karim Qassim, refused arguing that the 1937 agreement had been signed against their will at a time of unrest. Iran therefore refused to pay any tolls and insisted on piloting its own vessels. But with Iraq still weak and unstable (there were three coups and five governments in the years 1958–68) Baghdad was in no position to retaliate.

Disputes between the two countries were not yet critical, but the catalogue of disagreements was extended when it transpired that, from 1963, both countries were extracting oil from the same sector of the field on

the continental shelf at Khaneh and Naft-e Shah. An Iranian delegation visited Baghdad in February 1969 to offer a joint exploration of
the Khaneh field, resolve unsettled boundaries, and combine continental
shelf drilling. However, the Iranians again demanded the thalweg principle be applied to the Shatt al Arab. Baghdad refused. Yet, in March
1969, the Kurdish rebellion in the north of Iraq was reignited and, while
Baghdad was preoccupied, the Shah abrogated unilaterally the 1937
Treaty. Not only were Iranian vessels piloted by their own nationals, they
were escorted by gunboats. Iraq complained to the United Nations, but
no action was taken.

Seemingly powerless, Iraq resorted to punitive measures. It expelled
large numbers of Iranian residents of Iraq and began to offer active assistance to Iranian anti-Shah dissident groups. Baghdad revived the issue of
'Arabistan', arguing that Khuzestan was Iraqi territory surrendered under
the foreign mandate of the Ottoman Empire.[17] The Iraqis announced they
were forming a Popular Front for the Liberation of Arabistan, and established three anti-Shah radio stations to destabilise the Iranian regime.
The Shah responded in kind: according to the Iraqis, the failed putsch of
Major-General Abdul Ghani al Rawi on 21 January 1970 was backed by
Iran. Forty-four conspirators were executed. In fact, the Shah was certainly involved in destabilising Iraq, but his focus was on the Kurds. Iran
acted as the conduit for arms from Israel and the United States to the
Kurdish insurgents for many years. The United States no doubt hoped to
put pressure on the Iraqi regime and compel a successor government to
realign itself with the West and, typically in the Cold War, a variety of
diplomatic and clandestine levers were being used.

The Kurdish insurgencies and proxy war

The Kurds have long been conscious of their distinctive identity. They
were a people entirely distinct from Iranians and Iraqis, who descended
from tribes that settled in what is today south-eastern Turkey, north-
eastern Iraq, and north-west Persia. They trace their history to the Medes
of the seventh century BC, but they are thought to be descendants of the
Carduchi, possessing ethnic differences from Arabs, Persians and Turks,
and with their own language that is perhaps closest to Farsi. Although
there are possibly 27 million Kurds, they have always been a minority in
the countries of others. Most Kurds follow the Sunni tradition of Islam,
but there are significant numbers of Sufis too. These distinctions and the
long periods of alien occupation led to a frequent incidence of rebellion

in Kurdish lands. Unrest flared against the Ottomans on several occasions, and then in Mosul against the British Mandate in 1919 and 1922. After the First World War, the Sheikh of Qadiriyyah had been appointed by the British as an intermediary ruler, but he declared himself independent in May 1919. He was defeated a month later. Mahmud Barzani then declared himself the monarch of the 'Kingdom of Kurdistan' in 1921. The British, who were concerned about Turkish encroachments into Iraq, moved in and reappointed him as their leader, but he revolted against the British in the years 1922–24 in a more significant uprising. Once again he was defeated and the League of Nations formally awarded the region of Kurdistan to Iraq. Barzani remained resolute: there was a revolt in the Kurdish provinces of Turkey, which Iraqi Kurds joined in 1927–30, and Barzani made another unsuccessful attempt to eject the British in northern Iraq in 1930–31. With a smaller garrison, the British were dependent on the Royal Air Force to carry out air policing, and the rebels were crushed by ground attack and bombing missions. The Kurdish revolt on the north-western border was also defeated in 1935 by a joint Iraqi–Turkish campaign. The Kurds may have been condemned to remain a peripheral and largely unwanted provincial people but for the discovery of oil at Mosul and, subsequently, Kirkuk, in 1927, whereupon the area became one of strategic importance.

The strategic value of Kurdish lands was underscored in the Second World War. In Mahabad, Iran, in August 1941, a committee of professionals and tribal leaders was established during a popular uprising. They formed the Society for the Revival of Kurdistan, the Komelei Jiyanew-e Kurdistan, and elected Qazi Muhammad as their leader, seized the local administration and ran the area under their control for five years before declaring themselves entirely independent. The Soviets, who controlled the northern segment of Iran from August 1941, initially ignored the rebels but then gradually gave the 'republic' their support, providing transport, limited supplies and a cordon that prevented the Iranian army from retaking the area. Their intention was to incorporate the Kurds into the Soviet republic of Azerbaijan and consequently they opposed the declaration of independence made in December 1945. The Soviets had practically annexed neighbouring Iranian Azerbaijan, but the United States and Western Allies pressured Moscow to withdraw from all of northern Iran once the war was over.

After 1946, the Iranian government was therefore in a position to isolate and destroy the nascent Kurdish Republic. In fact, Qazi Muhammad was struggling to maintain support among his own people even without an Iranian offensive because of a blockade and the severance of Soviet aid. As a result, various tribal groups began to abandon the Barzani clan that stood at the centre of the resistance. However, when the Iranian offensive began in December 1946 it tended to increase the resolve of the remaining rebels. Nevertheless, with the rebellion weakened significantly, Mahabad was overrun in a matter of days. The Iranians set about a 'cultural cleansing' operation, banning the teaching of the Kurdish language, closing down Kurdish newspapers and destroying Kurdish books. Qazi Muhammad was captured and hanged in March 1947.

Not all the Kurdish fighters were captured or subdued. While some Iraqi Kurds retreated into Iraq, a party led by Mustapha Barzani filtered through the mountains into Soviet Azerbaijan, evading their Iranian army pursuers en route. In 1958, during the coup d'état in Baghdad, Barzani and his followers entered northern Iraq and supported the conspirators, under the banner of the Kurdish Democratic Party (KDP). Qassim, the leader of the Iraqi coup, reciprocated by granting recognition of the Kurds as a distinct minority, and he legalised the KDP, but their request for autonomy was refused. By 1961, Qassim, who was more secure in power, launched a campaign against Barzani and his followers, hoping to crush the party and reassert full sovereignty for Baghdad. Although Qassim was ousted in February 1963, the Iraqi government pressed on with its attempt to reassert its authority and Kurdish resistance intensified.

The fighting became so serious that three of Iraq's five army divisions were committed to fighting what had developed into a full-scale insurgency. In June 1966, in an attempt to end the conflict, a twelve-point agreement was reached between KDP and Baghdad.[18] The agreement included recognition of the Kurdish language in state business and offered proportional representation in the civil administration of the north. The Ba'athists, who seized power two years later, began implementing the twelve points, but the KDP was dissatisfied with the pace at which the reforms were being carried out and it suspected the Ba'athists would renege on the agreement at the first opportunity. As a result, the KDP returned to the armed struggle in March 1969 by attacking a Kirkuk refinery.

Baghdad sent the army back in to the Kurdish north, but the fighting was just as intractable as before. Indeed, so draining was the conflict that it was costing 30 per cent of the national revenue by 1970. The army had doubts that a decisive victory could be forthcoming and wanted to end the fighting, but even though the Ba'athists discovered the 'plot', they were compelled to conclude a fifteen-point plan in March 1970, with the objective of implementing its terms over four years. The agreement included autonomy for Kurdish provinces and their own vice-president. Baghdad refused to let the issue rest there, not least because three-fifths of its oil revenue came from the north and it could not afford to relinquish such a vital strategic asset. The agreement was allowed to fail from the outset. No census was held as promised and Baghdad set out to 'Arabise' the north, particularly around Kirkuk, by deporting 40,000 Fali (Shia) Kurds to Iran. Barzani, who did not trust Baghdad, also failed to keep his side of the bargain by expanding the guerrilla army and maintaining his contacts with Iran, the United States and Israel in order to obtain arms.

The Kurdish insurgency of the 1960s created a deep rift between the Kurds and the government of Baghdad in much the same way that the crushing of the Iranian Kurdish republic in the 1940s fostered bitter resentment of Tehran. Unrest among the Kurdish population offered an opportunity for the regimes of Iraq and Iran to exercise some strategic leverage against each other if they supplied the appropriate material support. Accusations of interference in the internal affairs of each state had been a frequent refrain historically, but in the insurgency that followed in the 1970s, both governments exploited the Kurdish question ruthlessly.

When Britain began to relinquish its power and influence over the Gulf, the question arose as to which country would replace it as the paramount authority. Britain aimed to leave the Gulf by December 1971 and the United States accepted that the Shah's Iran should represent the West's interests, while cultivating closer ties with Saudi Arabia and the Gulf states, although the so-called Twin Pillars strategy was not conceptualised until much later.[19] Iraq had remained immune to American efforts to rejoin a METO bloc, so the containment of Soviet influence was dependent on the strongest regional player at that time, namely Iran. The Shah decided to use his favour with the West to secure three strategically located islands in the Gulf, the Greater and Lesser Tunbs and Abu Musa, which had belonged to Gulf principalities. This meant that, along with control of the islands of Qeshm, Larak and Hormuz, Iran could dominate the entrance to the Gulf at the Hormuz strait. On 30 November, one day before the expiry of the British treaty, the Iranians invaded the three islands, with only token resistance encountered on Greater Tunb. Britain assisted the Shah by negotiating that Sharah's ruler, who owned Abu Musa, should receive an annual gift, indicating British complicity in the arrangement.

The Ba'athists of Iraq were furious that Iran had seized Arab territory. They were equally incensed that the Shah had announced he would not tolerate revolution on the Arab side of the Gulf, which the Ba'athists believed was a direct reference to them. They felt there was collusion by the Western powers with Iran which could only be directed at Iraq, and there was a general fear of CIA or MI6-inspired plots after the Mossadeq affair in Iran in the 1950s, when the prime minister had been deposed in a carefully orchestrated clandestine operation. Baghdad broke off diplomatic relations with Tehran and London and moved towards the Soviet Union to obtain support against an apparently imminent Western plot. The Iraqis quickly established a Treaty of Friendship and Cooperation, with terms that would last fifteen years, in April 1972. The Soviets and Iraqis agreed they would act against any state which threatened the peace of either country, they would not join an alliance directed at the other, and they would continue to develop cooperatively in the strengthening of their mutual defence capacity, which, in effect, meant Soviet aid and military equipment would be shipped to Iraq. To underscore its protest at Iranian actions in the Gulf, Iraq expelled Iranian theological students, pilgrims and businessmen, and then increased its secret military aid to the Popular Front of Arabistan.

The new Iraqi alignment prompted the United States to back Tehran more firmly. President Nixon announced that the Shah was entitled to buy any non-nuclear weapons he wanted and, in May 1972, he quietly assured Tehran that Washington would cooperate with Iran in the instigation of Kurdish insurgency in northern Iraq, in order to destabilise the regime in Baghdad. The Shah thought that the Soviets were intent on Iran's destruction and had backed Iraq on the western flank, while aligning with Afghanistan, and dismembering and weakening its partner Pakistan on the eastern flank. The Shah believed Iran embodied the monarchical order across the region, but Iraq regarded itself as the leader of militancy, revolution and republicanism and, furthermore, the champion of Arab nationalism. Ideological differences, underpinned by the sponsorship of the sharply divided Cold War protagonists, deepened the lines of division between Iran and Iraq.

Strategically, Iraq was in a weaker position. Its army was smaller than Iran's and, with only 40 miles (64 km) of coastline compared with the Iranian shores that extended down to the Arabian Sea, and a comparatively small fleet, it lacked the physical strength necessary to defeat Tehran. Kurdish unrest in the north of Iraq was far more serious than the Iranian Kurdish question and made that flank strategically vulnerable. Diplomatically, Iraq was relatively isolated since most of the Gulf states were in favour of the status quo and feared Iraqi revolutionary politics and the militancy associated with Arab nationalism. Iraq tried to persuade the Middle Eastern states that the Shah was the greatest threat to the region, but the outbreak of the Arab–Israeli conflicts in 1967 and 1973 convinced them all that the more significant and immediate problem was Israel. During the Yom Kippur War in 1973, Baghdad sent troops to the Syrian border and even managed to re-establish its diplomatic links with Tehran, but the issues of the navigation of the Shatt al Arab and anxieties about interference in internal affairs remained unresolved. The oil crisis that year, which quadrupled the price of a barrel of crude, enriched both nations giving them the power to purchase more military hardware and set the scene for an arms race between them.

It was the Kurdish question that worsened relations. In July 1973, the KDP had refused to join the Ba'athist Progressive National Front coalition and, sensing the insurgency was likely to recommence, Iran offered support to Barzani's faction. In March 1974, Baghdad began to implement the measures of autonomy stemming from the deal in 1970, but the Kurdish KDP was dissatisfied. The autonomy Baghdad offered seemed to exclude oil-rich areas like Kirkuk, Sinjar and Khanaqin; consequently the KDP wanted the implementation delayed until a census was carried out. When Baghdad refused, the Kurds returned to their guerrilla war.

The scale of the subsequent conflict was remarkable, as 45,000 insurgents fought four-fifths of the Iraqi army comprising some 100,000 men equipped with armoured and mechanised units and air power. Within weeks Barzani declared that 25,000 sq miles (64,750 sq km) of Kurdish lands had been liberated and, significantly, all of this territory was along the Iranian border. The Shah continued to make available American and Israeli arms and provided his own support, including artillery barrages across the border and a ready supply of anti-aircraft missiles. In January 1975, two Iranian regiments were driven into the 'liberated' Kurdish areas and border clashes between regular Iranian and Iraqi units soon followed.[20] This was in part a show of strength, but it amounted effectively to an undeclared war. In its own campaign of proxy war, Iraq tried to support Arab and Kurdish separatists in Iran. There was a significant danger of escalation, but Iraq believed it could not win a conflict against Iran and the Kurds at the same time, particularly as the fighting in the north had already caused heavy losses – there had been 60,000 military and civilian casualties in just one year.[21] Iran was also conscious that its oil installations and therefore its national wealth were at risk from a full-scale war, and Iraqi efforts to encourage separatism might escalate into an insurgency in a number of provinces in Iran. Both sides sought to scale down the fighting and seek a settlement, in which Turkey and Algeria mediated. Iraq was still the loser. For all the rhetoric of pan-Arabism, none of the twenty-one Arab league states offered assistance to Iraq. Significantly, the Soviet Union had not come to Iraq's aid in the crisis, despite the 1972 accord, and had not resupplied Baghdad's arsenal. It was even said that the Iraqi air force was down to its last few bombs by the time the conflict came to an end.[22]

The road to war: the Algiers Accord, 1975

The confrontation between Iran and Iraq was ended formally on 6 March 1975 at Algiers. The accord signed by Saddam Hussein, as vice-president of Iraq, and the Shah during the OPEC summit, agreed to the thalweg as the demarcation of the Shatt al Arab and the termination of subversive support in each country.[23] A new border commission was established to delimit a new portion of the border; Iraq was to get two villages in the Qasr-e Shirin area as compensation for the loss of the entirety of the Shatt al Arab. Iran had thus won, finally, recognition of the thalweg principle demanded sixty years before. Twice the Iraqis had had to concede to Iran because of internal weaknesses, namely either coup d'état or Kurdish insurgency. Military leaders in Iraq were deeply angered by the humiliation of the Algiers Accord.

Ironically, Iraq benefited from the conclusion of the confrontation. The insurgency in Kurdish areas subsided without Iranian backing, and the transfer of revenue from the fighting allowed economic development programmes to get underway both in the north and in the south among the Shias.[24] Baghdad had nationalised all foreign holdings in Iraqi oil production, increasing its revenue from exports, thus furnishing the development projects with more cash. The Ba'athists also became more established and secure in power, and consequently more self-confident in their socialist and secular ideology. By contrast, Iran's internal security began to deteriorate. The Shah headed a strong, centralised state, but, in contravention of the 1906 constitution, which held that Twelver Shi'ism was a state doctrine and only a Twelver Shia could become king, the Shah drove forward a Westernisation and secularisation policy. He was not backed by a party apparatus, and had no ideological counterweight to the Shia imams, relying on the benefits of Western capitalism and the distribution of Iran's increasing oil wealth. Thus, in just four years, the balance of power between Iran and Iraq was to be reversed, and Baghdad's political leadership, harbouring historic and recent grievances, looked to exploit the turmoil that subsequently engulfed the Shah.

The ideology of the Ba'ath

Formed in Damascus in 1947 as the Arab Ba'ath Party by Michel Aflaq, a Greek Orthodox Christian, Zaki Arsuzi, an Alawi or follower of Imam Ali, and Salah al Din al-Bitar, a Sunni, the Ba'ath was a small, clandestine organisation that aimed to create a unified and free 'Arab nation' within its territorial homeland.[25] In many ways the very existence of the organisation indicated a reaction to the domination of the Middle East by the West and by the Soviet Union. As a contrast to the superpowers, the Ba'ath believed in the 'special mission' of the Arab nation, to end colonialism and promote humanitarianism, through a political movement that was pan-Arab nationalist, socialist, populist and revolutionary. They claimed they wanted an end to class conflict, the promulgation of land reform, the public ownership of natural resources (particularly oil), transport, large industry and financial institutions. They wanted nationalisation in the economy, free trade unions for workers and peasants, the co-option of workers into management, and they accepted limited non-exploitative private ownership. Their socialist agenda put them in favour of representative government, freedom of speech and of association, within the bounds of Arab nationalism.

Their assumptions were that all Arabs belonged to one nation but they had been artificially divided into 'regions' (they did not recognise countries) by colonial authorities.[26] Their leadership, the National Command, would be a centralised executive for the entire Middle East. Below this, they envisioned Regional Commands, which would act like national governments, but only where the party was strong enough to justify it. Beneath these there were to be branches, sections, divisions and, ultimately, three-member cells. The language of the organisation, which was 'military-revolutionary' in tone, emulated the Marxist-Leninists, but their aspiration to achieve a pan-Arab 'empire' was far older and not unlike the dream of a united caliphate and single regional *umma* (community of Muslims) propagated by generations of militants. The recurrent theme of a desire for unity reflected the existence of internal divisions, which they regarded as the main source of weakness when faced by the external threats of the colonial powers, or the Cold War superpowers.

In 1952, the Arab Ba'ath Party merged with Akram Hourani's Arab Socialist Party of Syria, which necessitated the new title of Arab Ba'ath Socialist Party.[27] The merger gave the Ba'ath 500 members, but, while still small, there was a period of steady growth thereafter. The branch that opened in Iraq attracted 200 members in two years. When the pro-Western Iraqi regime joined the Baghdad Pact (1955) and refused to condemn the British–French–Israeli attack on Egypt in 1956, membership again increased. Nor were the Ba'ath mere theorists and agitators, they played a peripheral role in the overthrow of the Iraqi monarchy in 1958. However, the Ba'athists demanded that the new regime led by Qassim unite Iraq with Syria and Egypt, under Nasser's leadership, to create the United Arab Republic. When Qassim refused, they tried to assassinate him, but failed. Qassim consequently tried to suppress them, but their numbers continued to grow and, joining with other anti-Qassim groups, the Ba'athists overthrew him in February 1963. In the coup, they could claim 850 members and 15,000 supporters, with a paramilitary militia known as the National Guard. The idea of political-military militias in Iraq had a long history, dating back to the existence of the tribal militias in the 1920s, and there were continuities in the sense that clan and tribe allegiances influenced the membership of the organisation, despite the ideology.

On taking power, the Ba'athists were divided about whether to proceed with the unification with Egypt or not. Their main concern seemed to be the extent to which a unified polity would be truly socialist. The differences of opinion allowed Abdul Salim Arif to seize power in November that same year and throw the Ba'athists out. Although Arif died in an accident in April 1966, his brother, Abdul Rahman, maintained the exclusion of the Ba'ath. Rahman was then overthrown by a coup led by army officers and Ba'athists on 17 July 1968. The Ba'ath were not about to repeat their mistake of trying to share power. Within two weeks, the Ba'athists had eliminated or removed their former military allies. This rise to power was less ideologically motivated than had been envisaged in the early years, and the final stages of their ascent were marked by a pragmatic desire to obtain exclusive control of the state with promises of a programme of reform. This pragmatism proved to be an important legacy and the party would make more doctrinal sacrifices in order to stay in power in the 1970s and 1980s. The Ba'ath also learned to be better organised and, despite attracting almost 5,000 members to the party, they became even more conspiratorial and fearful of counter-revolutionaries. It was the secrecy that surrounded the movement which gave rise to the trend towards authoritarianism.

Divisions among the wider Ba'ath movement also became manifest in the mid-1960s, throwing the Iraqi branch of the party back on its own resources. The radical Syrian wing purged the older leadership at Damascus in February 1966, but the Iraqi faction continued to back Aflaq. The division became more permanent when the Iraqi Ba'athists held a separate national congress at Beirut in February 1968. The rivalry deepened to such an extent that later the Syrian faction gave its support to Iran during the Iran–Iraq War.

In Baghdad, the five-man ruling Revolutionary Command Council (RCC) had purged the senior command of the army and 117 of its own party officials who displayed insufficient commitment, while loyal party activists were placed into government departments to ensure that governance was dependent on trusted Ba'ath men. The army was also the primary target for party integration. Ba'ath members with recent military training were given authority in the armed forces and no crucial decisions could be taken without Ba'ath Party permission. The same rules were also applied to the domestic intelligence services. The senior commanders of the army were subsequently ordered to introduce Ba'athist ideological education, and party bureaux were set up. The RCC, it was decreed, was to have its members selected only from the Ba'ath Party. All RCC members had initially been serving military men, while the chairman and president, Ahmad Hassan Bakr, was a former army officer. The vice-president, Saddam Hussein, was neither a soldier nor a member of the RCC. The long-term objective of the Ba'ath became clear when they gradually replaced the military element of the RCC with their own men. The RCC thus became a fifteen-strong body, but all ten new members were civilian party loyalists.

Having secured power in the capital, the Ba'ath then infiltrated every organisation of the state, including government departments, the professions, trade unions, agricultural cooperatives and women's groups. All party affiliation had to be secret – an effective way of ensuring loyalty, as no one knew who was a party member and who was not. All reported to their headquarters independently and there was a graduated system of earning seniority over many years. By these means, an insidious surveillance culture began to grip Iraq and it would reach its ruthless apogee under Saddam in the years that followed. The whole apparatus was funded with the spectacular growth in oil revenue, which, during the oil crisis years of 1972–75, rose from $75million to $8,000 million. The regime thus possessed the means to increase popularity through wage increases to its supporters, and educational and health developments, while the party apparatus was able to purchase loyalty and expand its surveillance so that, even at street level, it seemed as if there were watchers everywhere. By 1978 it is estimated that one-fifth of all state employees were working for the intelligence and security services, giving it unprecedented levels of control.

A fifth column? Shia unrest in Iraq

Although Kurdish unrest in the north abated in 1975, Shia agitation in the centre and south of the country increased. An economic downturn in southern Iraq, caused by the onset of drought, led to a deterioration in conditions. Shia activists were also angry that as a sectarian group they were largely excluded from positions of high office and under-represented in the civil service and police. They were affronted by the fact that the Ba'ath movement was nominally headed by a Christian, Michel Aflaq, and that Ba'athists generally favoured secularism and a close association with communism.[28] In December 1974 a demonstration against the unequal distribution of wealth between Sunnis and Shias, a fact given greater prominence because of the dramatic increase in national revenues, turned violent and the regime reacted with significant repression. Twenty-five of the ringleaders were arrested, tried in secret, and five were executed.

Demonstrations are often the culmination of a deep-seated sense of grievance and, in 1974, a historic sense of injustice had resurfaced in a new form. In Mesopotamia under the Ottoman Empire, the Sunnis had kept the Shia out of public administration and they denied the Shia ulema the right to practise law, except within their own communities. The only significant concessions had been permission to run Najaf and Karbala, the holy cities that contained the shrines of Imam Ali and Imam Hussein, and issue fatwas there for the Shi'ites. However, when Iraqi Shia imams supported the revolt against the British in 1922, they were exiled to Persia. This, and the installation of a Sunni monarch, Feisal I (1921–33), broke up the channel of dialogue which hitherto had existed between the Shia population and the ruling elites and which had acted as a safety valve when grievances emerged.[29] The stage was set for the progressive alienation of the Shia population, but without the means to have their grievances redressed. When Qassim came to power in 1958, he was confronted by a Shia ulema fatwa that declared nationalisation and land distribution to be *haram* (forbidden). The Shia leaders organised a political movement to represent their religious interests, namely the Islamic Party of Iraq, and they stated that they were opposed to all forms of atheism and materialism. The party advocated its demands until it was banned in 1961. In 1964, Abdul Sarim Arif stepped up the pace of discrimination against the Shia, and when they attempted to organise an opposition movement, the Fatimiya, it was compromised by Iraqi intelligence and closed down. Iraqi intelligence established 'The Second Branch' specifically to deal with any other clandestine Shia organisations.

Many Iraqi Shi'ites felt that secularism and deterioration in religious observance were undermining and perhaps threatening the very survival of their denomination. The Ba'athist coup in 1968 led to a wave of new pressures. Religious publications were banned, Shia ulema were harassed, and the theological college in Najaf was shut down. Protests were quickly suppressed, leaving committed and increasingly desperate activists to consider a violent response. The Al Daawa al Islamiya (The Islamic Call), a clandestine and militant movement, was set up in secret in 1969 with the support of Ayatollah Muhsin Hakim, the senior authority based in Najaf. As the regime continued with its policy of eroding organised Shia opposition, insisting that Ba'ath political slogans be inserted into Shia prayers, for example, Al Daawa picked up more support especially from younger ulema, who used every opportunity to spread their resistance ideology. In essence, their message was that the Shia, the majority, were under the oppressive rule of the Sunni minority and should look to the example of al Hussein, who committed himself utterly to the struggle to regain authority from the caliph in the seventh century. The ability to tie their message to the central narrative of the Shia, namely the martyrdom in battle of Hussein in 680, was guaranteed to stir their supporters.

The demonstrations of 1974–75 were just the beginning of a more significant protest movement. In February 1977, the government sealed off Karbala, stating that a Syrian terrorist had been detected there. Searches of pilgrims sparked rioting, which quickly assumed an anti-government attitude. A police station was stormed at Haidariya, which prompted the decision to open fire on the rioters. Several were killed. News of these deaths ignited fresh disturbances in Najaf. For several days, the armed police battled with the protestors and eventually the army was called in. A number of Shia civilians were killed and there were over 2,000 arrests.[30]

The regime was shocked by the disturbances. It was unsure of the precise causes and there was some discussion whether the trouble was related to the four year Development Plan (1976–80) or the signing of the Algiers Accord. The president believed that some concessions to the Shia were desirable and that the Ba'athists might be able to incorporate Islamist ideology into their own. Vice-president Saddam Hussein disagreed and advocated complete repression of the protesters. The hardliners won the argument and the regime began its crackdown with a special tribunal, which tried and executed five Shia ulema and three activists. Saddam and his colleagues simply calculated that, since the Shia represented the majority of the population, concessions might lead to the end of the Ba'athists' grip on power. However, Saddam's group also knew that political repression alone would generate more resistance.

The policy that emerged was to pursue Al Daawa relentlessly and ruthlessly, but to offer economic incentives for the rest of the population in the south. Shias were permitted to join the rank and file of the Ba'ath Party, although senior offices were kept out of their hands. Formal constitutional arrangements were put in place to ensure the total control of the country by the elite of the Ba'ath Party, and this also gave Saddam Hussein, nominally the number two, considerable power. These moves came just before the Iranian Revolution. Had they not been made, it is just possible that the conflagration in southern Iraq may have coalesced with the revolutionary changes taking places in Iran, particularly because of the special status of Karbala and Najaf and the level of anger with secular dictators.

Ayatollah Khomeini had been living in Najaf during this period, having been exiled after protesting against the Shah in 1963–64. President Arif had given him sanctuary on the basis of 'my enemies' enemy is my friend'. However, when President Bakr had tried to enlist Khomeini's support in his dispute with the Shah, Khomeini had refused. The Ayatollah, disturbed by attacks on Shia clerics in Iraq, applied to leave for the Lebanon, but, with the regime eager to keep control of him, he was refused permission. Consequently, Khomeini was careful to avoid any association with the Iraqi Shia underground, realising the danger this would put him in. Nevertheless, he was genuinely committed to removing the Shah in Iran. When the Shah faced growing protest in October 1978, the Iranian government tried to persuade the Iraqis to clamp down on Shia dissidents and invoked the terms of the Algiers Accord, namely that all subversive activity likely to destabilise neighbouring states should be suppressed. Iraq complied willingly, eager to see the back of Shia leaders, and Khomeini was ejected. But Saddam caused further discomfiture by escorting the Shah's wife around the Shia holy places.

In France, Khomeini stepped up his criticisms of the Shah's regime and used the freedom to broadcast to great effect. He stated, with all his austere gravitas and certainty: 'Our future society will be a free society, and all the elements of cruelty, oppression and force will be destroyed.'[31] Khomeini condemned all governments that did not adhere to the precepts of the Koran as *taghutti* (tyrannical) and called for the liberation of the *mustazafin* (oppressed) everywhere. He denounced attempts to separate politics and religion as a device of imperialists, and called on the faithful to recall the fact that the Prophet did not deliver only sermons, but organised, planned and fought for a just society.[32] Khomeini claimed that his appeal was to all Muslims, but the greatest interest was among Shias in Iran.

The international situation for Iraq was then transformed by two 'strategic shocks'. The first, the overthrow of the Shah in 1979, meant the collapse of a major military rival on the eastern flank, and its replacement by a revolutionary regime committed to spreading its new doctrine. When the revolutionaries seized power, Khomeini was regarded as a hero among Shias not just in Iran but also in Iraq, placing the Ba'athist regime in the front line of the new challenge to the status quo of the Middle East. Ayatollah Muhammad Baqir Sadr in Najaf stated publicly that 'other tyrants have yet to see their day of reckoning'.[33] Any satisfaction the Ba'athists may have enjoyed when the Shah fled Iran had turned to anxiety. It was clear that urgent steps would have to be taken to dissuade the Iraqi Shias from similar direct action.

The Iraqis were also taken by surprise by Egyptian President Anwar Sadat's decision to sign a peace accord with Israel at Camp David, in the United States, in September 1978. Egypt had provided a counterweight to Israel, but the absence of a second front meant that Iraq might be the target of Israel's next offensive. The Ba'athists of Baghdad therefore approached the Syrians to suggest that Iraq and Syria should be united to confront Israel. Baghdad hosted the Arab summit and expressed Iraqi opposition to the Camp David agreement, but, just as it seemed to be making progress, the Iranian revolution split the sympathies of Syria and Iraq. President Hafiz Assad of Syria recognised the new regime in Tehran and welcomed the revolution, but Iraq did not.

For the Ba'athists, the Iranians were a threat because of their potential to ignite sectarian warfare in Iraq. The Iranian revolutionaries had overthrown one of the most powerful militaristic regimes of the region, undermining a security service and an army of 415,000 men, at a time of unprecedented economic growth. The revolutionaries championed the 'oppressed' against all wealthy and powerful oligarchs. They stated it was their duty to 'liberate' others across the world, and to support national liberation movements. They condemned other ruling elites of the Gulf region as 'corrupt' (referring to Saudi Arabia and the Gulf states), or 'atheist' and 'non-Muslim' (which meant Iraq). Moreover, the Iranians believed that the Shia Al Daawa movement was worthy of their support, which immediately abrogated the Algiers Accord of 1975. Iranian revolutionaries were eager to see Iraq 'liberated' and they believed that they could call upon the Shias of Iraq to show solidarity with the liberators in Tehran, and exploit the momentum of the Islamic Revolution.

Escalation to war

Four factors came together in 1979–80 to create the crisis conditions for war. First, in July 1979, Saddam Hussein acquired supreme power. It was his aggressive desire to see Iran humbled that, given the temporary chaos following the revolution, meant the two countries were unlikely to remain at peace. Second, an unsuccessful assassination attempt on Tariq Ali, the Iraqi deputy prime minister, followed by the execution of Ayatollah Sadr in April 1980, increased tension dramatically. Third, an attempted military coup in Iran, on 9/10 July 1980, was widely regarded in Iran as an Iraqi-inspired plot. Finally, the imperative of the Islamic Revolution to export its ideology, and 'liberate' its Muslim neighbours, created an irresistible momentum once Iran was locked into an international crisis. The more strident the rhetoric, the more the Iraqis believed that war was imminent and therefore some sort of pre-emptive strike became essential.[34]

For Iranians the causes of the war can be attributed to just one man: they firmly believe that the architect of this war was Saddam Hussein. It is clear that Saddam took the decision to launch an offensive into Iran, but a simplistic caricature of a ruthless tyrant does not help us to answer the crucial questions: what were his motives, and how far had his background or the context of events prepared him for this decision?

Saddam Hussein, born on 28 April 1937 to a landless family in Auja, near Tikrit, was raised by his uncle, Khairallah Talfa, an embittered man who had lost his post in the army for backing the nationalist Rashid Ali Gailani in the Second World War. In 1955 Saddam attended school in Baghdad and was involved in opposition activity; he joined the Ba'ath aged 20. After the coup of 1958 he was frequently involved in fights with Qassim supporters, and then took part in the unsuccessful plot to kill Qassim in 1959, injuring his leg in the escape attempt. He fled to Syria and then Egypt, where, in time, he studied law. Saddam returned to Iraq in 1963 after the Ba'athists had taken power. In Arif's time, he was involved in another coup attempt, but the failure of this conspiracy led to his imprisonment. He escaped in July 1966, and for his efforts for the Ba'ath, he was elected assistant general secretary of the Iraqi Ba'ath Party. In this role he helped to reform the party and its militia, learning the art of organisation and the management of personnel.

Once the Ba'ath returned to power in 1968, Saddam enjoyed close relations with the RCC former chairman Ahmad Hassan Bakr, a cousin of his uncle. This relationship helped him to get a place on the RCC just one year later. It was then that Saddam began to exercise power himself: he gradually had each of his rivals on the RCC dismissed. He also advocated a more cold-blooded resolution to the Kurdish problem, which earned him popularity among his comrades. He was admired more generally for his energy, ruthlessness and organisational powers. However, Bakr provided the reassurance to the older conservative members of the Ba'ath that their positions were secure and that this younger radical would not jeopardise party interests. Saddam was subsequently chosen as the delegate who signed the Algiers Accord, and no doubt he found the episode so humiliating that he harboured a desire for revenge. Yet, ultimately, his ruthlessness alienated his former champion. When he advocated a repressive line against the Iraqi Shia, it ruined his relationship with Bakr.[35]

To consolidate his power when he became president in 1979, he quickly identified 'a conspiracy' against him and the state, which involved sixty-eight leading Ba'athists. The tribunal to carry out the trial of the suspects comprised his closest allies in this 'Night of the Long Knives'. Twenty-one 'conspirators' were executed that August and it was clear that the suspects had all been rivals to Saddam. But the palace coup was not the end of the affair. Saddam went on to purge the trade unions, the Popular Army, student unions and local and provincial government. To maintain popularity, he increased salaries of judges, civil servants, the army, the police and the intelligence services, but his aim was to tighten his grip on power and make his subordinates dependent on him. He was, in fact, extending the policy he had advocated against the Shia, namely to crush the opposition leaders and give generously to the rest to buy support. As a result, $80 million was handed over to ulema of both Shia and Sunni denominations to maintain shrines, mosques or hostelries for pilgrims.[36] Loyal clerics got generous pay-outs, but he pursued Al Daawa and the new Mujahideen Movement mercilessly.

Saddam addressed religion carefully. He described Islam as the embodiment of civilisation and Arabism, arguing the ethos of Arab nationalism had existed long before Islam, but that, since the advent of Islam, Arab and Islamic identities had merged. This appeared to endorse the concept of a heterogeneous society of all faiths, and was designed to create a strong sense of Iraqi nationalism while supporting the concept of Pan-Arab unity. Aflaq, who had embodied the Ba'athist ideology, had stated that Ba'athist secularism liberated religion from the burden of

politics. Saddam used similar arguments to accuse Shia activists of trying to isolate the Ba'ath Party from the masses by the ill-disciplined use
of religion. He stated they had tried to provoke a heavy-handed response
that would deepen a sense of alienation. The separation of religion and
state was clearly important to Saddam but this may have been because he
realised the power of religious arguments and leaders to mobilise people
against the regime. He was to make a dramatic reversal in this secular
policy in the 1980s and 1990s, at least in terms of his public image.

Ayatollah Sadr, a leading member of the Iraqi Shia ulema, had con-
gratulated Ayatollah Khomeini publicly when he took power in Iran,
but such a warm declaration of moral support for a foreign leader made
Saddam's secret service nervous and he was subjected to close surveillance. In June 1979, he was placed under house arrest in Najaf and later
was moved to Baghdad to prevent him leading a delegation of Shi'ites
to meet Khomeini in person to offer their congratulations. Halting this
delegation led to rioting in the south of Iraq and also in some of the Shia
districts of Baghdad. This violence became so serious that the Iraqi army
was called in to restore order. Many protestors were shot and 3,000 were
arrested. Tehran exploited the unrest, using radio broadcasts to describe
Sadr as the 'Khomeini of Iraq' and to call for the Shia people to rise
against the Iraqi regime.[37]

Saddam ordered that there should be executions of some of those
arrested using the president's authority. The list Saddam submitted
included Shia leaders and also some army officers suspected as having
links with the militants. Understandably, President Bakr objected to the
names of the military men being included, fearing the effect this might
have on the army's morale. Saddam had him arrested, and later Bakr
'resigned on health grounds'. Saddam was consequently declared president on 16 July 1979, combining this position as head of state with his
role as the chairman of the RCC and the general secretary of the Regional
Command (Iraq) of the Ba'ath Party.

Saddam had been able to assume absolute power because of the nature
of the Iraqi state. The conspiratorial and putschist character of Iraqi
politics contributed to a lack of constitutional governance and account-
ability. Examples of this included: the army's seizure of power in 1958
led by Brigadier Qassim; the Ba'athists' attempts to assassinate Qassim
between 1961 and 1963, and their success in 1963; General Arif's court
coup, which threw out his erstwhile allies the Ba'athists; and the cooperation of the Ba'athists and Iraqi military intelligence to get rid of Arif in
1968. The presence of foreign agencies fuelled this sense of intrigue and
mistrust. When Qassim nationalised part of the oil industry, he angered

the West, and the CIA supported attempts to overthrow him. Fears of other CIA or Iranian plots created a political culture of anxiety and subterfuge.

Saddam inherited a significant level of ruthlessness in the system. When the Ba'athists took power, they eliminated their army allies systematically. Some were pursued even in exile as the political movement showed itself determined to assert and remain supreme over the army, just as the Revolutionary Guards were later to do in Iran. In 1979, when Saddam was 'selected' to lead the country, the apparatus of dictatorship was already in place. The purge he instigated was carried out by his brother and a quarter of the regime's former leaders were murdered. All this was possible only because the secret service and the party loyalists already regarded it as their modus operandi.

While many Iraqis and Iranians referred to the war of the 1980s as 'Saddam's War', many also believed that this was 'Khomeini's War'. Ayatollah Khomeini personalised the struggle, arguing that his role was to guide the people, even though he claimed he never wanted a political appointment. The consequence was that Khomeini's ideological opinions shaped the attitude of the Iranian people and their view of Iraq.[38] As we have noted before, Khomeini believed that religion and politics were inseparable. He refuted the idea that Islam could be reduced to a series of rituals and argued that Western imperialists had set out to do this so as to weaken the Muslims. What Khomeini offered was an agenda that put Islam at the very heart of the political culture of Iran, but Khomeini himself was more than that: he was regarded by many Iranians as an icon of socio-economic revolution, a representative of God's divine favour, the antithesis of grubby materialism and, for some at least, the embodiment of the transmission of God's 'divine light', the intimate and profound wisdom of the creator that was passed between carefully selected imams who had a mission to lead the Iranian people for the fulfilment of God's purpose. Khomeini was therefore a Mahdi, a messenger of God, and the success of the revolution seemed to many to be irrefutable proof of this singular reality.[39]

Khomeini had been steeped in a religious way of life. The son of a member of the ulema, his father was murdered while he was still an infant, a fact curiously similar to his nemesis, Saddam, whose father had also been killed while he was young. Khomeini spent his youth in study for a religious career, attending *madrasahs*, praying at particular mosques and learning Arabic. In 1941 he published a book attacking secularism and Reza Shah Pahlavi's dictatorship, and, by the end of the Second World War, he had qualified as Hojatalislam, which permitted him to acquire his own acolytes. In 1961, he published his interpretations of Islamic jurisprudence in *Clarifications of the Points of the Sharia,* which earned him the rank of ayatollah. In 1963, he gave a series of lectures at Qom attacking the Shah's 'white revolution' of reforms as a sham. He went on to make vitriolic attacks on the Shah's pro-Western policy, which attracted the attention and support of religious radicals. Periodically imprisoned, he was deported briefly to Turkey in 1964, before reaching Najaf in 1965 where he continued his verbal attacks on the Shah's regime.

After the Algiers Accord of 1975, Iraq permitted a greater number of Shi'ites to visit Najaf and Karbala as pilgrims. This enabled Khomeini to transmit his messages, often via tape recordings, the *i'ilamiya,* to his followers in Iran. One journalist remarked this was a 'revolution for democracy against autocracy by theocracy using xerocracy'.[40] Those who visited him testified that he was fearless, intolerant of secularism and pious. Others noted how he held his listeners in rapt interest, his voice firm but often quiet. He was absolutely determined not to compromise with the regime, as he believed other opposition groups had done, and this strength in his own convictions was to reappear during the Iran–Iraq War with significant consequences. In 1970 he had delivered a series of lectures while in Najaf, and published *Hukumat-e Islami* (Islamic Government, 1971). In both of these formats he called for the subordination of politics to Islamic injunctions and precepts. He argued that it was the duty of all Muslims to achieve an Islamic revolution in politics, to end injustice and corruption, and for the ulema to participate in the judiciary, legislature and executive of government. He did not call just for the fulfilment of some other-worldly paradise. He had spelled out the practical steps, the programme of action, needed to establish an Islamic state.

The concept of an Islamic state, utilising but subordinating the organs of a modern polity, was something of a pivot in history, because it acted as the inspiration not just for Shia Muslims but eventually for Sunni movements too. In the 1990s, Hizb-ut Tahrir, a global militant Sunni movement, for example, advocated the establishment of an Islamic state by a mass uprising, and bodies like Hamas and Hezbollah still look to the Iranian model. People, Khomeini argued, must become conscious of their oppressed nature and this is why the revolution must be led by clerics. He specifically called for the imposition of the divine law, the Sharia, which, since Allah was above the law, must be above the secular laws of the state. Transgressors of the divine law should be punished by Sharia, so this legal system had to be implemented fully. He advocated that the imposition of justice required the appointment of a *just faqih* (religious lawyer) who was expert on the interpretation and application of Islamic law. To assist him, a number of expert jurists were also required. Legislatures and an executive were required only to resolve disputes that could arise in the process of applying the Sharia. The *faqih* was also to act as a guardian to these other bodies, ensuring they did acquire too much power. The *faqih* himself had to be elected through the people and also through a selection process by the ulema.

This theocratic system alarmed neighbouring regional states not just because it required a revolution to establish it, and one that had overthrown a powerful Shah with a strong security apparatus at his disposal, but because Khomeini insisted on advocating a world revolution. On 11 February 1979, he announced: 'We will export our revolution to the four corners of the world because our revolution is Islamic; and the struggle will continue until the cry of "There is no God but Allah and Muhammad is his Prophet" prevails throughout the world'.[41] Khomeini also warned his critics that 'these American sympathisers and others must know that in a few hours we can throw them into the dustbin of annihilation any day that we wish to do so'.[42] He reassured his followers that Iranians who had recently been abroad after the revolution had returned with the news that 'all countries of the world love Iran'.

That a leading Shia theologian should become an advocate of reform and revolution was a sea change in Iranian political culture. When Shah Muhammad Reza had tried to modernise Iran after the Second World War, he had been opposed by Shi'ite religious leaders even though the landless rural population and urban workers had supported the Shah's policies. In the 1960s, the White Revolution was even more far reaching: land was redistributed, education expanded, new Western medicine introduced, civil engineering projects established, landowners compensated through oil revenue, and women were given a prominent role in public life.[43] The Shah enjoyed spectacular economic success with the development of the oil industry. However, his flamboyant and ostentatious display of wealth was less well-received. His references to the pre-Islamic era were unpopular and the Savak (Intelligence Service) was feared by everyone. Political power was centralised, and yet, ironically, the Shah had popularised politics by his reforms. The secularisation of Iran and fear of corruption played into the hands of the radical theocrats, and when Iran experienced high inflation, fuelled by increased spending on the army and changes in the economic climate, there were protests. Further concessions merely emboldened the critics and the demonstrations grew in scale. In 1978, seventy students were killed in a protest against the United States, and as crowds tried to protest about the killings on 8 September that year, the regime cracked down on the demonstrators. Black Friday marked the imposition of martial law and a wave of arrests. In response, there were strikes and more protests.

At this point, Khomeini's criticism became decisive. He articulated, through relentless rhetoric, the faults and inhumanity of the Shah's regime. The fact that Khomeini was a distant, almost mystical figure, added to his image as the moral antithesis of the Shah. Radical fighters set themselves up in his name and risked death in emulation of Al Hasan and Al Hussein, the 'founding fathers' of Shi'ism who had martyred themselves at Karbala. For the majority at street level, the historian Nikki Keddie notes that religion was less important. A cabal of left-wing activists, clerics and workers led the revolution for a variety of bread-and-butter issues.[44] The Shah fled, and Khomeini returned from exile amid hysterical crowds.[45] He quickly established theocratic oversight of a government with a radical revolutionary style. He and his followers also unleashed a reign of terror against 'counter-revolutionaries', which ensured that, despite the chaotic transfer of power, an inherent discipline was imposed on the political system from the outset.[46] This made subsequent opposition to the running of the war effort more difficult. A new politically correct language was imposed, opposing the 'corrupt West' and tyrannical regimes like Iraq. Amid the fervour of revolution, the US Embassy was seized and fifty-three hostages taken. When an American rescue attempt failed, relations between Iran and the United States were damaged irrevocably.

A fear of centralised power and the subsequent overlapping and competing groups in the Iranian political system created a 'polyarchy', which had a significant impact on the strategic direction of the war. Moreover, the fact that the revolution was a movement at street level influenced strongly the way that Iran would later fight the war. It would have been inconceivable for the new regime to have permitted the former professional army to conduct the fighting without its own revolutionary units and a directing hand over the war effort. Yet this very influence was to have disastrous consequences in the conduct of operations from 1983 to 1986, as practically untrained Iranian fighters hurled themselves at entrenched Iraqi troops.

During the revolution, Khomeini advocated that Arabs join the Shi'ite Iranians to establish an Islamic supremacy and eradiate differences on the grounds of ethnicity or nationality. At the same time he exhibited an extreme naivety in this regard: he did little to endear Arabs by condemning the Umayyads, the dynasty that inherited the Prophet's dominions whom many Arabs looked upon favourably, for distorting Islam. He equated Arabism with the 'state of ignorance' that had prevailed before the Prophet's revelations, and he claimed that the Umayyad dynasty had deliberately promoted Arabism over the interests of a united Islam in order to establish the first caliphate. This sort of litany of criticism was precisely the reason why Sunni Arabs detested the heresy of Shia Islam; they regarded the Shia as having departed from the true path of the Sunnah.

Khomeini's ideological pronouncements and the public criticism of the Iraqi regime prompted a response from Saddam. He tried to argue that a true Islamic revolution would embrace Arab interpretations and, indeed, the 'Arab Revolution', which was a description of Ba'athist revolutionary politics. Attempts to redefine a revolution in Iran as 'Islamic', he argued, could only be false if the revolutionaries there pitted themselves against the Arab revolutionaries and the Arabs themselves.[47]

Saddam increased the pressure by making a show of praying at particular mosques and shrines. He made a personal tour of Shia regions and announced further economic improvements. He symbolically declared Imam Ali's birthday as a national holiday. He adopted early Islamic ciphers in his propaganda. He pledged to 'fight injustice with the swords of the imams' at Najaf, and hinted at Shias sharing power. All theses moves were clearly designed to keep the Shia Iraqis isolated from the Iranian revolution. Saddam also maintained the pressure on underground movements. In March 1980, he ordered the execution of ninety-seven members of Al Daawa, stating that membership of this movement constituted a capital offence. Al Daawa had begun a campaign of attacks on police stations, party offices and recruiting centres of the popular army. Shocked by the executions, Ayatollah Sadr's verdict had been to declare any dealings with the Saddam regime as *haram*.

To interdict the militants and to send a strong signal to Iran, which he believed was weakened by its revolution, Saddam ordered the bombardment of Qasr-e Shirin on the Iranian border. Iranians were expelled en masse from the country, and 16,000 Iraqi nationals of Iranian descent were also thrown out. He added to the diplomatic offensive by demanding that the Iranians evacuate the Tunb islands and Abu Musa. In secret he ordered the execution of Ayatollah Sadr and his sister, hoping to silence his greatest critic, but the news of the event leaked out a week later and caused shock and revulsion in Iran. Khomeini raged that Saddam had declared war on Islam by his actions and he made a direct appeal to the Iraqi soldiers to disobey their dictator, and to the Iraqi people to overthrow their leader.[48]

More importantly, Iran began to train Shia Iraqis who were residing in Iran, some of whom had recently been exiled, and arranged for them to be inserted back into Iraq across the border. The Iranians had some experience of this with the Kurdish Democratic Party in 1979, but the training was clearly intended to create the conditions for insurrection in Iraq. Saddam, too, was engaged in a more determined war by proxy. Baghdad began to supply Arab secessionists in southern Iran and Iranian Kurds with arms and ammunition. Significantly, Iranian exiles from the Shah's era were permitted to remain in Baghdad, and to broadcast anti-Khomeini propaganda. Advice was offered openly to irregular fighters of the southern Iranian clans using these airwaves. In addition, border clashes increased with approximately ten incidents a month in early 1980. For their part, the Bakhtiari and Oveissi tribesmen wanted to establish a base of operations inside Iran so as to conduct a guerrilla war. The governments of both Iran and Iraq feared insurrection or counter-revolution, but both sides were making use of proxy forces as a means to topple their adversary's regime while avoiding a full-scale war.

The trigger for the success of the conspirators was to be foreign intervention, albeit of a limited kind. The Americans made an attempt to rescue their hostages on 24/25 April 1980 and this was also to be used by anti-Khomeini groups as the signal for a coup, but the plan had to be delayed when the rescue mission was aborted. The army attempted to stage its own coup d'état on 24 and 25 May, but it was defeated. Another attempt was made by army officers on 9 and 10 July, but this also failed. The death of the Shah on 27 July removed an important element of their movement, and they could no longer claim to represent a restoration. The failure of the pro-Shah forces and the Americans prompted Saddam to make more effort to deal with Iran himself. The main calculation was that acting sooner rather than later was to be preferred. Saddam and his elite believed Iran was weak. The Iranian army seemed to be suffering from low morale as it endured a series of purges. There were reports of shortages of vital military equipment, stores and fuel. There was news of conflicts between the president, Abol Hassan Bani-Sadr, and the ulema. Unemployment was rising, and there were shortages of consumer goods that might herald popular unrest. The professional middle classes were disaffected. Iran had angered the Gulf monarchies with its revolutionary rhetoric, and it faced an imminent economic embargo from the West. Moreover, the Iranians' relationship with the Soviet Union was a non-starter. The unrest in Iran had reverberated through Daoud's Afghanistan, prompting violent unrest in Herat. Soviet personnel were caught up in the fighting and the Afghan communist party, the PDPA, was paralysed by factional intrigue. The Soviet military intervention in Afghanistan in December 1979 was condemned by Iran as an assault on a Muslim country, marking Iran's complete isolation from the Eastern Bloc.

Saddam believed that he had to go to war with Iran for a variety of reasons. From an internal perspective, he was afraid of a revolt by the Shia in the south and the possibility of civil war. The only way to avert the threat was to destroy the Khomeini regime, which would otherwise provide a source of inspiration for dissidents in the future. Saddam expressed this view to his Ba'athist comrades at a meeting in July 1979.[49] There may have also been a calculation to act before the forthcoming American election in November. A new American president might try to make concessions to Iran to retrieve the hostages, he reasoned, and perhaps some other normalisation of relations that would make the opportunity for the defeat of Iran by Iraq impossible. This calculation might also imply that the Americans knew of Saddam's plans, but it also suggests, more prosaically, that it was only a matter of time before the Iranian regime got a firmer grip on power and consolidated its position, and this limited window of opportunity would surely end. An empowered Iran was a significant danger to Iraq.

Saddam knew that Iraq was wealthy and could afford a military option. Oil revenues had reached an unprecedented $30,000 million in 1980. Furthermore, Iraq enjoyed good relations with the other Gulf states, and Saddam travelled between them to discuss the possibility of military operations against Iran in August 1980. Iraq possessed a large field army and air force that could inflict a decisive victory. Iran was apparently in disarray. Former Iranian leaders had provided Saddam with invaluable information on Iranian defences and on the disagreements within the new regime. His assessment was that Baghdad would be able to call on some Iranians to support the Iraqi operations.

A war also held out the possibility that the Shatt al Arab dispute could be resolved in Iraq's favour with a successful conflict, and it would also provide a useful *casus belli*. A military victory meant that Iraq could resolve not only these local problems, but it could enable Saddam to look more broadly across the Middle East. Saddam knew that Egypt had lost its regional leadership role because of its unpopular settlement with Israel. A successful war in the liberation of Arabs in Khuzestan and the defeat of the radical regime in Tehran offered the chance of greater standing in the Arab world and all the benefits that implied. Moreover, the possession of the Khuzestan coastline with its oilfields and installations would give Iraq considerable wealth and a longer stretch of coast with strategic implications for control of the Gulf itself.

The support of the Iranian tribesmen and the Khuzestan 'Arabs' close to the shores of the Gulf was a key component in the Iraqi narrative and justification for war. Saddam convinced himself that his forces would be greeted as liberators. The areas freed of Iranian control were to be styled, the 'Free Republic of Iran' with the capital at Ahwaz. It was thought this success would set off other counter-revolutionary moves across Iran – tying down many more Iranian forces.[50]

Serious border fighting took place at Qasr-e Shirin between Iranian and Iraqi troops on 2 September 1980: Iran retaliated with the shelling of Khanaqin and Mandali on the Iraqi side of the border. The Iraqis claimed that the Iranian air force had also made air strikes against oil installations, but this was to be a war of claims, counter-claims and exaggerations throughout.[51] Even today, Iranians and Iraqis disagree about who started the shooting along the border, even if they concur on the strategic causes. Clearly when border guards came under fire, they retaliated, but the rapid escalation of the fighting suggests that both sides had anticipated an exchange of fire. Saddam, nevertheless, upped the stakes. On 6 September Iraq threatened to seize the Zain al Qaws area, which it claimed had, in fact, been awarded to it in the Algiers Accord, but which it had never taken possession. The Iranians allegedly replied by shelling more Iraqi border settlements. Between 7 and 13 September, Iraqi forces claimed to have overrun the border area around Zain al Qaws, but the Iranians were unable to offer any effective resistance at this point, and so their limited response using the local units available may be understandable.

Saddam steeped up the rhetoric on 17 September by claiming that Iran had violated the Algiers Accord by its persistent efforts to undermine the Iraqi regime, by backing guerrilla forces (namely the Kurds and the Al Daawa movement) and by refusing to return Iraqi territory. Saddam then announced that Iraq had abrogated the accord, dramatically tearing up copies of this and other treaties. He announced that Iraq now believed it had full sovereignty over the Shatt al Arab. When Tehran disputed the Iraqi claim, fighting broke out along the waterway. Iran mobilised its reserve on 20 September and two days later Iraqi armour rolled across the border.

The final catalyst for war

Saddam aimed for absolute political control of his own country and the aggrandisement of Iraq as the pre-eminent regional power. He had already achieved his first aim of becoming the undisputed master of Iraq. After Khomeini's revolution, he felt he could commence the next phase with the reduction of Iran. However, the decision to go to war was also based on anxiety. Saddam was concerned that the Shia of Iraq would join the Islamic revolution, or, at the very least, Tehran would attempt to support the Kurds and reignite the insurgency in the north. Saddam believed he had a limited window of opportunity. He was confident that Iraq was strong enough to tip the boiling cauldron of Iranian politics by a limited war, and Iran's diplomatic isolation encouraged him to believe that there was little risk of outside intervention. After all, the threat posed by the revolutionary zeal of the Iranians to the status quo of the Gulf regimes and to the oil interests of the Western powers tended to align them to Iraq. Most importantly for Saddam, the legacy of grievances and humiliations, including war by proxy, had created a desire to humble Iran. Southern Iraq was populated by Shias sympathetic to Iran, and this could be neutralised by absorbing parts of southern Iran, which would also include control over vital oil installations.[52]

The political culture of Iraq also contributed to this decision. Saddam's personal control of the most important offices of the state meant that his decisions determined all policy. Moreover, the narrow constitutional basis of support, because most of the Ba'athists belonged to a minority of Sunni clansmen in a country with a large Shia and Kurdish population, and the consequent concentration of power in the hands of a ruthless elite, favoured a decisive and militarist solution to political problems. The modus operandi of the domestic sphere was thus extended to the realms of foreign policy. Saddam believed that he could replicate the Israeli success of 1967, namely a surprise attack, and cause the collapse of the regime in Tehran, and thus the ceding of the territory of Khuzestan. This success would ensure his regime took the leadership role among Arab nations, as Nasser's Egypt had once done.

Ultimately, the trigger of the war was the dispute over the control of the Shatt al Arab, and the moment when Saddam felt he could repudiate the old agreements. The Iranians were already engaged in a war of words and they clearly regarded Saddam Hussein as an obstacle to the expanding revolution. Saddam had launched a propaganda campaign of his own, and the escalation of the border dispute, which led to a frequent exchange of fire, gave Saddam the opportunity to launch his offensive across the frontier. From then on, the die was cast.

Part II

The Early Operations

3

The Iraqi Offensive of September 1980 and the Failure of Saddam's 'Limited War'

The direction of the first Iraqi offensive was in the south-east, aiming to seize the Shatt al Arab, Khorramshahr and Abadan, and then to take Ahwaz as the capital of Khuzestan, and also Dezful. The concept of operations was to replicate the Israeli opening of the 1967 war – a lightning strike with air power to knock out the Iranian air force while it was still on the ground, followed by a swift land operation led by armoured formations. This approach would give the Iraqis air supremacy, enable them to overwhelm the Iranian resistance on the borders and create a psychological effect that would encourage the anti-Iranian government resistance and cause the collapse of the regime in Tehran. The Iraqi strategy also had to block any possible Iranian move in the north against its oilfields, and it had to safeguard all the approaches to Baghdad. In the south it had to cover the strategic ports and Basra. Success would therefore depend on a decisive result within the first few weeks and then negotiations could be opened from a position of strength. Saddam had no intention of pushing into the depths of Iran or of reaching Tehran; his calculation was that such risks would not be necessary.

On the night of 22 September 1980, Iraqi aircraft, in two waves, swept across Iranian airspace and struck at ten airbases and two air defence installations. The attack was a failure. Some bombs malfunctioned; others were simply way off target because of crew error, lack of experience and faulty Soviet technology. Nevertheless, Iraqi divisions crossed the border as planned at eight separate points and secured most of their initial objectives. In the north, an Iraqi infantry division moved into Iranian Kurdish Panjwin to block the any potential Iranian counter-attack from Sanandaj towards Suleimaniya.

In the centre, another Iraqi division took Qasr-e Shirin, driving out an Iranian armoured brigade. The division also secured the ridge that ran along the Baghdad to Tehran road. This put the Iraqis within striking distance of Bahktaran, a provincial capital that was protected only by a reduced Iranian armoured division. This move also secured the road back to Baghdad, which was just 75 miles (121 km) from the border.

To the south, another Iraqi infantry division took Mehran and advanced as far as the foothills of the Zagros mountains, effectively dominating the road network to the south-east, a hydro-electric power station, and an Iranian airbase at Vahidyeh. Still further south, the Iraqis pushed three armoured divisions and one mechanised division into Khuzestan, the flat country providing ideal conditions for a rapid advance. In divisional tasks, a two-pronged attack secured the road to Dezful, the other the route to Ahwaz, and by the 25 September the Iraqis claimed that they were laying siege to the cities. The other divisions focused on the security of the Shatt al Arab, Khorramshahr and Abadan. Control of the waterway required that the major urban areas be captured and the island of Abadan neutralised. At Ahwaz, this seemed a foregone conclusion as the Iranians could muster only one reduced armoured division. However, given the weakness of the Iranian forces, the Iraqis could hardly claim that they were victorious yet; the greatest test had not yet come (Figure 1).

The Iranian navy was the first to offer effective resistance. More numerous than their Iraqi counterpart, Iranian gunboats opened fire on Basra and Iraqi oil terminals at Fao, before imposing a blockade of the Shatt al Arab, confining the ships in Basra. Iraqi aircraft had not been trained to engage Iranian vessels and had difficulty reaching their target ports, most of which lay out of range.

The Iranian air force also retaliated with some effect. Most Iraqi airbases lay within striking distance of the Iranians so two-thirds of the Iraqi combat planes were moved to Jordan, Kuwait, North Yemen, Oman and Saudi Arabia. With just 332 aircraft and 38,000 personnel, in theory the Iraqis were outnumbered by the Iranian air force by almost two to one. The Iranians were able to launch up to 150 sorties a day and under this pressure the Iraqis were eager to preserve their air reserves. Although the Iranians had 450 combat aircraft, including 150 American F-4s and F-5s, only a portion of these could be used. A lack of spares and the death of pilots and senior officers in the revolution meant it was difficult to sustain intensive air operations. However, Iranian pilots, particularly those trained by the Americans, were highly skilled. By flying low in small

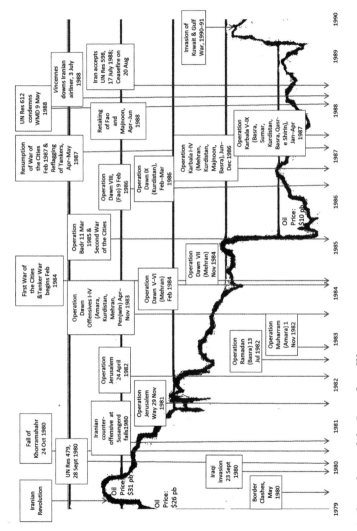

Figure 1   *A chronology of the Iran–Iraq War*

formations of four planes, they could avoid Iraqi radar and neutralise anti-aircraft batteries.

The Iraqis commenced their assault on Abadan on 25 September, hitting the refinery. In retaliation, the Iranian air force sent a huge armada of 140 aircraft to strike Iraqi oil installations in Basra and Zubair in the south and in Kirkuk and Mosul in the north. Oil exports were suspended after the attacks.

Resistance from the Iranians gradually stiffened as they recovered from the shock of the invasion. Aircraft strafed the advancing Iraqi armoured columns, slowing the offensives on Dezful and Ahvaz. Gunboats continued to pound the shoreline. Meanwhile Iraqi armour and artillery hammered each minor objective along its line of advance, and small detachments of Iranians defiantly opened up with small arms despite the odds against them. On 30 September, the Iraqis had reached the outskirts of their urban objectives. As the Iraqi troops made their final approach, Saddam attempted to negotiate from a position of strength. The United Nations (UN) had called for a ceasefire on the 28th, and Saddam had quickly responded with an announcement that he was ready to offer to end hostilities on the condition that Iran now recognised Iraq's full sovereignty of the Shatt al Arab and other territories that it had claimed. Saddam also demanded the evacuation of the three Gulf islands and an assurance that, never again, would Iran interfere in the domestic affairs of Iraq. He did not spell out the fate of Khuzestan, but referred only vaguely to 'usurped Iraqi territories'.[1] The Iranians simply refused to negotiate. They believed that Iraq did not yet possess the Shatt al Arab, not least because the Iranian navy controlled the mouth of the waterway and had blockaded it. Saddam may have hoped that an early settlement would avoid the costly battles for the streets of Iranian cities and achieve the strategic objective of making him appear to be the provoked victim of Iranian aggression and the magnanimous peacemaker. His willingness to negotiate was remembered by the UN and did much to preserve his reputation despite that fact that he had launched the war, but the Iranians now felt even more justified in their belief that the Iraqis and their allies were intent on the destruction of Iran and they were prepared to defend themselves.

In early October, the Iraqis attempted to take Dezful, Ahvaz and Khorramshahr. They began by sealing off the cities with entrenchments, then fired salvoes of artillery, mortar and tank rounds, and bombed the cities from the air. However, the cities were large and sprawling and it proved difficult to achieve the density of fire required to destroy targets of value. As so often in urban warfare, destroyed buildings provided just as much cover from fire as intact ones. Moreover, multi-storey concrete buildings proved resilient to heavy fire and provided ideal platforms for weapons and observation for the defenders.

The approach of the fighting caused most civilians to flee. One interviewee spoke of the terror that seized her and her family as they sought to escape to Tehran. Although a schoolgirl at the time, she found relating the experience harrowing even thirty-five years on. Another male interviewee told the author that, after experiencing the Iraqi air attacks at Khoramshahr he still flinches whenever he hears a jet aircraft overhead. With tears welling up in his eyes and clearly visualising the scenes of that time, he concluded, in a quiet voice, that war is a terrible thing to be avoided at all costs.[2] The plight of the evacuees like these, the sense of shock and anger at the invasion and the levels of damage inflicted on civil installations, including oil refineries, created a wave of patriotism across Iran. A spasm of national indignation replaced revolutionary zeal, and even surpassed it. While the revolution had divided Iranians, so the war united them. Hundreds volunteered for the war effort, and, as the civilians evacuated from the war zone, they were replaced with those eager to defend Iranian soil. By contrast, the Iraqis, who had expected to be greeted as liberators in Khuzestan by a grateful Arab population, found themselves confronted by resistance from both regular forces and irregular fighters.

The invasion also united the political and religious leaders in Tehran. The revolutionaries suspended the purges and executions. The army was no longer the target of their anger, despite the coup attempt of July 1980, because the regime now needed it. New weapons and supplies arrived from Syria, Libya and North Korea to augment the former Shah's arsenal, giving some hope that an effective resistance could now be maintained. Buoyed by the obvious support of the people, the Iranian armed forces started to recover. Khomeini made President Bani-Sadr chairman of the seven-strong Supreme Defence Council, despite his previous animosity towards him. Its terms of reference were simple: win the war.

On 11 October, the Iraqi army crossed the Karun river 10 miles (16 km) north-east of Khorramshahr, cutting the road to Ahvaz and effectively isolating the city. The Iraqis pressed on and cut off Abadan from the east. The only chance the Iranians had was to obtain supplies from the coast, or to hope for relief from the north and east. Dezful still held out, which proved a strategic disadvantage for the Iraqis; they could not push further east without exposing their forces to the risk of a counter-stroke from the north. The Iranian defence of the area was being sustained by the determined counter-attacks of the Revolutionary Guards.[3] Despite their inferiority in numbers and reliance largely on small arms, these highly-motivated fighters carried out infantry assaults, ambushes and longer range sniping against the Iraqis. They suffered heavy casualties, particularly in their close-quarter battles with the better equipped Iraqi armoured formations. The most effective Iranian equipment turned out to be helicopters, which they used as improvised gunships. Nevertheless, acting on local information, Iranian units continued to resist in any way they could.

The stiffening resistance, already much more robust than Saddam had anticipated, necessitated a revision of the date by which the war should have been won. Originally it was thought that Iraq would have achieved all its objectives by 20 October, Eid al Adha, but Saddam gave a television address on the 19th in which he excused the failure as the result of superiority in Iranian numbers and weaponry, and the fact that Iranian aircraft could reach deep into Iraq, whereas short-range Iraqi jets could not hope to have the same effect on Iranian cities, installations and military formations.[4] In fact, while the Iraqis indeed possessed fewer guns and aircraft, they outnumbered the Iranian armour by two to one. The truth was that Saddam had miscalculated. He had pursued a flawed strategy of a limited incursion into Iran, and now he had lost the initiative. Either the Iraqis had to increase their effort and restore a momentum into Iran, which was unlikely, or it would have to accept less ambitious results. Indeed, with the chance of a '1967-style' victory slipping away, he would either have to fight a longer and costly war, negotiate a settlement immediately from a position of relative strength, or accept an ignominious withdrawal.

There was also the option of pan-Arabism and the appeal of Islam. With great cynicism, Saddam, the arch-secularist, described the struggle against Iran as a jihad against Persian heretics. He told his countrymen to look upon the war as the 'Second [Battle of] Qadasiya', invoking the idea of Arab Muslims crushing the Persian Sassanian Empire in 637 AD. He referred to the Iranians as the descendants of Khosrow, the last Sassanian emperor, and of Rustam, the Persian leader who went down to defeat at Qadasiya. With one eye on the rest of the Arab world, he urged his troops to decapitate Iranians as if armed with 'the sword of Allah' and described the enemy as aggressors who followed the 'lunatic Khomeini'. To reinforce his personal message, Saddam organised the Sunni and Shia ulema into a pro-Iraqi war effort. They publically denounced the Iranian brand of Islam, and visited front-line units to stir the troops.

Initially, the increased Iraqi tempo appeared to be producing results. In just three weeks, the Iraqi forces pushed further into Iran. Heavy artillery concentrations were used in front of every advance, literally smashing resistance in their path. On 24 October, they bridged the Shatt al Arab and fought their way into the outskirts of Khorramshahr. Inevitably, once inside the urban environment, the pace of advance slowed. Saddam was anxious that fighting in built-up areas would dramatically increase the costs of the war and neutralise his temporary technological advantage. To make matters worse, there were reports filtering from the front line of some Shia Iraqi soldiers, who made up the majority of the army, firing on their own side. It appears these were not accidental 'friendly fire' incidents, but moments of crisis in the loyalty of Saddam's army.[5]

Distributed throughout buildings in Khorramshahr and Abadan, the Iranians could draw the Iraqis into close-quarter combat and create a stalemate. However, the resort to defending streets and houses with small arms, and the absence of any significant counter-offensive, was evidence of the confusion that reigned in Tehran. The only strategy appeared to be one of defending every inch of ground with what it had, while reinforcements filtered from the northern provinces. The new regime did not trust its armed forces and was reluctant to support them or to allow senior officers to direct the war. Khomeini even had to step in to demand that clerics stopped interfering in the direction of the fighting at a tactical and operational level. Rather than the Iranians seizing the initiative, they continued to react to events. Yet, Saddam was, in essence, now limiting himself. Believing that an assault on Abadan would cost too many lives, he decided instead to impose a siege. The siege was hardly effective, since Abadan retained its access to the sea and this the Iranians used to trickle supplies and munitions to their beleaguered garrison.

Taking stock

Little of the grim reality of the situation had appeared in the media in either country. In Iraq, there were triumphant broadcasts about captured territory (10,000 sq miles/25,900 sq km along a 735-mile/1,182 km front), about Saddam's brilliant leadership, and epic actions in the 'conquest of Persia'. There was little doubt this was Saddam's war. Having already established a leader cult, Saddam used every opportunity to identify himself with the successes of the war. He appeared in uniform more frequently, was filmed visiting headquarters, discussing the fighting with the generals, and conferring with the National Assembly as it rubber-stamped his utterances about the war effort. These broadcasts and a press conference on 10 November also indicated Iraq's emerging war aims. If Saddam felt any concern about the operational situation, he made no hint of that in his claim that, since Iran was the aggressor and Iraqis had been sacrificed in the defence of the nation, Iraq would put forward 'additional rights' which would be 'revealed' in future battles.[6] While assiduously avoiding the words 'territorial claims', and denying any intention to break up Iran, he nevertheless noted that he would support the ambitions of Arabistanis, Baluchis and Azerbaijanis, and, in a statement designed to appeal to the Arab world, he stressed his backing for the free navigation of the Persian Gulf, particularly the Strait of Hormuz. Tehran was determined to reject the first Iraqi overtures, and threw out the idea of either a ceasefire or negotiation. Drawing on its own Islamic rhetoric, the Iranian regime claimed it was compelled to fight as a religious duty. Khomeini consciously linked the despised Shah and Saddam together in the minds of the Iranian people, describing the struggle as essentially the same: against corruption, against oppression and in the defence of Islam.

In November, the rains set in and the Iraqi attempt to seize Susangard between the 14th and 17th failed, in part because of the difficulties in getting manpower and logistics across the mass of water courses in the area. By the end of the month, the Iraqis concentrated on digging in and consolidating, with a new asphalt road to link rear areas with the front lines through the winter. Iran prepared to strike back in a symbolic amphibious raid on 29 and 30 November at Fao and the Mina al Bakr terminal. The raid and combined air and sea operations effectively halted Iraqi oil exports in all but their Turkish and Syrian pipelines, cutting their revenue and reducing their pre-war export of 3.24 million barrels per day (bpd) to half a million. It was an indication that this war would be fought on several fronts: ideological, economic as well as military. But this was also to be a protracted war and the Iraqi National Defence Council was forced to set aside considerable revenue. Nevertheless, despite the failure to achieve their strategic objectives, the Iraqis felt confident about their position. They had an experienced, well-equipped army, and there was still strong congruence in the military-political elite. Geographically, they were in occupation of enemy territory that, for the most part, favoured armoured and mechanised divisions in which Iraq had the advantage. The Iraqis could boast twelve combat effective divisions of which seven were deployed against two weakened Iranian divisions in Khuzestan.

By contrast, Iran's armed forces were still reorganising, and there had been a purge of the senior leadership after a failed coup attempt in July 1980. To make matters worse, President Bani-Sadr, who was the acting commander-in-chief, disagreed with Mohammed Ali Rajai, the leading member of the cabinet who enjoyed the backing of the ulema, on the prosecution of the war. Rajai was able to control the Revolutionary Guards independently of the regular armed forces for a full three weeks until Khomeini stepped in. The compromise was to allow the Revolutionary Guards to defend the urban areas and villages, while the army concentrated on counter-attacks in rural areas, but there was little effective coordination with the result that, while stubborn in their defence of built-up areas, Iranian offensives failed.

The Iraqi army had been schooled in Soviet doctrine, with large-scale defence in depth and combined arms' thrusts while on the offensive. The Soviet system had been to concentrate great volumes of artillery fire on specific objectives to destroy static defences and to pour troops along relatively unopposed axes, the idea being to 'reinforce success'. Soviet doctrine also emphasised that urban areas were to be neutralised with fire and by-passed where possible. The problem was that the fighting revealed significant difficulties with the Iraqi armed forces. The army's combat experience was in fighting Kurdish irregulars in internal security operations, not the deep armoured battle. Moreover, the Iraqi air force, which Saddam feared might one day be the basis of a coup d'état against him, was directed one squadron at a time by Saddam personally. It lacked training in air-ground cooperation with the result that it failed to provide intimate support for the army. The army also lacked the command and control systems to organise air defence. Anti-aircraft missiles failed to function as expected, it had too few channels of communication with its air assets and there were inadequate air defences around its vital oil installations – with the consequence of a catastrophic loss of strategic export revenue.

To end the year, Saddam made an attempt to link up with Kurdish insurgents within Iran, but the penetration was checked. In Tehran, conscious of the domestic pressure to strike back and buoyed by the success of the Fao raid, the Iranian regime ordered a counter-offensive in the Dezful–Susangard area. Three weak armoured regiments, lacking infantry support, advanced to contact in a much-broadcast attempt to recover prestige. The Iraqis deliberately drew the advance into a killing area near the border at Hoveizeh. Tanks in hull-down positions, supported by entrenched infantry and some opportunist air strikes, blazed at the advancing Iranians, inflicting the loss of 140 vehicles. The Iranian counter-attack disintegrated and both sides settled down to endure the winter weather and await the arrival of spring.

From a strategic point of view, it was not so much weaknesses in the Iraqi armed forces as the errors in the campaign plan itself that accounted for the failure to achieve any lasting results in the war, and these were the responsibility of Saddam Hussein. He had expected the Iranians to negotiate once he had made a limited incursion into Iran, but this expectation was surely unrealistic, particularly when he had achieved no decisive victory. Moreover, if the intention had been to secure Khuzestan in order to secure its oil then the failure to protect Iraq's existing facilities once hostilities had begun seems like criminal neglect. If, however, the aim was to crush the revolution, then too little emphasis was placed on the propaganda effort or indirect means and too great an emphasis was placed on a military campaign which was bound to ignite Iranian nationalist sentiment against Iraq. If there was an expectation that the Sunni population of Khuzestan would greet the Iraqis as liberators, then this also appears to have been the very worst miscalculation. Indeed, one is led to the question: what was it that Saddam hoped to achieve? Even at the operational level, Saddam's planning was at fault. His attempt to secure Khorramshahr, Abadan, Ahwaz and Dezful at the same time could only have succeeded with a rapid and decisive military victory and the collapse of Iranian resistance. The focus on both port and inland oil facilities was based on the false premise, articulated by an over-optimistic intelligence service, that Khuzestanis would join Iraq willingly. The only operationally significant location was Dezful, because of its air assets and location at a nodal point in the Iranian transport and supply chain.

The Iraqis had also failed because, as the Americans put it, 'the enemy gets a vote'. Iranian resistance was far stronger than expected, and the 30,000-strong Revolutionary Guard Corps were highly motivated and willing to take significant casualties in their desperate defence. Moreover, a long war favoured the Iranians. Given time, they could mobilise up to 400,000 reservists and appeal to the patriotic sentiment of many troops who had been loyal to the Shah and who could be reconciled to the regime. Eventually they could call on a large population for recruits. They could also begin to organise their resources, particularly the large arsenal that had once belonged to the Pahlavi regime. Indeed, it was ironic but fortunate for the Iranians that their lack of preparedness had meant that few units were exposed to the initial Iraqi onslaught, and could be fed into the theatre of operations later. Once they had recovered from the shock of the invasion, the Iranians flooded certain areas to deny them to the Iraqis and began to organise their defence. Street fighting in Khorramshahr had taken the Iraqis by surprise, and Saddam's continued unwillingness to keep up any momentum or risk heavy losses in built-up areas, which he had made his objectives, gave the Iranians vital breathing space. Retaliatory Iranian air raids in September, the air and amphibious assault at Fao in November, and the Iranian navy's block-ade of the Iraqi flotilla, exposed Saddam to the realities of his war. As he himself admitted, geography did not favour Iraq, for Iranian strategic targets were dispersed over a wide area, while Iraqis ones all lay close to the Iranian western border and within easy reach of its air force.

Thus, while there had been three Iraqi thrusts into Iran which had led to the occupation of important terrain (Mehran, Dezful, Qasr-e-Shirin and Penjwin), and that seemed to amount to a victory, the flaws in Saddam's expectations were fully exposed as early as November 1980. Although soundly exploiting nationalist and religious sentiment, his decision to continue the campaign could not conceal the failure of his original objectives and put at risk everything he had achieved to that point. These traits of Saddam Hussein as a leader, particularly in light of his subsequent defiance of the international community, of weapons inspections, and his equally disastrous conflicts in 1991 and 2003, seem to be consistent themes of his entire career. During the Iran–Iraq War, his personality affected the Iraqi conduct of the war and he was, in short, lucky to survive in power. Yet the fact that he did survive indicates where his priorities lay. His subsequent appeal to the Iranians for peace, where he openly stated that his regime should be preserved (even at the cost of his national interests), reflects his priorities in the 1980s and after. Saddam understood the utility of propaganda and the nature of political power, but he was not always sophisticated enough to know how to use it effectively and as a strategist he had clearly failed.

The waning of the Iraqi offensive

In the winter of 1980–81, three organisations hoped to restore peace in the Gulf region. The first, the UN, represented the post-war aspiration that conventional wars and their associated costs could be halted or contained. The second, the Organisation of Islamic Conference (OIC), hoped to safeguard the interests of fellow Muslims by ending divi-sions between Islamic countries. The third, the Non-Aligned Movement, looked to reject the Cold War, bipolar domination of East and West so as to champion the interests of less-developed countries, particularly by avoiding wars in which the West or the Soviets might intervene. There were high hopes among delegates that a negotiated settlement would be preferred by both belligerents. On 1 March Khomeini met with the OIC and called upon it to condemn Iraqi aggression, while a similar message emanated from Baghdad condemning the Iranians. On 5 March, the OIC put forward its peace plan, which involved a ceasefire effective in one week's time, to be followed by an Iraqi withdrawal from the occupied territory. Iran rejected the plan and Iraq refused to accept any withdrawal until Iran recognised Iraqi rights.[7] Both rejections were based on specific calculations. Khomeini believed that Iraqi willingness to negotiate revealed Saddam's weakness and the merit in pushing Baghdad harder with a military solution. Saddam was looking for the Iranians to cave in and settle given their position of weakness, but, sensing that insufficient pressure had been applied, he highlighted the point by launching an attack on 19 and 20 March to capture Susangard. The failure of the operation undermined Saddam's position. It gave the impression that the Iraqis were at the limit of their capacity and the Iranian defences were too strong for them. Even the use of Frog-7 surface-to-surface missiles, a weapon that potentially can carry nuclear or chemical warheads, against Dezful and Ahvaz, failed to make any impression on the Iranians.

Instead there was just a hint that Iran actually enjoyed Syrian backing. On 4 April 1981, an Iranian air strike was made against the Iraqi bomber base at Walid, close to the Syrian border, and in the raid, conducted below radar level, forty-six Iraqi aircraft were destroyed.[8] The Iraqis claimed they had been able to track the raiders and that they had made use of Syrian airspace and perhaps even refuelled there. The Syrians denied the accusations, but had clearly benefited strategically from the neutralisation of the Iraqi bombers so close to their own frontier. The war of words continued. Iraq dropped any pretence about Khuzestan and argued that it would be content to see Iran dismembered. In response, the Iranian parliamentary speaker, Hojatalislam Ali Akbar Hashemi Rafsanjani, stated that the deposing of Saddam Hussein was now a strategic objective on which there could be no compromise.

Spring floods on the Tigris–Euphrates had prevented much of a buildup for new offensives until the end of March 1981. The delay added to a sense of frustration on the Iraqi side with a lack of progress. Further pressure was added by Khomeini's repeated appeals to Shia troops in the Iraqi army to rebel against infidel, oppressive and Ba'athist leadership. Today, it is easy to discount the appeal of rhetoric, but, so soon after the revolution, the sheer resonance of Khomeini's voice, with all its bleak austerity and gravitas, was hard for many Shi'ites to ignore. Several officers were later accused of having formed an anti-Saddam faction that was preparing a coup d'état. Its discovery by Iraqi military intelligence in June 1981 served the purpose of tightening discipline and loyalty to the regime at a time of considerable doubt and anxiety. Whether the conspirators were really behind five assassination attempts in as many months was not the point. Conscious of the need to bind the army to him personally, Saddam attempted to win it over by increasing compensation, awarding land and, bizarrely, television sets to the families of war dead, now styled exclusively as 'martyrs'. The media went into overdrive: posters of Saddam, the 'greatest Arab since the fall of Baghdad to the Mongols in 1257' and the 'symbol of the Arab revival', were distributed, and his birthday became a national holiday.[9] A film, *The Battle of Qadasiya*, portrayed the Iraqis as victors because of their nationalist, Arab and Islamic convictions. Promotions and decorations were presented more frequently. To show solidarity with the national effort, Saddam even deployed elements of the Popular Army, the loyalist Ba'ath Party militia, to the front. The Popular Army never lost sight of its primary function, namely internal security, and it kept the Iraqi officer corps under close surveillance.

Saddam's main measure for improving the army's loyalty was to give it military success. Instead of dissipating effort across the entire south-eastern front, the focus was to be Abadan. Control of the island would enable the Iraqis to gain full access to the Shatt al Arab, thereby bringing to an end dependence on land-based supply routes and Arab neighbours. By the middle of the year, Iraq had concentrated 60,000 troops and 1,000 tanks around the city. The Iranians had no more than 10,000 available, consisting of a mechanised brigade, an armoured regiment with 50 tanks and a naval battalion. Their lines of communication depended on one road, to Khosrowabad, and the river to Bandar Mashahr.

On the eve of the battle for Abadan, the Iranian army and the clerical leadership appeared to have settled some of their differences, the war against Iraq having provided a common interest. President Bani-Sadr was removed, and Rajai succeeded him, which created a more united chain of command. The armed forces responded, declaring their loyalty to Khomeini. There was consequently more tolerance for the Islamic Revolutionary Guards and their volunteer militia, the Basiji Mustazafin (The Mobilised Oppressed). For all newly raised units, Islamic education was a prominent feature. The ulema stressed the historic nature of the war, arguing how it was a re-enactment of much earlier struggles for the defence of Islam and Shi'ism. Saddam's aggression, they were told, constituted an attack on Islam itself, since Iran was the first properly constituted Islamic state. Martyrdom in battle compelled an enthusiasm for the war that was barely understood in the West at the time. Soldiers created wills which testified to their willingness to go to the deaths for the sake of Islam. There was significant prestige for families who lost a male relative, with official blessings and material benefits. The government established the Martyrs Foundation which gave widows or parents $3,300 a year with an additional child allowance of $670. Military personnel received a grant of $24,000 and servicemen's families got preferential treatment in the allocation of scarce goods or services, from a motorbike to a car, and from jobs to university education. More importantly, the war effort was increasingly better organised. The battle of Abadan was to be the first test of that coordination.

To draw Iraqi troops away from their objective, in July and August the Iranians made a series of small probing attacks. Keeping up the distraction, the Iranians pushed two light infantry divisions across the Bahmanshir into Abadan at night. Elements of the garrison then made a series of daring attacks, pinning the Iraqi strong points while penetrating into depth where resistance was light. The Iraqis were surprised by the sorties and several posts were overrun or capitulated when they were encircled; some 1,500 were killed. Iranian losses were also heavy, with about 3,000 dead, an unsurprising outcome given their infiltration tactics against entrenched positions. The Iranians succeeded in persuading the Iraqis to pull back across the Karun and to terminate their plans for a final assault on the city.

Saddam would not countenance a withdrawal to the Shatt al-Arab but, as yet, the Iranians lacked the strength to drive the Iraqis out. Indeed, the Iraqis still had the capacity to inflict significant damage on the Iranians. An air strike on the Iranian oil terminal on Kharg Island in October caused considerable disruption and a loss of much-needed revenue, at a time when oil exports were struggling to reach ten per cent of the pre-revolution levels anyway. Iran had imposed strict regulations over imports, but it could barely afford even essential goods. Only a campaign against 'consumerism' and the ruthless application of rationing in rice, sugar, cooking oil and, perhaps more surprisingly, petrol, enabled the regime to survive the crisis. In one respect it had an abundance of resources, and that was manpower. With unemployment at 15 per cent and a larger population than Iraq, the Iranian regime could afford to use this resource to its advantage on the battlefield. Conscription was doubled at the outbreak of war, sweeping up thousands of young men of military age. These men were not reluctant fighters, and they were often highly motivated. Inspired by the injunctions to defend Islam and the sovereignty of Iran against Iraqi aggressors, they sped through their training with genuine eagerness to get into the war.

The Iranian counter-offensives

The Iranians launched a counter-offensive strategy in three phases. The first phase lasted from mid-November 1981 to February 1982, the second from March to April 1982, and the final phase took place in May 1982. The first phase, fought throughout the wet weather, consisted of a series of small-scale attacks on Iraqi positions. Little by little, they compelled the Iraqis to pull back their most forward outposts from Abadan and the area to the north of Susangard, and from the central front around Qasr-e Shirin. With these constant off-balancing attacks, the Iranians hoped to conceal the concentration of their main effort: a full seven divisions were amassed in the Dezful–Shush area. Two of them were armoured divisions and two consisted of Revolutionary Guards and Basiji militia. Opposite these formations lay three tired Iraqi divisions and eight separate brigades, complacent in their belief that the Iranians would not attack on the eve of a major holiday period. On 19 March, with commandos making attacks deep behind Iraqi lines, the two armoured divisions spearheaded a surprise assault on two axes.

The 'break-in' battle was a success and the Iranians chose to keep up the momentum by a shift in tactics. To exhaust Iraqi ammunition and manpower, waves of Revolutionary Guards light infantry armed with small arms and shoulder-launched rocket propelled grenades dashed forward in battalion strength, each 1,000-man group separated by a gap of 500 yards. Iranian regular troops followed on with heavier weapons. These waves overwhelmed some positions, albeit at a heavy cost. Where Iraqi armour was concentrated in a hull-down posture, Iranian armour was brought in to pound these static positions. According to Iranian sources, the Iraqis lost 300 tanks destroyed while a further 350 fell into Iranian hands. Tehran also claimed to have killed 10,000 and wounded a further 15,000, with 15,450 taken captive. Their own losses they put at 4,000 with 8,000 wounded. Such estimates seem optimistic in a war characterised by inflated claims of success. The Iranians put great emphasis on the recovery of lost territory as a metric of their success. The expulsion of the Iraqis from Iranian soil was a key motivating factor in the national war effort and so the regime had to show that its leadership was effective and capable of producing tangible results.

The Iranians, perhaps fatally, believed that the dash and courage of their light infantry, especially the Revolutionary forces, had been the basis of the *Fatah al Mobin* (Clear Victory). Such a view fitted with their romanticised notion of war fighting and Persian patriotism. They could even believe their cause was righteous and enjoyed divine support. But the more prosaic analysis would reveal that this was a battle of mass: greater firepower, concentrated locally; greater manpower, which stretched and spread thin Iraq's defensive firepower; and the logic of a perimeter line overrun and thrown into confusion by penetration into depth.

Both sides had prepared for the air battle and had expected air supremacy over the entrenched lines. The Iraqis had lost more than 100 aircraft to date in the war and new French F-1s were purchased to restore capability. There were extensive sorties, but Iranian air defences, including Soviet SAM-7 and masses of anti-aircraft guns, made headway difficult.[10] The Iranians, too, had suffered heavy losses in the first phase of the war, with 175 aircraft downed and of the 250 planes remaining only half were airworthy. With no means to acquire or manufacture replacements, the Iranians had to marshal their dwindling air fleet. They resorted to equipping helicopters with heat-seeking missiles as the means to provide intimate support to infantry against Iraqi armour.

As the war began to turn in Iran's favour, Syria took advantage of the situation. It announced the closure of the Iraqi–Syrian border and severed oil pipelines to Banias and Tripoli. Iraq's oil exports, already much reduced, were slashed by two-thirds to just 600,000bpd, causing chaos in the economy. Frantic diplomatic efforts were made to open new exports routes through the Gulf states, especially Kuwait and Saudi Arabia. Syria was persuaded to reopen the pipelines with lucrative transit fees and, by September 1982, Iraq had restored its output to about half of its pre-war level. Then Kurdish groups grew restive in the crisis and a new front appeared to be opening to the north.

As Iraq struggled to maintain its control of the home front (see Chapter 8), the Iranians launched their third offensive in late April–May 1982. On 29–30 April, the assault known as Bait al Muqaddas (literally, Sacred House, or, more colloquially, Jerusalem), opened with an advance south from the Dezful–Shush area on three axes. Seventy thousand troops and 200 tanks used the same tactics as before: a night assault by infantry to break in to the Iraqi positions, with armour used against fortified positions. After daybreak, there were further attacks spearheaded by tanks and armoured vehicles, with support from a handful of attack helicopters. Having suffered from these types of attacks in the preceding months, the Iraqis manoeuvred their armour rather than remaining in static positions, and larger Iranian armoured formations gave the Iraqi pilots more targets, so they scored some successes with the new French aircraft they had just purchased. However, the Iraqi Popular

Army was a disappointment. Poorly trained and badly equipped, they were often too ready to surrender.

The Iranians were able to sweep forward in most sectors of the southern front. The Iraqis recovered sufficiently to deliver a counter-attack on 3–4 May and succeeded in retaking some lost ground. The Iranians then switched the direction of their assault and seized the Iraqi border town of Fakeh on 9 May, which had the effect of severing the Iraqi supply route to the east. To save two divisions, the Iraqis were forced to suspend their counter-offensive to tackle this problem. Yet the Iranians were able to press on, recapturing the area to the north of Khorramshahr before reaching Shalamche on the Shatt al Arab, just short of Basra. On the 13th, Shalamche fell to the Iranians.

This development occupied the Iraqis' attention while the Iranians were focused on the retaking of Khorramshahr. By the middle of May, the Iranians had taken all of the roads into the city, and, since the city was entirely surrounded by marshland, the Iraqis were dependent on the Shatt al Arab as their sole line of communication. The city was protected by three lines of entrenchments and minefields, with a garrison of 35,000. Even if the Iranians were able to penetrate the defence lines, the street fighting would inevitably be bloody for both sides. At least that was the expectation. Having assembled a force of 70,000, the Iranians began their assault at night on 22 May. It took 36 hours for them to fight through the defence lines at some cost. The Iraqis, once again hoping to preserve their manpower, chose not to fight for the streets, but to conduct a tactical withdrawal. Losses were heavier than expected and the Popular Army in some sectors simply gave up. About 12,000 Iraqi prisoners of war were taken, and there are lingering allegations that 2,000 of these men were summarily executed in revenge for rapes of Iranian women. Such accounts are almost impossible to verify among the claims and counter-claims. What is clear is that the city was utterly devastated and resembled the ruins of Berlin or Stalingrad in the Second World War. The destruction seemed to take on a poignant symbolism for the Iranians, as if one of their cities had shown courageous defiance and had been 'martyred'.

The result of the offensive was that the city was retaken and the Iranians were jubilant. The achievement seemed to fit with the regime's narrative of 'liberation' and religious victory over apostasy and secularism. For the Iraqis, there was little to disguise this defeat. Two of its four armoured divisions were severely depleted and the army as a whole was reduced to from 200,000 to 150,000 combat effective personnel. The Iraqi air force had suffered significant attrition since the beginning of the war, with 100 serviceable combat aircraft left from an original fleet of 335. Some senior officers were in prison for their failures, others had been executed, but the effect of this was to make the entire command system more cautious and less likely to act boldly or with resolution. Tariq Aziz, the Iraqi foreign minister, told journalists: 'There were mistakes by some commanders, negligence by others, and especially incompetence and lack of composure in the [southern] sector.'[11] Worse, Iraq appeared to be isolated from the Arab world, contrary to its expectations. Saddam's appeal to the Arab League's Joint Arab Defence Agreement of 1950, to give military assistance to another League member at the height of the battle for Khorramshahr, was ignored.

Yet there were other reasons for the Iraqi setbacks. The emphasis on operating deeper inside Iran and on a wider front than the logistical chain could support, the unwillingness to organise a defence in depth and the difficulty in deploying artillery concentrations in the marshy terrain had been contributory factors. The most disturbing feature from the high command's point of view was the lack of commitment among the Popular Army personnel and the rumblings of discontent among some regular units. Regular army officers did not trust the Popular Army, even as a reserve, and the surrenders at Khorramshahr seemed to create a cyclical argument. In fact, Saddam's instruction in May 1982 that all deserters were to be shot increased the likelihood that they would surrender to the Iranians. On 30 May, riots broke out among Shias in the southern Iraqi cities of Basra, Karbala, Hilleh and Nasiriyeh, and in Shia districts of Baghdad. Absence without leave among Shia soldiers had increased, and the regime had been forced to make concessions, including a military ordinance that deserters were not to be punished as long as they rejoined their unit within a month. Al Daawa stepped up its campaign amid the unrest. Arms and volunteers from Iran enabled the group to carry out sabotage attacks and assassinations. On 28 May 1982, they detonated bombs in an ammunition depot and fuel storage tanks near Baghdad airport.[12]

New efforts were made to punish dissidents and to reconcile the Shias to the regime. The Ministry of Waqfs [religious endowments] and Religious Affairs was expanded. More funds were allocated to the renovation and repair of mosques. Five million copies of the Koran were printed for free distribution outside Iraq. In speeches, including that on the anniversary of Imam Ali's birthday, Saddam stressed the importance of the southern Shia cities as Arab and Iraqi settlements and invoked the idea that Imam Ali was an Arab ancestor not an Iranian one. There were more appearances of Saddam as the pious Muslim, more efforts to portray him as the friend of Shia ulema, but equally more surveillance of suspects, both Shia and Sunni, especially in the holy cities of the south. The Committee of Religious Indoctrination, made up of 'reliable' ulema, monitored sermons. The Popular Army's efforts in this regard were stepped up with regular patrols. However, Shia dissidence could be just as effective when unspoken. Ayatollah Abol Qasim Khoei, the most senior Shia figure in Iraq, had supported Saddam publicly before the conflict, but he remained silent on the issue of the war. Saddam responded by having some of his students arrested.

The Iranians stepped up the pressure on Saddam by stating that they would only negotiate a peace settlement if Saddam was deposed. President Assad of Syria and King Fahd of Saudi Arabia responded to this injunction with a spate of diplomacy: Assad suggested that Ahmad Hassan Bakr should be made president, while Fahd thought Shafiq Daraji, the Iraqi ambassador in Riyadh, would make a better choice. What they could agree on was that the Gulf Co-operation Council (GCC) should oversee a Gulf Reconstruction Fund, to be financed by the GCC, as a means to pay for Iranian reparations. The GCC also put forward a peace plan on 2 June 1982. This called for an immediate ceasefire, a withdrawal by both sides to the 1975 borders and the initiation of negotiations to address the causes of the conflict. These efforts were overshadowed by the Israeli invasion of Lebanon on 5 June 1982.

There is some evidence to suggest that Israel was provoked into action by Iraq. The attempted assassination on 3 June of Shlomo Argov, the Israeli ambassador in London, was orchestrated by Nawal Rosan, a colonel in Iraqi Intelligence. It was hoped that the Israelis would assume it was a Palestinian strike and would use the assassination as the grounds to attack the Palestinian Liberation Organisation in southern Lebanon. The Iraqis attempted to deflect attention from themselves by calling for an immediate end to the war in order to confront Israeli aggression. The OIC, indeed, called for a ceasefire and Iraq was the first to respond positively. In a carefully stage-managed event on 9 June, the Revolutionary Command Council and Ba'ath Party leaders met to consider and then approve the move, signalling its approval to move back to the 1975 borders as a gesture of goodwill and to accept an inquiry into the causes of the war made up of delegates from the Muslim world. Saddam did not attend. Some international observers assumed that Saddam was being sidelined and that a change of leadership was imminent. Khomeini gloated and, believing Saddam was on the verge of being purged, refused the Iraqi peace offer again. Instead of conciliation, he likened Iraq to

Israel, arguing that both states sought to invade others' sovereign territory and then negotiate from a position of strength. He rejected Iraq's offer to transport Iranian volunteers to Lebanon, arguing that their primary duty was to liberate Iran first. He then committed a strategic error. He demanded that the Ba'ath be rooted out of Iraq, and the country liberated 'from the accursed party'.[13]

This one comment had the effect of driving the Ba'ath loyalists ever closer to Saddam and, more importantly, it persuaded the armed forces that only by supporting Saddam and the regime could there be any chance of success in mobilising the country and of giving the armed forces the tools they needed. Saddam detected this mood in the conversations he had with senior officers at the front. Far from being ousted, Saddam had deliberately avoided being personally associated with offers of peace knowing that, if they failed, he could distance himself from any blame. He instead embarked on the withdrawal of his forces from southern Iran. The decision was inevitable given the state of his army and the likelihood of further crippling Iranian offensives in the future. He calculated that defending Iraqi soil would galvanise the army and the people to fight more determinedly. It would also shorten the supply lines and make defence in depth a reality. Saddam tried to conceal the failure of his original strategy, arguing that Iraq had never intended to retain the southern Iranian territories. His intention, he continued, had been to smash the Iranian armed forces and this plan remained extant. To effect the strategy, it was necessary to withdraw from certain points in order to consolidate and strengthen more important areas.[14]

In late June, Saddam held a secret conference among the Ba'ath regional party congress. In the opening session, some of which was later published, he accused 'enemies of the Ba'ath' of infiltrating the party. He drew attention to the students and workers branches of the movement, which had not shown sufficient resolve or support for the party. The incompetence of certain officials was to be tackled and more robust local leadership was needed, and particularly greater willingness to heed the high command's rulings. These chilling remarks were not misunderstood by any of the 250 delegates; the Saddam dictatorship was going to punish dissidence more severely, starting with the party itself. A new discipline was imminent. Saddam was pulling the party more tightly to him, to snuff out any chance of conspiracy or coup. Riyad Ibrahim Hussein, the health minister and a proponent of bringing former president Bakr into office to replace Saddam, was sacked and subsequently executed in October that year '*pour encouragez les autres*' [to encourage the others]. The Regional Command Council was reduced from seventeen to nine men, consisting of Saddam's most trusted aides and relatives. His step-brother, Barzan Tikriti, was retained as chief of intelligence. The deputy commander-in-chief of the army and defence minister was his cousin and brother in law, Adnan Khairallah Tulfa. Sabawi Ibrahim, another stepbrother, was chief of police. Just two of the inner council were Shia and one was Kurdish. Of the new men brought in, four were Shia, but all were grateful for their posts and therefore loyal. Saddam also reorganised provincial and local party leadership, with a group of new men looking to prove their loyalty where others had failed. No one would associate Saddam himself with the failed strategy at the opening of the war; they blamed the sacked party functionaries for that.

However, Saddam was not safe. As he and his escort drove through Dujayal, north of Baghdad, Al Daawa attempted to assassinate him in an ambush of machine guns and rocket-propelled grenades. Ten of Saddam's bodyguards were killed, but in the reprisals 150 people were killed and parts of the town were demolished. Despite references to the need to Islamicise the mobilisation of the Iraqi people and therefore gird their resistance to Iran, the regime clearly did not subscribe to the sort of revolutionary idealism that inspired Al Daawa and its backers in Tehran. Saddam referred to the need to invoke Islam in order to strengthen a nationalist cause and the idea of pan-Arabism, but he saw no central role for religion in politics, and certainly not a theocracy. Saddam also used a variety of other tools to denigrate the Iranian war effort. Khomeini was regularly caricatured, but the Iranian rejection of the peace offer was portrayed as evidence of an Iranian–Israeli plot. These two states, he argued, sought to weaken Iraq and ultimately destroy its independence in order to further their own regional hegemony. Indeed, the change of the tide in the war was attributed to the arrival of foreign, namely Israeli expertise.[15] The emphasis on a secular, but still largely Sunni-orientated solution was appealing to the party and other loyalists. None wanted to see a victory for the brand of Islamic fundamentalism propagated by Iran and they had seen the consequences of defeat in the riots in the Shia cities of the south. The armed forces wanted a strong and unified civilian leadership, willing to keep the party out of military affairs and eager to guard their reputation whatever their fortunes in battle. Saddam was the one figure they felt could protect their interests and guarantee a full prosecution of the war.

Yet the assassination attempt at Dujayal also had the effect of increasing the reach and power of the intelligence services. Already renowned for their ruthlessness, they would surpass themselves in rooting out dissidence. Two more assassination attempts in July 1982 ruled out spontaneous visits to be photographed and filmed with the Iraqi people. Events were carefully stage-managed. The grandiose cult of personality, already well developed before the war, increased in momentum, such that statues and portraits of Saddam, often on a vast scale, protruded from hoardings, buildings and every public space across the country. The media broadcast songs, poems and letters of praise. As the circus of Saddam reached new heights, so the morale of the Iraqi people correspondingly suffered. The effect of the towering images of Saddam merely increased their fear that his intelligence services were everywhere. Saddam's own security was tightened, with palaces becoming fortified and large numbers of troops marking the presence of the leader. There were frequent changes in location, to throw assassins off the scent and to disrupt their plans. The traditionally secretive Ba'ath Party seemed more akin than ever to its Stalinist model, seeing enemy agents and assassins everywhere and creating a thick atmosphere of fear in all public and private life.

At the end of June, while Iraq consolidated its position on the domestic front and along its new defence line, the Iranian regime debated its response to the situation. Effectively it had to decide whether to begin negotiations for a final settlement with Iraq, or to advance into Iraqi territory to bring down the man they regarded as the architect of the war but also the personification of tyranny, cruelty and evil. The leaders in Tehran felt that Iran was certainly strengthening. It had overcome the Iraqi armed forces on the battlefield at Khorramshahr, it had crushed a Mujahideen-e Khalq revolt in June 1981 and survived the death of some of the leadership, including President Rajai and the prime minister, Muhammadjavad Bahoner. Its experiment with sales or barter agreements with developing countries had been suspended as it sought new military hardware for the war, but it had overcome the West's reluctance to buy Iranian oil, caused in part by world overproduction, by selling below the OPEC agreed price of $30 a barrel. In addition, its measures to control imports, namely the nationalisation of foreign trade, had produced more revenue for the war effort. Now the Iranian leaders had to decide how to prosecute the war.

4

Human Waves: Iran's Counter-Offensives into Iraq

The decision by Iran to take the war into Iraq was not a simple one. Operations had already been carried over the border, but, despite the offensives of September 1981 to March 1982, the Iranians had not yet recovered all of their own territory. The Supreme Defence Council in Tehran carefully weighed up the limitations of Iran's armed forces and the risks inherent on any attacks deeper into Iraq. The senior officers of the regular armed forces argued that Iran simply lacked the hardware, particularly armour, artillery and fighter aircraft, to defeat the Iraqis on their own soil. Moreover, logistical arrangements were inadequate, the country having barely managed the crisis of defence in 1981. Diplomatically, they risked squandering any sympathy they possessed against Iraq, which could mean the Libyans and Syrians might cut off existing and much needed supply of arms and ammunition. The ideologues on the council nevertheless argued that Iranian revolutionary zeal had already produced battlefield successes contrary to professional military advice. They believed, wrongly, that the Shia population in Iraq was on the verge of revolt against Saddam. Iraq, they reasoned, would be crippled by insurrection. Moreover, they argued that Iran need only occupy some of Iraq's oil fields to create a diplomatic advantage at the negotiating table. They won over many waverers by pointing out that Iraqi artillery still shelled Iranian settlements and only by driving them well back inside their own territory could Iran be freed from the bombardment. There were other, less attractive arguments that were no less important. Rising oil revenues gave Tehran a surplus with which to wage war, and the continuing high unemployment rates provided a pool of available young manpower. Moreover, since the outbreak of the war, many Iranians felt they had to support the regime. An early settlement of the conflict might reopen old fissures in Iranian society and end the unifying effect of the war.

When Rafsanjani finally announced the Iranian terms for a ceasefire on 9 June 1982, there was little expectation they would be accepted by Iraq, and some hope they would not. Tehran demanded the restitution of the terms of the 1975 agreement, which placed the Shatt al Arab in Iranian hands; the repatriation of 100,000 (Shia) Iraqi citizens; Iraqi acceptance of war guilt; the punishment of Saddam Hussein as a war criminal and the payment of a mammoth $100 billion in reparations. The UN responded to the Iranian demands by passing a Resolution on 12 July 1982 calling for an immediate ceasefire and a withdrawal to the pre-war borders. Tehran rejected the UN proposal and overnight launched its next major offensive: Ramazan-ul Mubarak (Blessed Ramadan).

Operation Ramadan

The focus of the offensive was Basra. The Iraqi defences consisted of successive lines of barbed wire, earthworks and entrenchments. Minefields and zones for the concentration of artillery fire covered the approaches. Machine guns and other weapons were sited for maximised fields of fire. More importantly the Iraqis knew the Iranians were coming. Broadcasts about the forthcoming offensives had been made quite publicly in Iran.

However, while the area immediately to the east of Basra was secure, to the north of the city, five Iranian divisions punched about 10 miles (16 km) into the Iraqi defences. The intention had been to cut access to the city from the north, the likely direction for any reinforcements. Pasdaran infantry led the assault, many units emerging from the Howizeh marshes. The Iranian infantry were soon pinned down or slowed as they tried to pick their way across a maze of obstacles. Carefully timing their response, the Iraqis counter-attacked with four divisions, spearheaded with armour. The Iranians found that their flanks were vulnerable and Iraqi units began to feel their way into a pincer. The Iranians fell back to their start line and the battle turned into a pounding match that lasted a week. Iraqi helicopter gunships and aircraft made resupply and concentration for the Iranians extremely difficult. Significantly, some Iraqi artillery fired CS gas (tear gas) to break up Iranian infantry waves and this proved so effective that the chain of command noted the results carefully. The Iraqis suffered heavy losses among two armoured brigades in their counter-attack, but the Iranians had suffered the gravest losses.

Two divisions had been badly affected, and their armoured and artillery elements had been significantly reduced.

The Revolutionary Guards, the Pasdaran-e inquilab-e Islami, were originally established to serve the clerics of the regime and it was envisaged they were to be deployed in a purely internal security role against the Kurdish minority and 'counter-revolutionaries'. The war transformed them and the auxiliaries or militia, the Basij, into military forces of considerable size. Tehran consistently denied that it recruited child soldiers into its forces, and that all its personnel were over the age of 16, but UNHCR reports provided contrary and empirical evidence.[1] Western media carried reports of the accoutrements they carried, including the plastic key as a symbol of entry to paradise.[2] Recruitment appeared to start as early as May 1982, suggesting that young people were not recruited as a measure of last resort to cover a gap in manpower.[3] Veterans have found it difficult to describe the experience of taking part in a human wave attack, but all accounts verify the heavy losses, the clearance of minefields by men running through them (ostensibly to save precious armoured vehicles) and the weight of Iraqi fire.[4] The Iranian newspaper *Ettela'at* stated: 'We had child-volunteers: 14, 15, and 16-year-olds. They went into the minefields. Their eyes saw nothing. Their ears heard nothing. And then, a few moments later, one saw clouds of dust. When the dust had settled again, there was nothing more to be seen of them. Somewhere, widely scattered in the landscape, there lay scraps of burnt flesh and pieces of bone.' The papers' authors then noted: 'Before entering the mine fields, the children [subsequently] wrap[ped] themselves in blankets and they roll on the ground, so that their body parts stay together after the explosion of the mines and one can carry them to the graves.'[5]

The Iranian leadership nevertheless believed that their tactical advantage lay in resolution, and that they had anticipated heavier losses than they could inflict on the Iraqis. The battle was to be decided, they believed, by breaking the Iraqis' morale. Consequently, without hesitation, they launched their second phase of the offensive on 21 July, just 12 miles (19 km) to the south at Zaid. As expected, the Iranians made their initial thrust at night but on two axes. Once again they pushed aside the perimeter line and penetrated into the Iraqi defensive belt. For a second time, the infantry were held up by Iraqi obstacles and intense fire and they were forced to fall back to avoid envelopment as the Iraqi armour lumbered into position on the flanks. Iranian airpower was so limited they could not hope to gain air superiority to cover their attacks and they lacked an adequate number of guns to neutralise Iraqi armour, (Iran had about 900 to Iraq's 1,800). Iran possessed only 900 tanks against Iraq's 3,000 and in the battle the Iranians could field only one armoured division. With 10,000 killed and wounded, the Iranians needed to rethink this entire offensive, but a third attempt was made to break into the Iraqi defences on 1 August 1982 between Zaid and Mashwa. This attack achieved even less, with the entire operation stalling and falling back in just three days. The total butcher's bill for Iran was in the region of 20,000 killed and severely wounded and a quarter of its precious equipment destroyed in just two weeks. Operation Ramadan was, by any standard, a criminal failure of leadership and strategy. There were rumours that the old divisions between the ulema and the regular army had reappeared, at least at a local level.

The Iranian leadership in Tehran still clung to the idea that the Ramadan Offensive had been a success because of its demonstration of resolve and the attrition of the fighting. Iraq, they argued, could not sustain the losses in the same way that Iran could, although their estimate of 7,000 Iraqi killed and wounded was double the actual losses. Moreover, given Iran's evident material weakness compared with Iraq, they believed that hurling swarms of infantry at Iraqi defences was bound to produce results eventually. The early successes they had enjoyed in the offensive known as Operation Jerusalem, they reasoned, had been achieved using precisely these methods. Anthony Cordesman accurately summed up the Iranian misconception:

> Iran's basic strategy was roughly equivalent to trying to use a hammer to destroy an anvil. Iran eventually broke its forces on this anvil by hammering away at Iraqi defences, scoring largely symbolic gains, and then pausing for months while it recovered its offensive capabilities. These repeated attacks also depleted Iran's cadre of leaders, skilled manpower and equipment. They deprived it of the tools it needed to take advantage of its superior manpower, and they undercut popular support for the war, military morale and Iran's recruiting base.[6]

To this one must add Khomeini's own convictions, which permeated the direction of the war. His deeply held faith in the moral value of martyrdom and sacrifice, forged in the crucible of the struggle, was designed to build a nation and stiffen revolutionary convictions as much as it was designed to win a war. It was extremely difficult for other members of the Iranian leadership to challenge such beliefs without appearing to undermine the legitimacy of the revolution, or the war effort. Mehdi

Haeri Yazd, a philosopher and Islamic jurist who had once studied with Khomeini, visited the Iranian leader at the height of this phase of the war. Haeri found Khomeini alone in his garden and used the opportunity to express his anguish at the human costs of the war, stating boldly that 'hundreds of thousands are dying in a war that has no end and no good purpose'.[7] Khomeini had, 'in reproachful tones', asked: 'Do you also criticise God when he sends an earthquake?' Perhaps Khomeini made the remark to suggest that he was not in control of such an event, but Haeri was 'shocked at Khomeini's implicit comparison of himself to the Almighty'. It was clear to Haeri that Khomeini believed he was so close to God that he was, in effect, God's lawgiver on earth, uniquely qualified and chosen to carry out God's purpose with an almost exclusive grasp of the truth. The idea that faith was sufficient to guide the Iranian forces was manifest in the absence of proper training for the Pasdaran. Their poorly coordinated attacks and brave, but inadequate tactical leadership had also been a cause of the Ramadan disaster.

By contrast, the Iraqis were making every effort to improve their technical and logistical advantage. To improve links to the front line, new roads were built, while tank transporters were purchased to save wear on armoured vehicles. Every effort was made to acquire the latest hardware in terms of weaponry and equipment, with stockpiles built up where possible. Training was continual. More importantly, the successful battle for Basra had demonstrated that Iranian offensives could be checked and defeated. Saddam, who had so carefully cultivated his image with the fortunes of the war, succeeded in getting the credit for the battle. He could also claim with some justification that the Shia of Basra had not risen up in revolt against Iraq, but had remained loyal. In fact, many had made the calculated judgement that an Iranian victory would offer no political benefits and all of the material costs of occupation, revolution and defeat. Moreover, it was difficult to contemplate, let alone organise a revolt when the Iraqi Popular Army and secret services were doing their utmost to snuff out dissent. Had Basra fallen to the Iranians, the situation may have more closely resembled that of 2003. Indeed, some Basra Shia Iraqis interviewed in the wake of the Coalition occupation expressed their sense of relief tinged with the fear that the Saddam loyalists and Ba'ath might come back to power and wreak their revenge against them.

In the 1980s Iran had gone to some lengths to rouse the Shia of Iraq to rebellion. Hojatalislam Baqir Hakim, the exiled Iraqi Shia ayatollah, had travelled to the front line, and, with Khomeini, had made dramatic calls on the Iraqis to overthrow Saddam. The effort failed just as Saddam's attempts to mobilise the Arab population of Khuzestan had failed, for the simple reason that national identity, local networks and personal survival determined their decision-making. Nevertheless, the Iraqi withdrawal to their own border had brought the Iranians within range of some densely populated areas. Even before the withdrawal, Iranian units had got to within 13 miles (21 km) of Basra. Now the second largest city of the country was within range of Iranian guns.

Saddam again stepped up the effort to improve Iraqi morale. With almost a third of the army depleted, he curtailed announcements of battle casualties in the media. Desertion, which remained a problem even though the front line was on Iraqi soil, was tackled with a new decree: absence for longer than five days was to be punished by the perpetrator being shot when caught. Those who had previously enjoyed exemption from military service were called up, including college students. The Popular Army was opened to non-Ba'ath membership to create a force of 400,000 and some specialist units were rotated through the front line. Promotion in the regular forces no longer relied on Ba'ath membership, but all ranks were subjected to a political education programme. Saddam made several visits to front-line headquarters and gave the impression that he was scrutinising every officer. He sought out those who exhibited courage and resolve against the Iranian attacks for rewards and promotion, and denigrated those who failed to achieve success. Army officers found it difficult to contemplate any resistance to Saddam, since everyone's career appeared to depend on him alone and any collective action seemed impossible.

The shelling of Basra, which the Iranians saw as retaliation for the damage done to Khorramshahr and other cities, was an illustration that they had failed to secure the city, but Saddam believed that he could not remain inactive. With the land campaign now in a stalemate, the obvious choice was to widen the conflict against Iranian economic assets, namely vulnerable oil installations in the Gulf. On 12 August 1982, he announced the northern Gulf waters, 30 miles (48 km) east of Kuwait and due south of the thalweg line, were a 'maritime exclusion zone'. All Iranian ports and vessels within the zone were therefore legitimate targets of war. This move enabled Saddam to avoid antagonising foreign powers further down the Gulf coast, but it enabled him to raid the Iranian ships and ports, including Bandar Khomeini and Kharg Island, causing a 55 per cent fall in exports of Iranian oil.

In September, Saddam kept up the diplomatic pressure by attending the Arab League summit in Morocco and accepting all of the Saudi peace-plan proposals. This allowed for a ceasefire during the haj period, evacuation of Iranian territory and, now, an Iranian withdrawal from Iraqi soil, with compensation to Iran through the Islamic Reconstruction Fund financed by the GCC. Tehran, predictably, rejected the terms, believing it could still win the war and set its own conditions later. In fact, the Iranian revolutionary government was at that stage battling with the Kurdish minority in its own country as it sought to consolidate its grip on power. The Kurdish Democratic Party of Iran was the target of an Iranian offensive, launched as a joint army-Pasdaran mission close to the Iraqi border. The operation soon degenerated into protracted fighting as the Kurds adopted guerrilla tactics and bad weather in November brought the whole effort to a standstill. However, in the south, a more sustained and conventional operation was prepared that was designed to engulf Baghdad itself.

Operation Muslim Ibn Aguil

Operation Muslim Ibn Aguil, launched on 1 October 1982 around Naft-e Shahr, involved 40,000 Iranian troops, a mixture of regulars and Pasdaran, with a single armoured brigade in the vanguard. The aim was to take the Sumar hills that overlooked the Iraqi town of Mandali, the road south-west to Baghdad and north-west to Kirkuk, and also the Iranian plains to the east. The Iranians took time to concentrate such a large force and the build-up was detected by the Iraqis who despatched elements of the 2nd Army to the area. The Pasdaran calculated that an attack on a broad front might either envelop the Iraqis or stretch them so thinly that they would be able to infiltrate their positions using the broken upland terrain. Although pressed back, the Iraqis carefully sited each new position to cut down as many 'human wave' assaults as possible. As each attack petered out, the Iraqis would gather local units to launch counter-attacks and try to retake positions that had been lost. By this means they slowed the Iranian advance significantly. The battle continued until 6 October, with the Iranians barely a few kilometres into the hills and certainly nowhere near their objective. The day before, the UN Security Council had issued another call for an end to the war, a withdrawal and a ceasefire. Iraq accepted the latter, but Iran again rejected the entire resolution.

To exert more pressure on the Iraqis and to break their resolve, the Iranians reopened the Basra front on 1 November in an operation entitled Muharram al Harram. The intention was to draw Iraqi forces away from the Sumar hills, to retake Iranian territory lost in 1980 and to finally cut the Basra–Baghdad road. The Pasdaran made use of the marshy ground and launched their first attack at night with the element of surprise. The soft ground did not favour armour and most of the fighting, which lasted a week, consisted of infantry assaults and counter-attacks. The Iranians managed to reach the Iraqi border by crossing the Doverijch river. The nature of the ground meant that some Iraqi units were left behind, and some artillery, which was difficult to move, was overrun. The Iranians claimed to have taken some 3,000 prisoners and a number of armoured vehicles. To maintain momentum, the Iranians attacked again at the Sumar hills on 7 November, but after ten days of fighting, which was brought to a halt by torrential rain, neither offensive had produced either the decisive breakthrough or the breaking of the Iraqi army.

Despite all the rhetoric from Tehran, unsupported infantrymen simply could not prevail against heavy machine guns, tanks and artillery. Increasingly, it was evident that the Iraqis were prepared to increase the technological element in their defences. There were reports that the Iraqis had again experimented with gas to break up Iranian attacks and they had launched Scud missiles with conventional warheads at Dezful, killing 21 civilians.

On the Iranian side, there were more air attacks on Iranian oil facilities at Kharg Island, but the Iranians had hardened their defences, adding more anti-aircraft weaponry, bunkers and shelters. Consequently, inexperienced Iraqi pilots found it difficult to locate, hit and destroy their targets. The journalist and historian Dilip Hiro, in contrast to Cordesman's conclusions on the autumn offensives, drew attention to some other Iranian successes. He argued that the Muharram al Harram offensive had reduced Iraqi reserves to a single army corps south of Baghdad and two armoured brigades in the north.[8] He pointed to a significant loss of helicopters and aircraft, the loss of the Bayat oilfield and a moment of crisis for the Iraqis when the Iranians drew close to Mandali. He also noted that about fifty well heads were taken near Tib. Cordesman concluded that the Iranians made 'token gains' for 'heavy losses'. While the Muharram al Harram offensive gave the Iranians 350 square miles (906 sq km), 3,000 prisoners and 140 captured tanks, Iraqi counter-attacks were effective at stemming the flow of Iranian deep operations.[9]

Saddam used this Iranian offensive to draw the Iraqi people into a patriotic stance: he called for a referendum asking whether the Iraqi people would prefer Saddam or Khomeini, adding that Iran was trying to occupy Iraq regardless of whether Saddam remained in power or not. An 'informal' and apparently spontaneous referendum in Baghdad on 13 November emerged as a 'popular' march in favour of the leadership.

The crowd chanted 'yes, yes, Saddam/this is our referendum'. Saddam responded by modestly promising to remain in power even if the war lasted another ten years. The images of popular support and patriotic sentiment nevertheless encouraged the troops at the front. Tib was retaken.

Saddam did not miss the lesson. Pan-Arabist ideas were dropped from the official discourse, and now the emphasis was purely on Iraqi nationalism. All members of the Ba'ath Party were now expected to join the Popular Army. Saddam encouraged people to feel that their problems were to do with bureaucracy and he encouraged them to complain if there were administrative failures, carefully distancing himself and his paternalist credentials from the people's grievances. Socialist equality was also sacrificed for the sake of the war effort. The state sector was geared to war and the private sector was encouraged to fill the gap, while foreign military imports continued to arrive, albeit without a clear or smooth procurement plan. At the front there were also developments that combined the priorities of bolstering morale and the war effort. Throughout the wet months, the Iraqis used the opportunity to build better and more sophisticated defences on the eastern front. Artillery fire was directed more accurately, tanks were dug in and barbed wire obstacles festooned the lines. Minefields extended around their positions, while trenches were augmented with concrete strong points and bunkers. Below ground, rest facilities were built for the benefit of the troops, with television rooms, clinics, education and fitness areas.

Iraq also kept up its air campaign. Taking delivery of French fighters, Chinese MiG 19s and Egyptian MiG 21s, the Iraqis could still muster 332 combat aircraft despite suffering a loss of 117 planes during 1982.[10] It used these to strafe Iranian front-line units and also to strike economic and strategic targets deeper inside Iran or along the coast. By contrast, Iran had only a quarter of its pre-war fleet intact, about 100 aircraft, with which to contest its airspace. Short of spares and unable to purchase replacement planes, the Iranians focused their efforts on the defence of airbases, oilfields and ports. Consequently, the Iranian air force could offer mere token air cover to its ground units. Nevertheless, the Iranians were about to restore momentum to the war with vast ground offensives.

5

Escalation: Operations Wa al Fajr and Khaibar, 1984

On 7 February 1983, the Iranians launched yet another massive offensive. Entitled Wa al Fajr (By the Dawn), the offensive was directed towards Amara on the Basra–Baghdad road from the Fakeh region of Khuzestan. Six Iranian divisions, a total of 100,000 men, poured across the border line, with the first 40,000 striking along two axes. Rafsanjani described the attack as 'the final move towards ending the war'. Expectations were high.

Facing the onslaught, Major-General Hisham Sabah Fakhri's Fourth Corps at Basra called on Iraqi air support with some effect, and 150 sorties a day pounded the Iranian formations. One Iranian armoured brigade got too far ahead of the supporting infantry, was lured into a pre-prepared killing area, and destroyed.[1] Air strikes and machine-gun fire from helicopter gunships further slowed the Iranian advance and gradually the Iraqi armour and infantry could begin to push the Iranians back. The Iranians were able to recover some of the remaining ground lost in 1980, but they had again failed to effect the breakthrough they had planned for. In March, the Iraqis tried to off-balance the Iranians and disrupt any preparations for another offensive by making their own attack at Miqdadiya on the central front, but its effects and gains were limited.

On 10 April 1983, the Iranians made another giant attack, part of the Wa al Fajr-I, west of Ein Khosh, in the hope of reaching the Baghdad–Basra highway. The fighting lasted a week and once again Iraqi air power helped turn the tide. The Iranians were turned back again, occupying positions largely along the international border. Rafsanjani excused the lack of progress with the remark that: 'our forces ... returned to positions more easily defendable' and claimed that the time 'was not yet ripe' to tell the nation what had happened. It was becoming more difficult to disguise the failures. The Iranian army were well aware that they lacked the guns, ammunition, aircraft, armour and logistics to succeed. They wanted more limited tactical objectives, not the flamboyant gestures of trying to reach positions deep within the Iraqi defence zone. The ulema and the Revolutionary Guards' leaders were impatient and wanted to maximise the use of surprise and the fighting spirit of the volunteers, using massive numbers to overwhelm the Iraqi positions and then penetrate deep into the Iraq rear where, they assumed, panic would set in among their adversaries.

The waves themselves were often successful, at least initially. Darkness enabled them to approach close to the Iraqi perimeters and then swarm into their defences. However, there was a physical limit as to how far and fast they could run and fight. Without follow-on waves in the right place and time, the attacks petered out as the leading elements were shot down or collapsed through exhaustion. The enthusiasm to keep moving forward meant that too few men were left to hold the Iraqi positions they had taken and inadequate logistics meant these were not consolidated with heavy weapons and ammunition resupply. As a result, when the survivors of the first waves were being pursued by an Iraqi counter-attack, it proved difficult to hold their positions.

The absence of concentrations of reserves was not simply inadequate planning. The Iranians on the front line were well aware that any large force held in reserve was a target of Iraqi airpower. Moreover, American satellite surveillance information was being passed to the Iraqis via Saudi Arabia, so the preparations for the offensives were almost invariably known to their enemies in advance.[2]

The commencement of the Wa al Fajr offensives

The failure to break through did not deter the Iranian Supreme Defence Council where the mood was even more grim and determined. Given the difficulty of concentrating forces and the Iraqis' ability to check assaults at particular points in the line, the strategy was altered to attack as many points along the border as possible. This would have the effect of stretching the Iraqi lines and weakening them. Moreover, by holding their nerve and continuing with a war of attrition, they would continue to exhaust the Iraqis until eventually their defence line snapped. The final element of the new thinking was to probe the Iraqis at their weakest point, among their Kurdish minority, to compel them to divert forces to hold down a portion of their own population.

Consequently, on 22 and 23 July 1983, Wa al Fajr-II was opened on a 48-mile (77 km) front, along the road that linked Piranshahr in Iran to

Rawandoz in northern Iraq. To add credibility to the idea of Iranian 'liberation' forces coming to the assistance of the oppressed Kurds, Kurdish Democratic Party [of Iraq] (KDP) members and Iraqi Shias, known as Al-Mujahideen, joined the Iranian forces crossing the border.[3] The KDP proved to be a useful asset as they knew the terrain and were able to communicate in the local language with the civilians en route. With a four-to-one advantage in numbers, the Iranians advanced 9 miles (14 km) into Iraq, severed the Iraqi supply route to the Iranian Kurdish militias, which had been fighting against the government in Tehran, and took the town of Hajj Umran. Piranshahr was taken by infiltration prior to the main attack. The Iraqi counter-attack was a failure. The mountainous terrain made movement for the armour more difficult and Iranian troops had more cover in the broken ground. Iraqi infantry, which had lost the high ground of Mount Karman, were pinned down as they struggled to ascend the slopes. As the Iraqi forces fell back, the Iranians moved quickly to establish an alternative government on Iraqi soil in Hajj Umran. The grandly named Supreme Assembly of Islamic Revolution in Iraq was convened by Hojatalislam Baqir Hakim, with representatives of Al Daawa, al-Mujahideen and its political wing, the Islamic Action Organisation or SAIRI. The Iraqis were concerned with more practical issues. They were compelled to deploy elements of their forces to protect the strategically important oil pipeline into Turkey, and hoped to stem the Iranian onslaught.

The next offensive on 30 July 1983, Wa al Fajr-III, was launched from Mehran on the central front. The Iranians drove 6 miles (10 km) into Iraq, and were assailed by waves of Iraqi air strikes and every mile was bitterly contested on the ground. Iranian Pasdaran forces were protected by the broken nature of the terrain. When the Iraqis attempted to make a counter-attack with combined infantry and armour, they were checked and forced to withdraw, which caused confusion. Fighting went on in this sector until 10 August as sub-units struggled to control features of tactical value. There were reports that the Iraqis used poison gas, particularly mustard agent, delivered from helicopters and aircraft.[4] If the objective had been to neutralise Iranians on hilltop positions, then too little attention was paid to the wind direction and the 'heavy' nature of the gas which caused it to sink downhill into Iraqi positions. The Pasdaran had managed to take more territory with their human wave assaults, and these were effective when delivered in close country or at night, and when they avoided frontal assaults on Iraqi positions. The human cost was once again high. Figures were disputed, but the butcher's bill was in the region of 12,000.

While many Iraqis admired the armed forces and Saddam's determined leadership at this moment of trial, the old doubts had not entirely disappeared. The Iraqi intelligence services revealed another plot on Saddam's life in the spring of 1983 and in May the President's step-brother published a bizarre book about assassination attempts against Saddam. The idea was to convey the efficiency of the intelligence services and thereby deter further attempts. In fact, the majority of plots and conspiracies were political manoeuvres and may have been a convenient excuse to continue to push out those who showed insufficient loyalty to Saddam. The president himself spent more time bunkered down than before. He curtailed visits to the front line or Ba'ath Party events, and contemplated how to survive the new Iranian strategy.

Enduring the monthly offensives on the eastern border was absorbing the army's resources and much of the air force, but the Iraqi advantage in numbers of aircraft and the vulnerability of the Iranian oil industry suggested a strategic move in the Gulf could break their momentum. The Iraqi air force concentrated on attacking Iranian ships, claiming in early December 1982 to have sunk six Iranian merchant and naval vessels between Bandar Khomeini and Kharg using French-made Exocet missiles.[5] In January 1983, the Iraqis knocked out the Iranian *Nowruz* oil rig. Naval and air attacks were also made against the port and installations of Bandar Khomeini. That autumn, the Iraqis threatened that their new French Super-Etendard aircraft and Exocets would soon be deployed against Kharg Island.

The Iranians responded by threatening the Western powers and others who supplied Iraq, by stating they would cut them off from their oil resources, referring to a potential closure of the Strait of Hormuz. This was a significant escalation of the conflict and could have created a coalition of states against Iran in the war. There was no question of this being empty rhetoric. Iranian troops were moved to the Larak, Henquin and Sirri Islands in the Hormuz Strait. Anti-aircraft guns and artillery batteries were moved to the Tunbs and Qeshm. It was clear that Iran was contemplating making the Hormuz Strait too dangerous to shipping that attempted to move oil supplies through it. In the 1980s, some fifty ships a day used the channel, including up to twenty tankers carrying 8 million barrels of oil. Approximately one-fifth of the world's oil was transited through this waterway. France responded immediately, offering $500-million-worth of missiles and bombs, including more Exocets, to Iraq. Bahrain mobilised, Qatar closed its borders, and Oman deployed its armed forces to Ras Masandam on the western shore of the Strait of Hormuz.

The defiance shown by Iran reflected a new discipline in the regime. In May 1982, the government imposed Islamic law throughout the legal system. All secular laws were abolished in August. The personnel of Mujahideen-e Khalq (MEK), who were regarded as a serious threat from the outbreak of the revolution until the autumn of 1982, were condemned as 'agents of Saddam' by a desperate propaganda agency. The party was consequently broken up and the MEK leader, Sadiq Qutbzadeh, was executed in September. New, more intensive Islamic education was introduced into the Revolutionary Guards while Islamic associations of dedicated ulema were despatched like commissars to the front-line units. Their role was to ensure compliance with the 'right' way of thinking, to make sure that government policies were not challenged, to raise religious consciousness, to pass on intelligence about 'dissidents' and to look after the spiritual welfare of the units under their care. The Revolutionary Guards were reorganised like regular battalions, which assisted the planning of operations and helped the regular army to accept them in the order of battle and the chain of command. Some of the 150,000-strong force remained as independent brigades, but some were integrated into larger army formations. The Revolutionary Guards also acted as an internal security force, largely hunting down and fighting the remaining MEK.

More popular was the notion that, simply by dint of their own efforts and guided by the righteousness of their Islamic revolutionary cause, the people had overthrown a powerful dictator, thrown the Iraqi invaders out of the country and were rebuilding the economy. Like the communists of the 1920s, much was made of the startling improvements to the economy to 'prove' the correctness of the political agenda. Enemies of the state were by the same token enemies of the people and of the revolution, and could be dealt with severely. This brutality was condemned overseas, but there was a growing sense that Iran was isolated anyway and would have to continue to rely on its own resources. Defying the world with a threat to the Strait of Hormuz merely reflected this feeling.

On 19 and 20 October 1983, the Iranians made another attempt to stretch the Iraqi land formations. Wa al Fajr-IV was designed to build on the success of the first northern offensive. Iraq's First Corps was driven back by yet more waves of Iranian light infantry from three divisions and they withdrew 25 miles (40 km) westwards from Baneh and Marivan. Wagner and Cordesman noted:

> Iran's initial success showed that the proper use of volunteers to charge machine guns or walk over minefields still made sound

military sense if it was directed at achievable, well-defined, and practical goals, kept within careful limits, the resulting penetrations were properly exploited, and the fighting had a well-chosen and meaningful objective.[6]

Meeting these criteria was difficult in the extreme. Saddam, clearly under some pressure, sent the elite Republican Guard to drive the Iranians back, but they were not successful. The Iraqis also made use of mustard gas, but with limited tactical effect. The arrival of more reinforcements and a bitter struggle for Panjwin eventually contained the Iranian attack. Some Kurdish conscripts in the Iraqi army began to desert. Of the 48,000 who fled the Iraqi army, a significant number joined the growing Kurdish insurgent forces. The Iranian strategy at last appeared to be paying off. Already pressed for manpower, the loss of the Kurdish personnel seemed to be a point of crisis for Saddam's regime.

The Iraqis retaliated at this obvious attempt to undermine the civilian morale of the country by firing Scud missiles at five Iranian towns and cities. The action reinforced the view of the Iranian public that Saddam was a war criminal. Al Daawa then detonated five bombs in Kuwait to drive off this staunch ally of the dictator, which killed six and injured eighty, so Saddam ordered that five more Scuds be fired into Iran. There were 21 deaths and over 200 wounded. The Iranians fired their artillery on six Iraqi towns near the border, but the number of civilian casualties was not recorded. To Saddam, the Iranians were using terrorism and irregular revolutionary warfare methods against him and his country, which, in his mind, necessitated fierce reprisals to create a deterrent. To the Iranians, Saddam's deliberate targeting of civilians was further evidence that only by deposing him could Iran and the region be safe. He was portrayed by propagandists as the personification of evil.

The Iranians looked now to reopen the central and southern fronts. The Iraqis had attempted to flood and drown Iranian infantry by diverting the Tigris into their positions, so the Iranians prepared the battlefield by digging a 36-mile-long (58 km) canal to drain the floodwaters into the Karun. They trained their troops in crossing water obstacles, with the specific intention of carrying out a daring, deep strike into what they perceived as a vulnerable zone in Iraq's defence lines: the Majnoon Islands. The Iranians had been fought to a standstill by the end of the year, but there was every prospect that new offensives would push the Iraqis to the limit and everyone expected that 1984 would be the year of decision in the conflict.

The Khaibar (Majnoon) offensive and chemical warfare

The Iranians planned to make three large-scale offensives during the year, continuing their strategy of stretching Iraqi defences along their border with a series of probing attacks. In the north, the Kurdish guerrillas had already tied up a large number of Iraqi troops. The goal of the first new attack was, again, the Basra–Baghdad highway, the severing of which would cut off the Shia south from the Sunni-dominated centre. Nevertheless, the Iraqis knew the direction of the attack and the likely objective. When the Iranians crossed the start line on 16 February 1984 in Wa al Fajr-V, near Mehran, the Iraqi Fourth Army was prepared. The Iranians were halted and pushed back relatively quickly. Neverthless, it had achieved is objective, which, like the subsequent Wa al Fajr-VI, was designed to put further pressure on the Iraqis diverting more reserves away from the main effort, which had yet to come.

The second phase of the offensive was thus more determined and effective. Beginning on 22 February under the title Operation Khaibar (named after the Jewish settlement captured by the Prophet before he turned his attention to Mecca), several divisions of Revolutionary Guards emerged from the Haur al Hawizeh, the marshes that extended westwards from the Tigris to the junction of the Euphrates and the Shatt al Arab. The Iraqis knew that the Iranians could not cross the area swiftly and would be unable to use heavy guns or armour there and so it was only lightly held. However, the Iranians made use of many small boats and inflatable dinghies to ferry their troops through the marshes, and small plank tracks to pick their way through the reeds and islands, and they covered their advance with helicopter gunships. An estimated 100,000 troops swarmed through the marshes, with another 100,000 held in reserve ready to exploit success. The marsh assaults, entitled Fatima al-Zahra, preceded the main thrust, which was to be delivered in three waves.[7]

Just short of Qurna, on the Basra–Baghdad road, lay the islands of Majnoon, which were artificial mounds built by engineers to facilitate the extraction of oil. The outbreak of the war and the difficulty in access meant that the well heads had been sealed. Held by a token Iraqi force lacking in armour and artillery support, the Revolutionary Guards made use of the difficult ground and their preference for highly devolved command to seize the islands in close-quarter combat. The Iraqis' command and control was too slow and cumbersome to manage the surprise assault, and the positions were abandoned on 27 February. Two days later, the Iranians had reached the outskirts of Qurna and could bring small arms fire to bear on the highway. In doing so, they had left the relatively good cover of the marshes and were now confronted by dug-in Iraqi positions.

More importantly, the entire sector was now alert and making preparations for a counter-attack. The local Popular Army units and the Iraqi regulars were thrown into the gap together. Artillery was rushed into the sector and was used to bombard the Iranians who were struggling to concentrate enough manpower for the final push into Qurna. Aircraft and Iraqi helicopter gunships were brought up and added to the fusillade of firepower raining down on the Iranian formations. Chemical weapons were deployed as part of the Iraqi last-ditch defence plan. Despite the shelling and air attacks, the Iranians managed to establish a bridgehead across the marshes and rolled forward two Revolutionary Guards divisions with armour and combat engineer units. However, these were soon depleted by Iraqi fire, and their attack on Qurna was stalled.

The Iraqis hoped to turn the extended Iranian thrust to their own advantage. The problem was that they could not bring sufficient mass to bear anywhere along the front. The Iranians darted through the marshes on motorbikes, on foot or in small boats, making ambushes and then changing position. This was infantry-fighting country, unsuitable for Iraqi armoured units. Iraqi progress was therefore slow, but they retook the southern section of Western Majnoon Island, effectively putting the Basra–Baghdad highway beyond the reach of their enemy. For three weeks, 300,000 Iranians and 200,000 Iraqis floundered through the marshes in attack and counter-attack, much of it at a small tactical unit level. Twenty thousand Iranians were killed in the fighting along with 7,000 Iraqis.[8] In March, the Iranians attempted to restore momentum by committing another armoured division, this time from the regular army. It, too, was consumed by the fighting in the marshy terrain and failed to reach its objectives.

The Iraqis made more use of chemical weapons, especially mustard gas and Tabun nerve agent to defeat the Iranian infantry. Mustard gas was deployed on 25 and 26 February and again through the first few days of March, but the effects lasted far longer.[9] Sinking into the marshy water, the agent continued to cause blistering of the skin, eyes and lungs of all those who came into contact with it. A classified CIA report noted that the Iraqis used both a liquid and a dust form of delivery of Mustard agent. The dust form had an almost instantaneous effect on respiratory systems but the liquid form took up to four hours to incapacitate a soldier.[10] Medical services were said to be 'overwhelmed' by the numbers of injured. The Iranians claimed that 1,200 men were killed by the Iraqi chemical weapons and a further 5,000 were otherwise incapacitated. In a war where casualty figures were notoriously inaccurate, it is difficult to be certain about the claim, added to which the effectiveness of chemical warfare has often been exaggerated throughout the history of its practice. Nevertheless, few would dismiss the grievous effects on the victims. Tehran protested and pointed to the fact that Baghdad was a signatory to the Geneva Protocols of 1925, banning the use of such weaponry. The Swedish Peace Research Institute investigated and found that casualties and sites did indeed exhibit plenty of evidence of particular chemical agents.[11] More startling was the apparent presence of mycotoxins, biological agents, but there was insufficient evidence to prove that they had been weaponised and used by Iraqi forces. Indeed, given the circumstances – namely to retake Majnoon – it seems unlikely that Iraq would have risked the unintended infection of its own scarce manpower, but the source of the toxins was never established.[12]

What mattered to the Iranians at the front was the effect such weapons could have on the morale of their troops. The Iraqis' use of chemical weapons contributed to the decision not to make a second major attack in the area. Nevertheless, the Revolutionary Guards had, throughout the operation, exhibited their usual courage and determination. The chief problem was still a conventional one: emerging from the Howizeh marshes into open ground, unsupported by either their own armour or heavy weapons, and without adequate air cover, their attacks failed just like the others before them for much the same reasons. Here perhaps the war resembled the battles of the first half of the First World War in Europe more strongly than anywhere else: troops entrenched behind barbed-wire entanglements cut down lines of assaulting infantry as they struggled through clouds of poison gas, boggy terrain and with ill-coordinated artillery, air and armoured support.

By mid-April, it was apparent to the Iraqis that the Iranians meant to try again in the same sector. Judging that they had assembled some 300,000 troops in the marshes ready to try once more for Qurna, the Iraqis made use of the rising waters of the Tigris to flood the marshes along the southern and western periphery. Consequently, for the rest of the summer months, it proved almost impossible for the Iranians to push on with the offensive.

The prolonged fighting, its tempo around Majnoon, the reckless courage of the Iranian Revolutionary Guards and the Iraqi use of chemical weapons all contributed to a strong sense of bitterness on both sides and a tangible decline in respect for the enemy. Major-General Mahir Abdul Rashid, the Iraqi commander of Third Corps, used the rhetoric typical of the time to describe the defeat of the third Iranian offensive in his sector: 'We have destroyed thousands of these harmful magian insects . . . we will turn what is left of these harmful insects into food for the birds of the wilderness and the fish of the marshes.'[13] At the time, the Iraqis denied they had used chemical weapons, and the same senior Iraqi officer merely quipped that, if he had been issued with pesticide, he would have used it willingly against the 'insects' that confronted him.[14]

6

Foreign Intervention, 1980–84

The superpowers

Saddam Hussein had been aware that Iran had isolated itself diplomatically prior to the outbreak of the war. Iran had condemned the Soviet invasion of Afghanistan in December 1979 and had taken hostages from the American Embassy, thereby breaking international protocols and alienating the two superpowers. When Iraq invaded Iran in 1980, the superpowers were officially neutral. The United States had no embassy in Iraq, but its interests were represented by the Belgian Embassy in Baghdad. The Iranians, perhaps predictably, argued that they had evidence of collusion between Iraq and the United States through transcripts of meetings between Iraqi, American, French and Israeli officials with dissident Iranian officers. It was further alleged that the United States had passed on information to Iraq that emphasised Iranian military weakness and therefore encouraged an invasion. The internal assessment was, apparently, that Iran would require spare parts within three weeks of the outbreak of war for its largely American-manufactured munitions, planes and equipment, and these could be swapped for the American hostages. If this was the calculation, then it misfired as the Iranians looked initially to Vietnam to supply former American spare parts, albeit ones that were already obsolete in most cases.

In fact, the American line on Iran and Iraq was consistent. It favoured neither side and was eager to keep Soviet influence out of both countries. This meant that, should either belligerent get the upper hand, some effort could be made to attempt to re-establish a balance. Having both parties weakened would serve American interests, but an outright victory for one, or the total collapse of either was certainly not to Washington's advantage. This may help to explain the curious and apparent contradictions in US foreign policy. According to Dana Steinberg, a researcher for the Woodrow Wilson International Center, the CIA may have warned

Iran of the impending Iraqi attack a full year before operations began, but the Iranians took no action and the taking of American hostages ended any prospect of future cooperation.[1] Gary Sick, a former aide in the National Security Council, states that Saddam had met King Hussein of Jordan a year before the war in the presence of the CIA and having had no 'red light' from the United States, believed that amounted to a 'green light'. However, Sick argues that this hardly constituted a US-backed war against Iran. Saddam, he pointed out, had his own reasons for starting a war with Iran regardless of American interests.[2] Despite the later 'tilt' towards Iraq, American priorities were clear: the United States threatened the Soviet Union against any invasion of Iran, stating it would defend Iran by force in the event of Soviet intervention.[3] Gulf stability, which included safeguarding energy reserves and denying the space to the Soviets, was far more important than the individual fortunes of Iran or Iraq.

After the hostage crisis had begun, the United States tried to keep the 'back channels' of communication with Iran open. President Carter was particularly keen to recover the hostages to assist with his forthcoming election campaign. He was prepared to announce that Iraq should withdraw its forces, and the US secretary of state pointed out that Iraq's action had threatened the stability and security of the Gulf. A few days after these statements, the American ambassador to the UN stated that the Iraqi invasion of Iran threatened Iranian national integrity. On 28 October 1980, it is alleged that Carter even offered to airlift $300–500-million-worth of arms and spares, which Iran had already ordered and purchased under the Shah, to Tehran in return for the release of the hostages. Carter apparently also hinted that the United States might back Iraq if the Iranians were uncooperative. However, Reagan's Republicans were eager to derail this effort and had already met Iranian officials to agree not to release the hostages before the election, but to do so afterwards in return for the direct supply of arms. When Reagan won the election, he publicly announced the end of sanctions, agreed to honour Carter's offer and, by definition, agreed the clandestine transmission of weapons and spares to free the hostages.

The Soviet Union was understandably anxious about the Iraqi invasion of Iran. As the principal supplier of munitions, it was bound to be assumed by the United States that Moscow was somehow behind the attack, at a time when many Americans thought that the Iranian revolution might in some way be communist inspired or would at least be exploited by them. The Russian newspaper *Izvestia* had announced that the 'Iraqi operations against Iran will enable the West to achieve changes in Iraqi policy in the West's favour' and 'will reduce the ability of the republic of Iran to resist imperialist pressure'.[4] Moreover, the invasion of Afghanistan appeared to the rest of the world as a blatant onward march of Soviet socialism rather than, in the Kremlin's view, a rather defensive, reactive measure to stabilise a state which, allowed to collapse into Islamist turmoil, might jeopardise the stability of the southern Soviet Union. The official Soviet response to the outbreak of the Iran–Iraq War was to be found in the Tass news agency announcement on 28 September 1980 in which Moscow urged restraint and argued that the war was threatening the idea of national liberation in the face of 'imperialism and Zionism'. The Soviets brought their arms supplies to Iraq to an abrupt halt, even turning around a ship in the Strait of Hormuz with 140 armoured vehicles on board.[5] However, Soviet neutrality in the conflict enabled Tehran to move its reserves of troops from the north to the south, thus altering the course of the war.

Growing Soviet concerns that Iran might lose the war and open the way to Western involvement in both Iran and Iraq, led to President Brezhnev's decision to sell weapons to Tehran. According to Muhammad Ali Rajai, the Iranian prime minister at the time, his country rejected the Soviet offer because of the occupation of Afghanistan. In fact, the rejection was purely a gesture. Iran accepted airlifted Soviet supplies via Syria and Libya. The Soviet military newspaper, *Krasnaya Zvezda*, stated that Iraq's territorial claims and its growing alignment with the United States marked its culpability for starting the war. The Iranians concurred with the idea of a US-inspired Iraqi invasion. Given the smaller population and territorial resources, Iraq, they reasoned, could only have chosen to attack Iran with American connivance and encouragement. Yet the Soviet Union stopped short of severing its ties with Baghdad, hoping for some restoration of the *status quo ante-bellum*. The Iraqis complained that Moscow was not fulfilling its pre-war agreements and had ceased its military support in defiance of the terms of the Treaty of Friendship of Co-operation of 1972. The Soviets argued that military supplies could only be offered if the weapons were used in a purely defensive manner. In fact, Iraq continued to receive Soviet weapons and munitions via Somalia, North Yemen, Egypt and Poland, most of which were shipped through Saudi Arabia. Iraq knew it could pressure the Soviets only so far and the subterfuge by Moscow allowed it to reassure *Kayhan*, the Iranian newspaper, that arms shipments to Iraq had ceased.[6]

The Israeli airstrike against the Iraqi nuclear reactor at Osirak in June 1981 and the obvious defeat of the Iraqi invasion changed the

Soviet position towards Saddam. In mid-1981, the Soviets announced a willingness to 'broaden trade and economic relations', which was a coded reference to the supply of more arms. The priority for the Soviets was to preserve Iraq against an Iranian onslaught and was not unlike the American objective of preserving the balance of power in the Gulf region. The United States was eager to keep the Gulf waters open for the supply of oil on the world's markets. Carter had announced that he had ordered the establishment of a joint Rapid Deployment Force for use in the Gulf.[7] With the collapse of one of America's 'twin pillars', namely Iran, the United States was looking to strengthen its other one, Saudi Arabia, and sent four Airborne Warning and Control Systems (AWACs) aircraft for its protection. He stated the United States would look favourably at requests for assistance from non-belligerent Gulf states, and he sent a total of thirty-seven US Navy ships to the waters of the Persian Gulf and Indian Ocean.

In June 1982, when an Iranian counter-offensive against Iraq seemed imminent, Moscow urged restraint on Tehran. Iran nevertheless publicly denounced the Soviet Union as a threatening superpower like the United States. Khomeini believed that the Islamic Revolution could provide the means for a truly independent foreign policy and could eventually draw on the strength of the entire Muslim world. By contrast, he believed that Iraq was entirely dependent on foreign support. It was a naive assumption that would be exposed the moment the United States believed their primary interest, namely the security of the Gulf, was threatened more directly. In practical terms, Khomeini's views owed more to rhetoric than reality. Without foreign arms and munitions, its war effort would have been particularly short-lived.

The Gulf states at the outbreak of war

On 5 August 1980, before the outbreak of war, Saddam had met the leaders of Saudi Arabia to discuss their shared concerns about Iran. Ever sensitive to criticism of the Saudi monarchy, the king and his ministers were angry about Tehran's war of words against the 'unIslamic regime in Riyadh', its corruption, and its willingness to serve the interests of the 'Great Satan', America, by selling oil. Saddam had assured the Saudis that he would use military force if all other avenues of diplomacy had been exhausted, but that Iraq would pursue a 'limited war' strategy. The Saudis were particularly worried that Iran might disrupt the haj due in October that year, but they were prepared to commit, secretly and in league with Kuwait, the revenue from increased oil output to Iraq. The increased volume would amount to an extra 1 million Saudi and 800,000 Kuwaiti barrels of oil per day, valued at about $54 million.[8] Saudi Arabia was eager to avoid an overt anti-Iranian policy, lest it attract unwelcome military action against its vulnerable offshore oil installations or stir the antagonism of its small but vocal Shia minority (a community which had rioted in 1979). Moreover, it could hardly be seen to be standing in opposition to an Islamic state and it had few arguments that it could use ideologically against the rhetoric of the Iranian regime, other than a vague pan-Arabist sentiment. Consequently, the public announcements of Saudi Arabia called for a speedy end to the war between brother Muslim nations, while it quietly permitted Iraqi aircraft to over-fly or even take refuge in Saudi Arabia, and it permitted Iraqi vessels to use Red Sea ports to transit its goods and war materiel. Most significantly, it loaned Iraq at least $10 billion in 1981 alone.

Kuwait felt more exposed than Saudi Arabia. A quarter of its population was Shia and its installations, within range of Iranian aircraft or missiles, were even more vulnerable. Iran threatened all the Arab states that cooperated with Iraq and made air strikes against Kuwait as early as 12 and 16 November 1980. Kuwait broadcast its moral support for Iraq, but essentially did nothing that would implicate it as directly involved. Yet, when Iraq was compelled to withdraw from Iranian territory, Kuwait increased its logistical support to Iraq with hundreds of truck-loads of supplies and three tranches of interest-free loans of $2 billion in 1980, April and December 1981. The last of these was inspired by the Iranians' air strike against a Kuwaiti refinery at Umm Aayash on 1st October, which, while denied in Tehran, had been tracked by Saudi-based AWACs flights.

Bahrain, Qatar and UAE were more cautious in their attitude towards the war. For UAE, the constituent states were divided on the issue, with two said to be pro-Iraqi and three pro-Iranian. Abu Dabai and Ras al Khaima, which favoured Baghdad, loaned between $1 billion and $3 billion in 1981, and Qatar added a further $1 billion. These generous loans enabled Iraq to maintain its pre-war economy and shield the Iraqi people from the true costs of the war, with an increase of $5 billion worth of imports. Oman was more genuinely neutral, and stood to lose much if the fighting spread to the Strait of Hormuz.[9]

Iran realised that the West was only likely to get involved if the Strait was threatened and so Tehran announced that it would guarantee that the Strait would remain open to free navigation. This led to the Western decision to localise the fighting and keep it out of the Hormuz area. Consequently, when British intelligence discovered Iraqi plans to use Oman as a platform to attack Abu Musa and to seize the Greater and Lesser Tunbs, the British and Americans urged the Omanis to stop the operation. Meanwhile, Britain and France encouraged the Saudis to take the lead in forming a Gulf Co-operation Council (GCC), which would call upon Western support if one of its members was attacked. Hitherto such an organisation had proved impossible because of Iraqi–Iranian–Saudi rivalries. In May 1981, the GCC was created in Riyadh with the objectives of improving internal security, coordinating arms procurements, national economic activity and settling border disputes. On external security, Kuwait favoured a joint military command that was entirely Arab-based. Oman, with closer ties to the West, believed an Arab joint force could only defend strategic sites of interest like Hormuz with the full cooperation and support of American and British naval forces. The solution to this difference of opinion was for Saudi Arabia, Oman and Bahrain to seek bilateral military and intelligence ties with the United States. In February 1982, Saudi Arabia agreed to form a joint Saudi-American Military Committee. America, while officially neutral, had taken another step towards safeguarding its interests in the region and dealing with the challenge posed by the Iranians. While the GCC member states believed they could remain neutral in the conflict, Iran saw the new alliance as little more than an Iraqi-inspired front.

The Iraqis, ironically, felt snubbed by their exclusion from GCC. Saddam was irritated that the Kuwaitis had not permitted the Iraqis to use the islands of Bubiyan and Warba, which would have given Baghdad more access to the coastline of the Gulf. He began to argue, in what was to become a common refrain, that Iraq was bearing the brunt of an Iranian–Israeli offensive while other Arab states stood idly by.[10] He publicly praised pro-Iraqi states like Jordan, North Yemen and Morocco, but stated that Saudi Arabia and Kuwait had made contributions 'much less than their duty dictates'. He described Syria and Libya as 'traitor states', and remained privately furious with Algeria and South Yemen for their refusal to break off relations with Tehran. For Egypt's President Anwar Sadat, the Iran–Iraq War opened up a new opportunity. Having been ostracised, suspended from the Arab League and boycotted for the signing of a peace deal with Israel in 1979, Sadat condemned the war. However, he readily sold arms to Iraq as a first step in his rehabilitation with the Arab world.

Jordan was perhaps the most enthusiastic supporter of Saddam Hussein. Before the war, Jordan had been the beneficiary of generous aid from Iraq, and King Hussein was particularly angry about Khomeini's attacks on the institution of monarchy. He offered public support to Saddam, and moved 40,000 troops to the Iraqi border. He opened Mafraq airbase to Iraqi fighters, and Aqaba became an important logistics hub for both civilian and military supplies, just as it was to be again in the 1990s.

By contrast, Syria's President Hafiz Assad was an irreconcilable enemy of Saddam. Assad had been ideologically opposed to Iraq from the moment he gained power in 1970, was the first to recognise the legitimacy of Khomeini's seizure of power in 1979 and he condemned Saddam's invasion of Iran as a futile distraction from the main effort, namely combating Israel and Zionist imperialism. Yet Syria went further, supplying Soviet weaponry via airlifts to Tehran, offering intelligence on Iraq, and its air force made incursions into Iraqi air space to divide Saddam's forces. In October 1981, Syria signed an arms deal with Iran which was extended into a ten-year trade agreement in March 1982. Iranian oil was sold to Syria in return for cash, manufactured goods and agricultural supplies. No longer dependent on Iraqi oil, it cut Baghdad's pipelines on 10 April 1982 and declared dramatically that it would support the Iraqi people in any attempt to overthrow Saddam.[11] Libya, too, threw in its lot with Iran. Colonel Qaddafi believed that America was behind the Iraqi invasion as an attempt to end the charismatic revolution in Iran and it, too, became a staging post for weapons destined for Tehran.

More importantly, Syria and Libya rather punctured Saddam's claim to be representing the Arab world against Iranian aggression. The failure of many Muslim states to step forward to defend Iraq against the 'heresy' of 'Shi'ite Iranian aggression' was striking. The suspicion across the Muslim world that the hand of America lay behind the decision to invade Iran was certainly difficult to eradicate. Ironically, Saddam was correct in his accusation that Israel was assisting the Khomeini regime. There was no ideological connection, of course; it was a case of realpolitik. Israel supplied arms to Iran simply as a means of keeping the war going, to exhaust both belligerents.[12]

Europe and the outbreak of war

At the outbreak of war, the British, which had been Iran's second largest arms supplier in the 1970s, refused to continue its sales or to ship the vehicles, weapons and parts already paid for by Tehran. That did not stop private companies from making attempts to circumvent the official position, and one firm was accused of shipping tank engines in July 1981. In the spring of that year, the government was prepared to sell only technical equipment to the Iraqis, but not weapons. It was not until February 1982, when the war had swung in Iran's favour and it looked as if a radicalised regime threatened the stability of the Gulf, that London changed its line and permitted repairs to Chieftain tanks the Iraqis had captured from the Iranians.

France, by contrast, was far more overt in its support for Iraq. While refusing to ship the missile patrol boats Tehran had paid for, it rushed weapons and spares to Baghdad in November 1980. The pay-off was a series of lucrative construction contracts for the French, including a nuclear reactor and Iraqi oil. Sixty Mirage fighter planes arrived in January 1981, and in 1982 the Iraqis put orders for military hardware worth $660 million to France.[13] Iraqi oil also proved to be a useful lubricant to obtain weapons, vehicles and parts from Austria and Spain and, outside Europe, from Brazil (Figure 2).

Arms Sales to Iraq
(Figures: SIPRI)

Year	Soviet Union & Warsaw Pact	France	China (PRC)	United States	Egypt	Others	Total
1973	1,321	5	0	0	0	0	1,326
1974	1,471	5	0	0	0	0	1,476
1975	1,087	35	0	0	0	0	1,122
1976	1,161	119	0	0	0	0	1,280
1977	1,062	106	0	0	0	0	1,168
1978	1,827	26	0	0	0	20	1,873
1979	1,108	78	0	0	0	17	1,203
1973–79	9,037	374	0	0	0	37	9,448
1973–79	95.7%	4.0%	0%	0%	0%	0.4%	100%
1980	1,665	241	0	0	12	114	2,032
1981	1,780	731	0	0	46	182	2,739
1982	2,023	673	217	0	71	227	3,211
1980–82	5,468	1,645	217	0	129	523	7,982
1980–82	68.5%	20.6%	2.7%	0%	1.6%	6.6%	100%
1983	1,898	779	745	21	58	773	4,274
1984	2,857	883	1,065	6	0	116	4,927
1985	2,601	700	1,036	9	32	116	4,494
1986	2,663	251	918	9	70	86	3,997
1987	2,719	214	887	30	114	157	4,121
1988	1,202	355	301	125	118	196	2,297
1983–88	13,940	3,182	4,952	200	392	1,444	24,110
1983–88	57.8%	13.2%	20.5%	0.8%	1.6%	6.0%	100%
1989	1,319	113	23	0	47	67	1,569
1990	537	281	0	0	0	33	851
Total $'s	30,301	5,595	5,192	200	568	2,104	43,960
Total %'s	68.9%	12.7%	11.8%	0.5%	1.3%	4.8%	100%

Figure 2   *Arms sales to Iraq*

The Gulf states after the Iranian invasion of Iraq, 1982–84

The southern Gulf states had no reason to get involved in the war with Iran, providing their national interests were not threatened. For Saudi Arabia and Kuwait, Iran posed a direct challenge to them, ideologically, militarily and economically. However, both powers had no wish to become embroiled in the fighting and preferred to use Iraq as a bulwark, but neither country wanted to antagonise Iraq, since its military power was also a threat to them, particularly if Baghdad won a decisive victory. Consequently, Kuwait agreed to deliver 130,000bpd of oil on Iraq's behalf and guaranteed the balance for any foreign country signing contracts with the Iraqis. The Saudis could afford to support Iraq more directly, and periodically warned Iran that the defeat of Iraq would rouse the entire Arab world against the regime in Tehran. The Saudis offered moral support to Saddam: King Fahd telephoned Saddam to reinforce that support at the height of the Iranian offensive of October 1982. Yet, much more important to Baghdad was Saudi Arabia's material support. In January 1983, the Saudis permitted an oil pipeline to be constructed through their territory for Iraq's use. The Saudis agreed to increase its production by 200,000bpd, selling the product as Iraqi oil, despite a lower OPEC quota. It was the Saudis who negotiated on Iraq's behalf to secure five state-of-the-art Super Etendard fighter jets from France, purchasing the aircraft with Saudi oil. They also guaranteed Iraqi contracts for foreign companies and agreed to pay the first 10 per cent on any deals.

Kuwaiti and Saudi intolerance of Iran increased after terrorist bomb attacks in Kuwait in December 1983. While denying responsibility, Tehran was regarded as the architect of the attacks which had targeted American and French embassies, the international airport and an American residential complex. Coming at the height of the unrest in Lebanon, which had also targeted US forces, the Kuwaitis believed that Iranian residents were a fifth column and hundreds were deported. Iraqi air strikes against Iranian cities as retaliation were applauded in Kuwait. Subsequently, when Iraq lost the Majnoon islands in 1984, the Kuwaitis announced a Mobilisation Plan, although they stopped short of a declaration of war. GCC representatives at the Arab League summit called for a ban on all arms sales to Iran. GCC member states then formed a Joint Rapid Deployment Force and staged a high-profile military exercise in the UAE desert in October 1983.[14] Tehran was under no illusion that it was the target of the manoeuvres and, while condemning the posture, reiterated its commitment to non-aggression and non-interference in the internal affairs of the GCC states. Indeed, in the summer of 1983, the Iranians had stated they had no territorial claims to GCC lands, and offered to protect their sovereignty against 'arrogant forces'. Many states therefore exploited the war. UAE was officially neutral, but while Abu Dhabi gave financial aid to Iraq, Dubai maintained its trading relations with Iran. For Iranian businessmen in UAE, there was considerable money to be made.

Iraq turned to Egypt as a regional partner and its arms purchases helped to overcome earlier rivalries. Although Saddam had advocated Egypt's expulsion from the Arab League in 1978 after Sadat's deal with Israel, now Baghdad extolled the virtues of Egypt as a staunch pan-Arab ally. In just three years, Iraq purchased $2.7 billion of arms and ammunition, and eagerly accepted the 15,000 Egyptian 'volunteers' and military advisers that came to aid the war effort. Egypt's President Mubarak had no love of Khomeini's revolutionary politics, but equally he was looking for a counterweight to Libya, a country that was supplying Iran.

Meanwhile, in January 1983, Iran, Libya and Syria held a conference of foreign ministers and announced their joint condemnation of Iraqi aggression and their desire to support Iran. There was no mention of the far more important arms sales that accompanied the conference. Syria, for its part, saw strategic advantage in supporting Iran against Iraq. With Saddam occupied on the eastern border, Syria could intervene more directly in Lebanon, which had been invaded by Israel in June 1982. Iran reciprocated the support, offering oil for cash, including a grant of $200 million to help Syria fight Israel.

Yet, ironically, Israel, among others, was also selling weapons to Iran. Since the United States had embargoed military supplies to Tehran, the Israelis used Portuguese, Italian and Cypriot intermediaries.[15] It is suggested that perhaps $100-million-worth of arms and components were shipped between mid-1980 and mid-1981, the transfers being designed to keep Iraq occupied in a long-term conflict and therefore give Israel a free hand in Lebanon. Moreover, since Israel regarded Iraq as an ally of the Soviet Union, preventing an Iraqi victory also played a part in the Cold War. Finally, offering assistance to Iran constituted insurance in Tehran for the future. Although the Iranians would remain ideologically opposed to Israel, they could see that, for geo-political reasons, Iran made a useful counterweight to other states in the region. The priority though, as a consistent element of Israeli foreign policy, was its security and it was prepared to defend itself, covertly if necessary, but using all means. In June 1981, it had made an air attack on the Iraqi nuclear reactor at Osirak. When it was revealed in 1984 that the Iraqis had built a chemical weapons factory at Rutba, it seemed likely that another attack would be forthcoming. The Iraqis therefore made strenuous efforts to get the United States to intercede on its behalf, and made direct warnings to Israel. Given the change in the tide of war by that stage, namely the Iraqis on the defensive against Iranian attacks, the Israelis may have felt that no immediate action was necessary. The potential consequences of an Iraqi attack were nevertheless illustrated by the 39 Scud-B strikes on Israel in 1990, which resulted in the deaths of 74 civilians.

The changing positions of the United States and the Soviet Union, 1982–84

Despite the antagonism between Iraq and Israel, a close ally of the United States, in January 1983 Saddam published the essence of his conversations with Stephen Solarz, a US Congressman who had visited Baghdad in 1982. In the text, Saddam expressed the view that Iraq had never been part of the Soviet orbit in the region and had always sought to have the Americans present if the Soviets tried to increase their influence. The publication clarified the Iraqi volte-face which had taken place since the outbreak of the war, from a pro-Soviet tilt to a pro-American one. The announcement was welcomed in the Reagan administration, which saw an opportunity to strengthen its regional influence against the Soviets without a full commitment. It agreed to offer support that was non-military: commercial helicopters and credit of $460 million for the purchase of American rice. Given the economic crisis in Iraq at the time, the gesture was received warmly.

American calculations about the war are fascinating. In 1983, the National Security Council felt that Iraq would be unable to win the war and there were two possible results: one, the Iranians would overrun Iraq; or, two, a long stalemate. If Iran defeated Iraq, then it seemed likely that weaker military powers, such as the Gulf states would also be overwhelmed. Some of these might become Islamic republics which, although unlikely, could look towards the Soviet Union for assistance. More importantly, they would seek to cripple the West by interfering with the flow of oil from the Gulf, which constituted half of the world's proven reserves. Memories of the 1973 energy crisis were recent.[16] This was a major threat to American interests.[17]

The National Security Adviser issued a directive, classified as secret, which translated this assessment into policy. The US armed forces were to prepare contingency plans to assist Iraq to secure the border area, which could include the deployment of A-10 'tank buster' aircraft, other ground-attack aircraft and air-defence weapons.[18]

The United States' public condemnation of the Iraqi use of chemical weapons came as a shock to Baghdad and even when relations were put on a more formal diplomatic footing in late 1984, the Americans insisted on their condemnation. Iraq did agree to condemn the use of terrorism as an instrument of policy. This freed the Reagan administration from restrictions on trade, and opened the possibility of sending 'dual-use' technologies.

Terrorist attacks, by groups thought to be sponsored by Iran, in Kuwait in December 1983 and more directly against US Marines in Beirut in October that year, brought US–Iranian relations to a new low. Over 200 American servicemen on a peacekeeping mission died in a single devastating blast. Operation Staunch, the banning of arms trading with Iran, had been initiated in the spring of 1983, but now America stepped up the pressure on its allies and partners to do the same. Private companies that had circumvented the regulations were prevented from continuing their commerce with Tehran, at least, officially. Some companies continued to flout the embargo. The Americans continued to supply military intelligence to the Saudis knowing this material was being transferred directly to Baghdad (Figure 3). Nevertheless, the Iranians did not give up their quest for American parts with which to repair their aircraft, vehicles and equipment. They set up front companies in America or continued to work on intermediaries. The Americans were prepared to turn a blind eye to this as long as the United States benefited financially and there was no change in the balance of power in the Gulf.

There were, however, limits to Iranian freedom of action. The United States was simply not prepared to tolerate Tehran's announcement that it could close the Strait of Hormuz against any countries supplying Iraq. Reagan reiterated his warning that the United States would intervene to keep Hormuz open. To underscore his resolve, the number of American warships in the Gulf increased. The British and French also increased their naval presence, while the Soviet Union maintained its fleet of twenty-six vessels in the Arabian Sea.

The Soviet position had been radically transformed. Its initial disapproval of Iraqi actions in 1980 was tempered by the obdurate Iranian rejection of the United Nations Security Council (UNSC) resolution which had called for a ceasefire in July 1982. Tehran's continuation of the war, as far as the Soviets were concerned, merely gave the Americans and Israelis an opportunity to increase their power and influence in the Middle East. The Israeli movement into Lebanon and increase in

· **THE WHITE HOUSE**

SYSTEM II
(91372 Add On)

WASHINGTON

November 26, 1983

*National Security
Decision Directive 114*

U.S. POLICY TOWARD THE IRAN-IRAQ WAR ~~(S)~~

I have reveiwed and approved the Terms of Reference to govern our political and military consultations with our key Allies and the Gulf Arab states. Political consultations should begin immediately followed by military consultations with those Allies and regional states which express a willingness to cooperate with us in planning measures necessary to deter or defend against attacks on or interference with non-belligerent shipping or on critical oil productions and transhipment facilities in the Persian Gulf. ~~(TS)~~

In our consultations we should assign the highest priority to access arrangements which would facilitate the rapid deployment of those forces necessary to defend the critical oil facilities and transhipment points against air or sapper attacks. Specific recommendations bearing on U.S. plans and force deployments should be submitted for approval following the consultations. ~~(TS)~~

It is present United States policy to undertake whatever measures may be necessary to keep the Strait of Hormuz open to international shipping. Accordingly, U.S. military forces will attempt to deter and, if that fails, to defeat any hostile efforts to close the Strait to international shipping. Because of the real and psychological impact of a curtailment in the flow of oil from the Persian Gulf on the international economic system, we must assure our readiness to deal promptly with actions aimed at disrupting that traffic. The Secretary of Defense and Chairman, Joint Chiefs of Staff, in coordination with the Secretary of State, are requested to maintain a continuing review of tensions in the area and to take appropriate measures to assure the readiness of U.S. forces to respond expeditiously. ~~(TS)~~

Ronald Reagan

Figure 3   *National Security Division Directive, 26 November 1983*
These materials are reproduced from www.nsarchive.org with the permission of the National Security Archive.

American naval power in the Gulf seemed to confirm this anxiety. With Iraq under pressure, the Soviets looked to restore closer relations with Baghdad. It made secret arrangements to supply armour and aircraft which had been ordered before the war, although Saddam announced the deal publicly in an attempt to deter the Iranians from another offensive. As it turned out, the Soviets were not concerned that the arrangement had been made public. Despite the rhetoric of revolution in Iran, the

Soviets felt threatened because of the ideological threat of Islamic militancy that might affect the Central Asian Soviet Republics. The effect of such unrest was already evident in Afghanistan, where a surgical operation to restore the authority of the Afghan communist government had gone disastrously wrong by 1982. Factionalism among the Afghan communists, and a growing insurgency inspired by nationalism and Islamism was proving an unwelcome and complex problem, and the Shia Afghans were undoubtedly looking to Tehran for leadership and support.[19]

When the Iranian offensive of November 1982 failed, Tehran put the setback down to the Soviet war supplies that had been shipped in. They were also on the receiving end of Scud and Frog-7 surface-to-surface missiles and artillery concentrations made up of Soviet guns and shells. The Soviets increased their sales to Iraq to include Mig-23 and MiG-25 fighters, new T-72 tanks and surface-to-air missiles. In total, the Soviets sold Iraq a staggering $20 billion worth of munitions and weapons during the war years. The Iranians could only express angry disapproval with gestures. It banned the communist Tudeh Party and expelled eighteen Soviet diplomats, accusing them of espionage and supporting 'mercenary agents'. By 1983, relations between Iran and the Soviet Union were irreconcilable. In January 1984, in an attempt to mend fences, both sides expressed a formal solidarity against world imperialism, and Rafsanjani announced that Iran was 'active in Lebanon against the Western occupiers and Israel', but it was mere window-dressing and nothing came of it.

Curiously, it was North Korea and China, the former being the state that acted as an intermediary for the latter, which offered material support to Iran. It is estimated that $1,080-million-worth of arms and ammunition were shipped to Tehran between 1981 and 1984, with Iranian oil sold in return.[20] SIPRI, the Swedish peace research institute, estimates that China had provided $2.2-billion-worth of arms during the war and North Korea a further $927 million, making them the largest donors to Iran.[21]

France was much more overt in its position regarding the war. President Mitterrand announced in December 1982 that Iraq's defeat would not be in the national interest because of the huge investment in the country. While the United States has often been criticised for its tilt towards Iraq in the 1980s and its foreknowledge of the Iraqi chemical arsenal, the United States publicly and consistently condemned the use of weapons of mass destruction by Iraq in the war. France, on the other hand, supported Iraq much more directly. Forty per cent of French military exports went to Iraq. Until 1985, it was the largest supplier of arms and munitions other than the Soviet Union, with a total of $17.1 billion invested during the war.[22] It supplied $2.5-billion-worth in 1984 alone. The decision to lease five state-of-the-art Super Etendard warplanes was criticised in other European countries and the United States, but the Iraqis announced that they would engage the French in business contracts after the war. There were approximately 1,000 French businesses active in Iraq, and 6,000 specialists, and the announcement was clearly intended to tempt other European nations into assistance to gain similar benefits. The French believed that the Iraqis would soon purchase more Exocet missiles to furnish the new warplanes and tried to justify their actions as supporting the security of the Gulf, which was in the interests of all Western powers. The British, West Germans and Americans felt that the action, which would almost certainly cause production at Kharg to cease, risked pushing the Iranians towards an attempt to close the Strait of Hormuz, and that would necessitate Western naval and air operations.

The French strategic motive for supporting Iraq was larger than protecting its investments. It believed that support for Iraq gave France a higher standing in the Arab world, and would pave the way for commercial and strategic benefits in the future. However, the obvious support for Iraq created a strong reaction in Tehran. French goods were blacklisted and French banks no longer enjoyed any preferential status in Iran as they had before. When French troops were deployed into Lebanon as peace-keepers in 1983, they were the target of a Lebanese Shi'ite truck bomber. While no direct link was established at the time, it was widely believed that the Iranians had sponsored the attack, not least because Rafsanjani had announced that same month that the sale of Super Etendard planes to Iraq made France 'Iran's enemy'. Fifty-nine French soldiers died in the terrorist attack. In France itself, French intelligence detected a growing network of affiliates to the revolutionary regime in Iran. In December 1983, eight Iranians were deported amid suspicions of terrorist planning.

The Swedish firm Bofors-Nobelkrut, which was allegedly supplying Iran clandestinely through intermediate companies and countries, apparently sought the cooperation of the French company Société nationale des poudres et des explosifs (SNPE) in 1983 and a cartel of businesses from fourteen other countries. It is alleged their sales included explosives for small arms and artillery shells. If true, all the companies involved were it seems motivated purely by the profits to be made from larger and larger orders. For small-scale industries, these sales would have been regarded as a financial lifeline and their efforts were concealed successfully for some time. As with state calculations, self-interest may have determined their positions relative to the combatants.

The United Nations Security Council

Collective action by the UN has often proven difficult, and, while dominated by the United States and Soviet Union, caution about the likely reaction of each superpower could delay or even prevent the resolution of specific conflicts. There were no less than twelve UN Resolutions during the course of the war, the majority of which called for an immediate ceasefire and withdrawal to the original borders ante-bellum. However, the UNSC had first called for a ceasefire when Iraq still occupied Iranian soil, and Tehran was irritated that the UN had failed to condemn the Iraqis' action. Iran felt the UN, as an institution, opposed their revolutionary regime and generally favoured Iraq. In fact, the UN was unable to determine quite how the conflict had begun and it dared not risk a full condemnation of Iraq without being sure that it had not acted in self-defence. Moreover, its calculation was not to give encouragement to a regime like that in Iran. After all, it had breached diplomatic protocol by storming the American Embassy and it seemed determined to alter the status quo of the region by force. This attitude was reinforced by Iran's subsequent invasion of Iraqi territory in 1982. UN Resolution 479 was passed on 28 September 1980, just a week after the invasion, and was accepted unanimously. It called for an immediate cessation of hostilities, and demanded that both sides submit their grievances for mediation in order to avoid spreading the conflict across the region. Neither of the superpowers wanted to be drawn into the war, and the Western states were particularly anxious to prevent any impact on the Gulf coast.

Two Resolutions were passed in 1982: 514 (12 July 1982) reiterated the call for an immediate ceasefire, which Iraq accepted, while 522 (4 October 1982) added that observers should be deployed to monitor any withdrawal. The personal efforts of mediation by the UN Secretary General, Javier Pérez de Cuéllar, were praised and he was urged to continue. Resolutions 540 and 552 in 1983 and 1984 respectively called on the belligerents to respect freedom of navigation because of attacks on Gulf installations and shipping. In these, there was a failure to condemn Iraqi attacks in the Gulf, which Iran used as evidence that the UN favoured Baghdad. In fact, Iraq was not making attacks on Kuwaiti and Saudi shipping as Iran was, and it was these two Gulf states that had called for a Resolution. Moreover, there was little progress towards a ceasefire because Iran believed it could still win the war. Nevertheless, the Resolutions did not enjoy unanimous support.

In 1986, until the end of the war, there was an increase in the tempo of Resolutions being passed. In February, Resolution 582 deplored the attacks on neutral shipping, the escalation of the conflict, the bombardment of civilians in cities, the violations of international law and, most significantly, the use of chemical weapons. In October, Resolution 588 urged the implementation of a ceasefire and the exchange of prisoners of war, but the Secretary General subsequently reported that neither side was willing to negotiate a peace at this stage, largely because of Saddam's determination to recover Fao, and the Iranians' belief they could secure Baghdad within weeks. The following July, Resolution 598 reaffirmed the details of 582, but added that an impartial body, acceptable to both sides, be appointed to mediate, ascertain responsibility and find solutions to the issues which had caused the conflict. In 1988, Resolution 612, following the report on the use of chemical weapons, condemned their use and called on member states to exert stronger controls on their supply, but there was still no progress towards a final settlement.

The breakthrough came after the shooting down of the Iranian Airbus 655 over Hormuz. Resolution 616 ordered an investigation on 20 July. On 9 August 1988, a further Resolution, 619 reiterated the calls for a ceasefire to two sides that were finally prepared to discuss an end to the war. The UN called for a Ceasefire Monitoring Group to be appointed to supervise a phased withdrawal. A final Resolution on the war, 620, reaffirmed the condemnation of the use of chemical weapons in light of the attacks on the Kurds.

With each of the Resolutions, criticism still prevails that the UN did not do enough, and that, under American influence, it 'favoured' Iraq. Yet, it is difficult to see quite how the UN could accommodate Iran when Tehran consistently rejected any conditions for peace. Saddam, while clearly in breach of international law in 1980, had nevertheless sought to escape the consequences of the conflict by accepting UN terms each time they were presented. His own overtures of peace, however strategic they may have been, were also acknowledged favourably by the UN.

Part III

The Search for a Decisive Result

7

Turning Point: Operations Badr and Fao, 1985–86

The Iraqis used the lull in the Iranian attacks in 1984, thanks to the flooding of the western and southern portions of the marshes, to build up a stronger network of defences around Qurna and along the axis of the Basra–Baghdad road. To speed up command and control in the new vulnerable sector, a separate East Tigris chain of command was established, followed by the creation of a distinct Shatt al-Arab Command in May 1984. By the autumn, the system of defence was a formidable mass of entrenchments, barbed wire, concrete emplacements and killing zones. The defensive belts were organised in four layers in depth. A vast number of guns, situated on higher ground, had registered all their likely targets. To assault such a position, the Iranians would have to cross a lake 8 miles (13 km) long and 2–7 miles (3–11 km) wide, or risk fighting through waterlogged terrain to the south, which was dominated by a mass of concrete pill boxes. The Iraqi army was also much larger than before. The regular army was composed of 22 divisions, totalling 500,000 men; in other words, twice the size of the force that had gone to war in 1980. The Popular Army had also expanded to 560,000 and its tasks ranged from internal security to battlefield police in the rear areas of the front lines. Saddam wanted more of these men and authorised the forcible conscription of university students, and implemented man-hunts in residential areas. To equip these new forces, Iraq imported $7.7 billion worth of arms and ammunition that year alone.

Faced with such formidable obstacles and conscious of the failure to make headway with infantry that lacked adequate support, the Iranians set about increasing the size of the armed forces, making improvements to training, particularly in amphibious and combined arms operations. New roads were built into the marshes and across the southern sector, and there were fresh efforts to obtain tanks, aircraft, logistical support vehicles and armoured personnel carriers. The Iranian air force obtained trainer aircraft spares from Switzerland, while Chieftain tank parts were purchased from Britain (as part of a pre-Revolution contract), but the bulk of equipment was in the form of Soviet-built tanks from Syria and Libya. The Libyans also purchased arms on Iran's behalf from Brazil.

The new approach was tested in a limited operation on the central front at Saif Saad on 18 October 1984. Light infantry infiltrated Iraqi positions at night along a 12-mile (19 km) front. With the Iraqis unable to ascertain the main effort, the Iranians pushed the Iraqis back until a strong counter-attack deprived them of the ground that had been taken. The Iranians noted the results carefully. Brigadier General Qasim Ali Zahir Nejad, who had been dismissed for allegedly failing to show sufficient determination in the Majnoon offensive in February 1984, was reinstated as Khomeini's personal representative on the Supreme Defence Council. It was another indication that the government had realised that the sheer determination and courage of the Iranian volunteers was not sufficient to defeat the Iraqis.

At the end of the wet season the Iraqis believed the Iranians would launch another major offensive. To off-balance the attempt, they made their own attack north and east of Majnoon on 28 January 1985. The attack soon bogged down and the Iranians, who were also well entrenched, drove the Iraqis back. Another Iraqi 'raid' towards Said Saad, designed to retake the settlement, was also checked. However, the Iraqis were satisfied that their positions were secure and that they had seized the initiative from the Iranians. To cause disruption in depth, the Iraqi air force also made a series of sorties against targets in Iranian cities as part of the so-called 'war of the cities'.

Operation Badr, 1985

On 11 March 1985, the Iranians launched Operation Badr, which was the culmination of several weeks' preparations. The Iraqis had strengthened their defences west and north of the Howizeh marshes, with yet more extensive flooded sections and a chain of strong points to the south. However, from January, the Iranians had systematically pushed the Iraqis out of each position. Small patrols had attacked from the cover of the reeds, infiltrating, outflanking and raiding, often using patrol boats, convincing the Iraqis to move back to more consolidated positions in open ground to the west. The main offensive, involving some 60,000 Iranians, made further use of the small waterways to push boats and infantry up to and then into the Iraqi positions. As they advanced, they assembled pontoon bridges and brought in supporting arms. Instead of hurling unsupported infantry forward, they paused their main attack once the break-in had been achieved. More troops and logistical support was assembled before embarking on the second phase. The more scientific approach succeeded, and the Iranians managed to sustain intense fire from the Iraqi guns and tanks to drive 4 miles (6 km) into depth, which brought them, finally, across the Basra–Baghdad highway in strength.

The Iraqi response was immediate. Although anxious that their well-prepared defensive lines had been breached, they launched an immediate counter-offensive. Reinforcements were concentrated at Qurna, to the south of the Iranian breakthrough, and Uzayr, to the north. Employing massed artillery, repeated air sorties and clouds of chemical agents, the Iraqis began to close in on the Iranian salient from two directions. Saddam's Presidential Guard division was in the lead, and its armour pushed the Iranians back towards the marshes. Nine days of intense fighting brought the Iranians back to their start line, with something in the region of 20,000 Iranian and 14,000 Iraqi troops killed.

The Iranian strategists believed that their tactics had paid off. Infiltration, the use of cover and broken terrain, night assaults using the element of surprise, and the steady demoralisation of the Iraqis all contributed, they argued, to the eventual defeat of the Iraqi army. In many ways, this was simply wishful thinking. The Iraqis, even when thrown back, overwhelmed and forced to operate where their advantage in armour, artillery and air power were reduced, had rallied and counter-attacked successfully. The Iraqis did not appear to be breaking and their support for Saddam seemed as steadfast, relatively speaking, as ever. Indeed, Saddam was reassured that his strategy of holding the border-line was broadly correct. Maintaining a large reserve to plug any gaps in the south and centre had been proven to work. The only real cause for concern was the northern sector.

Two senior officers had also emerged from the campaign with some success: Major-General Hisham Sabah Fakhri (the deputy chief of staff who had checked the Iranian offensive of 1983) and Major-General Mahir Abdul Rashid (a relative of Saddam who had successively commanded First Corps in the north in 1983 and then Third Corps in Basra in 1984–85). Saddam praised these men in particular but, in fact, awarded decorations to all his officers in the high command. Saddam also felt more confident to devolve command decisions to these trusted lieutenants, and new officers were promoted on the basis of professional competence rather than purely on the basis of party loyalty. Saddam also felt more able to have himself identified with the armed forces once again, often appearing in uniform alongside them in the state media.[1]

In July and then into August 1985, the Iranians made further, smaller offensives, entitled Quds and Ashura, across the northern, central and southern fronts. Iraqi Kurds assisted the Iranian attack in the north, while in the south Al Mujahideen Iraqi exiles also fought against the Iraqi army. The gains were modest, with small sections of ground taken in all three sectors. Another attack around Rawandoz on 8 September gained more Iraqi territory, but, significantly, the Kurdish Democratic Party claimed that it now controlled all of northern Iraq up to the Syrian border.

The centre of gravity for both Baghdad and Tehran still appeared to lie in the south. The Iranians made an attack on 11 September to take the southern part of Western Majnoon Island as a prelude for launching an attack that would encircle the southern edge of Basra. The Iraqi Presidential Guard was selected to retake the southern portion of the island because of the difficult nature of the terrain. It was unable to dislodge the Iranians from their extended salient, but inflicted such destruction that the Iranians were unable to make use of the island as a launch pad for the second phase of the operation. Nonetheless, the marshes remained a significant problem for the Iraqi defence plan. The Iraqis constructed towers to overlook the reeds and marshes, deployed acoustic sensors and night-vision equipment, but it proved difficult to stop further infiltrations. The Iranians had specifically trained 1,000-strong teams of 'Special Forces' to operate in the marshland, and, further back, a new network of plank roads connected the small areas of high ground so as to move men, equipment and combat supplies forwards into the battle area.

To create the momentum for new offensives the following year, the Iranian regime continued to mobilise the population. In a campaign called 'Caravan to Karbala', Tehran set out to raise a million men. The notion of Karbala, where Imam Hussein had chosen to fight a battle in 680 knowing he would be killed rather than submit to the tyranny of the Arab caliph's army, was deliberately chosen to invoke a spirit of sacrifice and enthusiasm. In parts of Iran, Ali's last stand was always commemorated with a ten-day ceremony of self-flagellation, the cuts of Ashura being seen as a particularly blessed act of remembrance and spiritual solidarity. The Iranian people were going to be urged to make yet another bloody sacrifice against Iraq, despite the steady deterioration of their material capability and the sustained Iraqi air and missile attacks against their cities. Yet, for 1986, Tehran planned to outflank the Iraqis from the south with an audacious amphibious and hazardous river-crossing operation.

Operations on the Fao peninsular

Overnight on 9 February 1986, the Iranians launched their Wal-Fajr VIII offensive with two prongs directed at Basra and a third against the Fao peninsular. The northern thrust, in the Howizeh marshes, was checked, but Umm Rassas Island in the Shatt al Arab was secured. The unexpected success occurred in Fao, where Iranian troops in small craft, in driving rain and strong winds, crossed the 1,094-yard-wide (1,000m) waterway, and established six beachheads.[2] The Iraqis were thrown off-balance by this new front, and there was confusion as they tried to identify the main axis of the Iranian advance. The Iranians decided to push further on, off the waterway, which added to the chaos engulfing the Iraqi headquarters. The Iranians brought across more waves, and eventually established a pontoon bridge to increase the flow of men and materiel into the peninsular. Unable to ascertain whether this was a feint, and unwilling to be drawn further south before the main attack appeared around Basra, the Iraqi units were driven further and further back. In the withdrawal, some equipment had to be left behind.

The Iranians launched a new thrust near Basra on 11 February to divide the Iraqi reserves and so it was not until the 14 February that the Iraqi headquarters could be sure of the main Iranian effort and mount a counter-attack into Fao. By then, a significant proportion of the low-lying peninsular, an area interspersed with marshes that lies to the west of the Shatt al Arab and about 75 miles (121 km) south of Basra, had been overrun. The Iranians were aware that an Iraqi counter-offensive would be forthcoming. Having taken many fortified emplacements, they had decided to consolidate and dig in.

The Iraqis led their attack with three armoured columns in the centre and on either side of the peninsular, dragging up heavy guns to support the effort. Against the odds, the Iranians had managed to get heavy weapons across the Shatt and inflicted significant damage on the Iraqis as they were channelled into a narrowing zone, limited to a few roads or hemmed in by marshy terrain. The Iranians beat off the attack, and viewed the whole operation as a success.[3] They had captured the Iraqi coastline, a radar station, a missile battery and a significant amount of equipment that made useful war trophies.[4]

Saddam once again used his elite Presidential Guard as the spearhead of a new counter-attack, but this fresh attempt to retake Fao met with the same problems. The terrain was unsuitable for heavy armour. Artillery concentrations, when they could be mustered, proved less effective against Iranian infantry who were carefully dispersed. As the Iraqis tried to advance along the causeways, they were attacked by small parties of Iranians armed with anti-tank missiles from concealed entrenchments. The Iranians also made every use of the captured Iraqi equipment – including armour and personnel carriers. The Iranians kept up a steady supply of anti-tank weapons and troops, using the pontoons or small craft under cover of darkness. Continuing bad weather not only concealed these movements in daylight, they also degraded Iraqi air power to a significant degree. American or Chinese-made anti-aircraft missiles were also employed to take down hostile planes and the number of sorties that could be mounted by the Iraqis was reduced. Moreover, in the brief windows of good weather, the Iranians made a conscious effort to achieve some sort of air parity over the Fao peninsular by concentrating their best aircraft (including twenty-four F-14 fighters) in the far south. The Iraqi pilots responded by making more low-level flights, and increased their efforts to ground-strafe Iranian infantry. However, this tended to make them yet more vulnerable to surface-to-air missiles, and they suffered the loss of fifty-five planes and helicopters in just two weeks of fighting.

Despite these problems, the Iraqis kept up their efforts, making best use of artillery, armour and airpower to inch through the dug-in Iranian troops. The Iranians found it difficult to maintain the supply of their forward units, a fact made more problematic by their dispersal over such a wide area. By 18 February, both the Iranian offensive and the Iraqi counter-offensive had stalled, and on 21 February, the Iraqi Third Corps began to reinforce the existing units in the peninsular, while a large-scale chemical attack covered the move. In fact, wet weather reduced the effectiveness of this attack, and the Third Corps could not give its undivided attention to Fao because of Iranian moves on the Basra front. Here the Iranians withdrew from Umm Rassas Island, leading Iraqi planners to assume that this must be the prelude to another attack elsewhere. As a result, the Third Corps counter-offensive in Fao amounted to little more than an infantry assault supported by artillery. It was driven off with heavy casualties.

The next day, 24 February, the Iranians attempted to keep the Iraqis off-balance and prevent them from sending more reinforcements to Fao by attacking again in the far north. The so-called Wal al Fajr IX was launched just 14 miles (22 km) from Suleimaniya, where Kurdish insurgents had already been intensifying their attacks on Iraqi army units for the previous two weeks.[5] By the first week of March, the Iranians had acquired more ground in the north, and fierce fighting had erupted around the Darbandi Khan Lake and its strategic dam, which provided electricity for Baghdad. This action was countered by a series of Iraqi air raids on Iranian installations and tankers in the Gulf.

Saddam regarded the ejection of the Iranians from the Fao peninsular as his priority. By early March, the Iraqis had built a new defence line across the peninsular from which to launch a counter-offensive. An attempt to open a flank on the Iranians with an amphibious landing on 9 and 10 March went awry and the Iraqi force had to withdraw. In mid-March, the Iraqis tried to push forward in more conventional operations, but the Iranians, reinforced and prepared, checked their assailants with heavy losses. Saddam judged that the rising cost of casualties would have too high a political cost to be sustained and he called off the counter-offensive. The Iraqis had lost perhaps 8,000 killed in action, and the Iranians, who lacked the same firepower, had losses estimated at more than 20,000. The Iraqi air force had also suffered significant losses having flown a staggering 18,648 missions in just six weeks in 1986 compared with the same number of missions for the entire year of 1985.[6]

The Iranians, despite their ability to hold the Fao peninsular, were now in a precarious position strategically. They had to maintain two divisions across the Shatt al Arab, with a further five in reserve on the 'home bank'. This left the Iranians in an extended posture with a significant water obstacle at their back. If the defensive perimeter was in some way breached, the men in the peninsular had little hope of escape. In addition, they were not strong enough, certainly in armour or artillery, to push any further northwards towards Basra. Their ability to tie down Iraqi forces while another operation started from the Howizeh marshes was also somewhat limited and would probably result in heavy casualties. However, the possession of some Iraqi territory, along with that acquired in the north, did suggest that Iran could negotiate with a significant advantage in any final settlement. The problem was that the greater the achievement, the more tempted Khomeini and his allies became to continue the war to a final military victory.

Reflections on the operations in Fao produced different responses at the time. The Iraqis were irritated with the Americans for their 'intelligence failure'.[7] They had come to rely on support from their satellites to locate the concentrations of Iranian forces, but the bad weather had, in fact, obscured any opportunity to observe the Iranian movements. Iranian formation had also taken the precaution of using messages delivered by motorcycle couriers rather than risk signals' intercepts, and by these means had achieved a tactical surprise. The Iranians had benefited in other ways from the weather conditions and environment, especially in concealed movement, degradation of the strike capability of the Iraqi air force, and the canalising of the Iraqi counter-attacks in the Fao peninsular itself.

The Iranians had also managed to launch multiple offensives on several fronts in a coordinated fashion. They had demonstrated that where they could achieve surprise they could make some substantial gains. More importantly, they had made better arrangements to consolidate the territory they had overrun, adopting a posture of strategic offence and a tactical defence, and had made more strenuous efforts to build up logistical and manpower support behind the offensives. Yet many of the old problems continued. The Iranians were still dependent on infantry assaults and in open country they were particularly vulnerable to Iraqi firepower. They had no answer to Iraqi mobility or to the Iraqis' ability to operate on interior lines, reinforcing any threatened sector with their substantial reserves. While they had achieved local air parity, they still lacked superiority in the air on any front. Their weakness in air power left their cities vulnerable to an Iraqi offensive from the skies.

8

War of the Cities, Home Fronts, Internal Security and Insurgency

Both Iran and Iraq went to considerable lengths to sustain the war effort. First, they had to establish their ability to fight, in terms of national revenue and in the willingness of the populace to endure the conflict. This necessitated measures to protect the economy, to sustain the people's motivation to fight, and the suppression of opposition groups. Saddam was particularly concerned about public morale and the threat of Kurdish or Shia subversion. He tried to use the economy as a prop to the war effort, and for months hoped to shield the Iraqis from the full blast of a costly war. He also assumed that Iran faced similar problems and so he sought to terrorise or demoralise the Iranian public to such an extent they would turn on their government. The result was the 'war of the cities', an air and missile offensive against major Iranian urban areas. However, the Kurdish insurgency continued to develop through the war and threatened to overrun the strategic oil facilities of the north. As a result, Saddam had to intensify his efforts on the home front. The Iranians did, indeed, face several internal crises caused by the crippling economic effects of the war, but, despite severe losses, Iranian morale remained intact. Nevertheless, both sides were forced to introduce more draconian measures in 1986 and 1987. This chapter traces these developments in order to give a more rounded perspective on the history of the war behind the front lines.

The Iraqi home front, 1981–82

Before the war, Iraq's oil production totalled 3 million bpd, of which 2.8 million were exported. This gave Iraq about $26 billion out of a total revenue of foreign reserves of $35 billion with which to wage the war. From the outset, Iraq's installations were attacked and damaged, leading to a steep decline in output. Basra and Umm Qasr were either blockaded or became the scene of bitter fighting, preventing export shipping. The solution was to develop existing overland routes through Saudi Arabia, Kuwait, Jordan and Turkey, but it had to offer financial assistance to Jordan, settle long-standing border disputes in favour of its neighbours, and offer transit fees to persuade Syria to allow Iraqi oil to be pumped through its own network to Lebanon. Through these means Iraq managed to export 1.4 million bpd by the end of 1981, giving it $10.4 billion. The ability to wage war did not just depend on sufficient revenue, it required the willingness of the people to accept all manner of hardships and losses.

Saddam's anxiety about the loyalty of the Iraqi population was reflected in his measures to ensure that standards of living could be maintained during the war. He assumed that, even with a reduced export capability, the economy could continue to grow at 20 per cent per annum. There was a conscious effort to permit consumer goods to be imported, with an increase from $14 billion to $19 billion in payments, and there was a significant increase in development projects with an expenditure of $22.5 billion.[1] Foreign companies were persuaded to continue their construction work, including the highway from Baghdad to the Turkish border, housing in the capital and the underground system. Some $12 billion was spent on purchasing arms, part of which was paid for by securing loans from the Gulf states and from Iraq's own reserves, but even with these measures, Iraq would be unable to sustain a long war.

Consequently, in April 1982, with news that the Syrians had closed the oil pipeline to Iraqi oil, Saddam announced an austerity plan. Some foreign contracts were cancelled and new development projects suspended. The Five Year Plan was scaled back. Imports were cut, and only existing development projects continued so as to maintain the prestige of the regime. Yet the impact on the Iraqi public could not be disguised. The large numbers being called up into the armed forces caused a decline in production, and all government employees were compelled to work additional hours to make up for the shortfall in the state sector. Private sector operatives were, for the first time in the Ba'athist socialist regime, encouraged to develop business activities and to work in agriculture. The party's propaganda machinery absorbed the change without missing a step. Saddam's cult of personality was extended to new heights so that devoted Ba'ath Party loyalists organised demonstrations in favour of additional hours and the war effort. However, campaigns to raise money for the wounded enjoyed genuine public support and there was acceptance that, in wartime, material sacrifices were inevitable. Farmers and herders were delighted to see the back of the regime's cooperatives and the rise in demand.

A number of the Kurdish Iraqis regarded the war as an opportunity. The announcement that Saddam had offered to withdraw from Iranian territory in order to secure peace, and the withdrawal of some Iraqi units to fight the war further south, seemed to herald a weakening of the regime. The Kurdish Democratic Party (KDP), led by Masud and Idris Barzani, mobilised opposition, and the trigger for angry demonstrations was Baghdad's announcement that it had suspended 'cultural concessions' to the Kurds for the sake of national unity in wartime. There were outbreaks of fighting between insurgents and the Iraqi army in several Kurdish cities.

The Iranian home front, pre-1984

Iran had its own internal security problem as a residue of the revolution. The Mujahideen-e Khalq (MEK) was an armed organisation located in the centre of the country, and the Revolutionary Guards used the opportunity of the war to carry out ruthless suppression of the MEK movement between July 1981 and September 1982. In contrast, the Tudeh (the Masses) Party, ostensibly a left-wing opposition group, was permitted to function because it supported the concept of *inquilab* (revolution) and Khomeini's leadership, but, as a Marxist-Leninist organisation, it stood for secularism and therefore was at odds with the ideology of the theocratic elite. Moreover, it opposed the extension of the war by the invasion of Iraqi territory. When the USSR resumed its supply of arms to Iraq, the Iranian regime suspected that Tudeh's sympathies lay elsewhere. It decided to ban the party on 4 May 1982, shortly after Soviet-made missiles had struck Dezful. There was a wave of arrests, trials and executions, and many of the victims were members of the armed forces, thereby bolstering the narrative that Iranian military setbacks could be explained by the existence of these 'fifth columnists'. The only remaining opposition group, the Freedom Party, came close to being banned in 1982–83 when its leader, Mahdi Bazargan, not only criticised the invasion of Iraqi territory, but also condemned the regime's practice of labelling any critics as 'heretics'.

Nevertheless, there was genuine support for the government from the Iranian people when the Iraqis were ejected from Iranian soil and when the nation reached its economic targets through sheer hard work. There was a desire to demonstrate that, without the Shah, the Iranian people could thrive. The war thus had the effect of strengthening the government, or, more accurately, Khomeini's personal rule. The harsh treatment of the regime's opponents created a general sense of fear in the country that, nevertheless, lay alongside a desire to defend both Iran and Islam against the Iraqi 'aggressors'.

By the spring of 1984, it was estimated that 170,000 Iranians had been killed and more than 300,000 wounded. Iraqi losses were thought to have been about half of these figures. Demographically, Iran could sustain this ratio, which gave rise to Tehran's idea of fighting a war of attrition. While Iraq could count on 161,000 men each year reaching the age of conscription at eighteen, Iran could find 422,000, or about 1 per cent of the population. Raw numbers alone, however, cannot explain the motivation of the Iranians to fight and endure a long, costly war. The capacity to field a large force is not sufficient to sustain an indefinite strategy of attrition if the citizen-soldiers refuse to fight.

The usual explanation, and the one given by the regime at the time, was to attribute their endurance and willingness to take heavy losses as an expression of their distinctive Shia Muslim identity. Officially, the Iranian soldier believed that the war, as an extension of the Islamic revolution, would carry him to Najaf and Karbala, and thence on to Jerusalem, the Al Quds, or Bait al Muqqadas (the Holy House). At each stage, the idea was to liberate the cities from secularism and oppression, or in the case of Saddam, from evil itself. The campaign towards Karbala had to start with operations against Basra, on its route, but would culminate with a struggle that would recreate the battle in which Al Hussein had died. If one were killed in such a battle, then it would be a perfect emulation of the sacrifice of Hussein himself. Success in this military operation would also redeem the Shia and earn the particular blessing of this martyr. Iranian radio broadcasts reinforced the idea of holy sacrifice in war by urging listeners to 'wish death and welcome the afterlife'. It has been suggested that while Iran held 50,000 prisoners of war in 1984, the Iraqis held only 7,300, which represented the unwillingness to give in even when overwhelmed in battle. Iranians were also motivated by a strong sense of national and ethnic identity. The defence of the south against the Iraqi invasion was a defence of Iran and of being Iranian as much as it was about the revolution or religion.

On the home front, it was a different matter. When the regime abolished the idea of arbitrary arrest in December 1982, believing the revolution was secure, private entrepreneurs and retailers began raising their prices. In January 1983, in his usual stern and threatening delivery, Khomeini had to remind the public, and particularly retailers, that in the

Islamic War he expected everyone to make sacrifices and not to enrich himself from the struggle. This specific reference and the regime's reputation for ruthless punishment was enough to check the rise in prices.[2] The government continued to condemn 'economic terrorists', those who opposed the regime through economic or financial means. In July 1983 there were trials and punishments. Economic crimes were rooted out by 'assistants of God' who patrolled urban areas looking for war profiteers, although the criteria for such a crime remained conveniently obscure. Since high prices were also the result of uneven distribution of goods, the regime set up consumer cooperatives. All foreign trade had been nationalised, so the complete nationalisation of all domestic commercial activity seemed imminent. Interestingly, this was in contrast to Iraq, where private enterprise was encouraged and the regime relaxed its socialist economic agenda.

There were limits to what 'sacrifices' the regime could expect. The revolutionary regime did not make any changes to subsidies on foodstuffs for the poor or the social security system, which together cost the government $4 billion per annum. Rationing was introduced to support the poorest and when scarce imports arrived, priority was given to distribution in poor urban neighbourhoods first. The regime turned a blind eye to the black market so that those who could afford to pay did not get alienated entirely by the rationing system. Controls on imports, designed to help the war economy, were actually detrimental to industry, which could not obtain parts or raise foreign revenue. Skilled manpower was also lost to the war effort and, as a result, output fell in 1982.

There were some successes in the Iranian economy. Inflation remained steady at 20 per cent in the first years of the war and a rise in oil prices helped to offset the loss of revenue. Iranian oil output totalled 2.3 million bpd and oil sales also helped in raising GNP in 1982, the first time since the revolution, turning the deficit of $3.2 billion in 1980 to a surplus of $6.3 billion in 1984. Foreign debt fell from $15 billion to $1.1 billion. A drive for self-sufficiency helped in the agricultural sector where output rose by 20 per cent. These factors enabled Iran to sustain its war effort and to find some revenue for foreign weapons and equipment, when it could find states willing to sell. However, the Iranians were still forced to make desperate economies. The armed forces, Revolutionary Guards and Basiji militia, the war pensions, martyrs fund and the war reconstruction projects amounted to $15 billion, or 30 per cent of the entire budget.[3] Consequently, in the early years, conscripts were paid just $1 a day. The Revolutionary Guards were often equipped with captured Iraqi vehicles and weapons leading to problems of ammunition resupply and spares. The lack of spare parts also affected specialist units, including the armoured brigades and air force. The Iranian public was urged to give what it could for the national war effort, but the most abundant resource was manpower. The Basiji Militia, operating out of mosques and educational institutions, helped to mobilise and train 2.4 million men, and claimed to have dispatched 450,000 to the front line by mid-1983. The regime therefore placed a much greater emphasis than Iraq on sustaining motivation and a sense of religious-military mission. Yet, even here, by the eighth year of war, the country had reached its limits.

Invoking war in defence of Islam

Saddam was not prepared to be upstaged on the notion of an 'Islamic War'. He organised the Popular Islamic Conference in Baghdad in April 1983, inviting 280 ulema and scholars from over fifty countries, asking them to consider that Saddam, once he realised that the Muslim world wanted him to withdraw from Iranian soil, had done so. In return, he asked the Popular Islamic Conference to back Iraq's cause, which, with the skilful chairmanship of Sheikh Ali Kashif Ghita, a Shia and outspoken critic of Khomeini, it obliged to do. However, many Shia ulema of Iraq refused to attend the conference, including the family of Ayatollah Hojatalislam Baqir Hakim. The regime responded by arresting and executing six members of Hakim's family in May that year. Secret service surveillance increased in Najaf to the extent that virtually every public building, café and restaurant had intelligence coverage. Every religious service had to have state sanction, to ensure that each member of the ulema and every religious organisation were 'on message'.

Iraqi Shias were not automatic enemies of the regime, with several serving in high positions. Moreover, once the Iranians had invaded Iraqi soil, they demonstrated their allegiance to Iraq even where they feared Saddam's regime itself. There was little sympathy for Khomeini, who was feared, and the Al Daawa organisation's terrorist activities put Shias as much in the firing line as anyone else, so there was little popular backing for that movement either. The Islamic Action organisation was another group that claimed to represent revolutionary Islamic and largely Shia interests, but its short-lived bombing campaign against government buildings in November 1983 aroused little interest or support from Shia Iraqis.

A contributory factor to the loyalty of the people was the casualty toll. Few families were unaffected by 1983, but there was a genuine determination to see that they had not died in vain. Yet the regime was so concerned that morale was failing it banned all demonstrations of mourning. Propaganda messages stressed the value of service in the Popular Army, the courage of the armed forces and the gradual defeat of the Iranians. There were repeated film-clips of dead Iranian troops, references to less-than-human characteristics exhibited by Khomeini, and the achievements of Saddam Hussein. In September 1983, Saddam ordered that martial values were to be inculcated and encouraged in the Ba'ath and throughout government, emphasising loyalty, obedience, exhibiting high morale and endurance. To ensure the armed forces lived up to these values themselves, a Punishment Corps patrolled the rear of the front lines. Sensing that the younger generation were the most enthusiastic for action, in November 1983 the government encouraged 14–17-year-olds to get weapons training. It simultaneously called up men aged thirty-six, adding a one-year cohort to the conscription levy.

Yet the steady militarisation of Iraqi society had an adverse effect on the war economy. The decline in manpower continued to have an impact on the industrial sector and the decline in oil prices during 1983 caused a significant fall in revenue, reducing it by one third to $7 billion. By the end of 1982, the per capita domestic income fell by 12 per cent, adding to the 26-per-cent fall the previous year. From 1982, Iraq could no longer pay cash for its arms imports, and its foreign exchange reserve had fallen to $1.2 billion. In response, the government cut the development budget by a third in 1983, reduced the size of the civil service and cut public service salaries. Consumer imports were reduced by two-thirds, although military hardware coming into Iraq increased at the same rate.[4] Inflation soared briefly to 50 per cent in December 1982 before falling back to 25 per cent the following year.

To escape a fiscal crisis now that the balance of trade had tilted so significantly, Saddam raised fresh loans from the Gulf states, rescheduled debts and looked for moratoria on contract payments. Like Iran, it also appealed to the public for contributions. In June 1983, one campaign of this nature yielded $500 million and 8,800lb (3,990 kg) of gold and jewellery. Donors' names were publicised to encourage others. Foreign workers were a target, and they were prevented from sending home a third of the $4 billion that annually left the country for their place of origin. The unexpected effect was to prompt 700,000 Egyptian workers to leave, closely followed by other nationalities, which created a labour shortage in all sectors. Iraqi women were encouraged to take up a range of new employment opportunities so that, by 1983, they made up a quarter of the national work force.

War of the cities

On 5 March 1985, Iraq carried out air attacks against the steel factory at Ahwaz and the unfinished site of Iran's planned nuclear power station at Bushahr, which, it claimed, were legitimate military targets. Iran argued that these attacks violated the UN agreement of June 1984 not to attack population centres and in retaliation it shelled Basra. For their part the Iraqis believed it was the Iranians who had violated the agreement and they immediately carried out air attacks against Isfahan. The exchange was later referred to as the first 'war of the cities', even though urban areas had been the target of specific operations since the outbreak of the war. Iraq always maintained that its border settlements had been shelled by Iranian artillery and the Iranians pointed to the attacks on Khorramshahr and Abadan as evidence of unrestrained Iraqi aggression.

On 11 March, Iranian aircraft hit the suburbs of Baghdad, which led to a day of air raids on sixteen Iranian towns and cities. The Iraqis announced that, after one week of further attacks, all Iranian air space would be treated as hostile, which would prevent even civilian aircraft from flying. The Iranian response was characteristically defiant: they fired a Scud-B missile with a 1,000lb (454 kg) warhead at Kirkuk. When the Iraqis bombed Tehran the next day, the Iranians fired four more Scuds at Baghdad. When the UN Secretary General visited Iran later that month, the Iranians claimed that 1,450 of their civilians had been killed and a further 4,000 injured in Iraqi bombing. Bazargan, the leader of the Freedom Party, called for a ceasefire with Iraq, but Khomeini dismissed the request as defeatist. Indeed, despite a widespread fear of the air attacks, there was broadly a mood of defiance and certainly not a willingness to overthrow the government in order to end the war, as the Iraqis had hoped.[5] Both governments were sufficiently concerned about the long-term effects on morale that they agreed to a mutual suspension of attacks on urban areas when the UN pushed for a renewal of the deal on 6 April 1985. The Saudi foreign minister hoped this might herald a more general peace process, but his attempts to secure agreement in May failed.

When a suicide bomber detonated a car bomb in a clear attempt to kill the Kuwaiti leader, Sheikh Sabah al Sabah, on 25 May 1985, there was widespread agreement it was an Iranian operation. Saddam used the assault to resume strikes on Tehran and on Iranian Gulf installations. Kharg Island was subjected to several attacks, and the Iranian air force responded with air strikes against Saudi and Kuwaiti shipping along the coast of Qatar. When the Iranians announced they would stage a rally to mark the last Friday of Ramadan as Jerusalem Day, a reference to the objective of marching on the ancient city as the culmination of the Islamic Revolution, the Iraqis threatened to bomb Tehran and even named particular streets as targets. The Iranian response was a giant public demonstration, inviting, in a sense, a martyrs' climax to the holiest month in the Muslim calendar. The Iraqis did not make the air strikes, no doubt conscious of the international opprobrium the massive civilian casualties would create. Devout Iranians attributed the absence of Iraqi bombers as divine protection and therefore reinforced their convictions that this was a just war. The Iraqis announced a two-week unilateral suspension of air operations against Iranian cities, hoping the people would turn against the government, but also hoping, no doubt, to avoid any escalation against their own urban centres.[6]

Saddam continued to focus efforts on raising morale and cementing his leadership. A cadre of commissars toured military units and issued pamphlets containing Saddam's speeches and injunctions. By 1984, there were already 312 booklets of this type in circulation. The commissars were often drawn from the Presidential Guard, itself an organisation that recruited largely from the Tikrit area (where Saddam's own clans originated). They grew to the size of a division and eventually expanded to cover all seven army corps by the end of the war. The rest of the army in Iraq grew to one million in strength, although its ranks were not always enthusiastic about military service. As early as 1982, the death penalty was imposed on deserters and those 'absent without leave', and new legislation was created to encourage those going absent without leave to return to their service before this draconian measure was implemented. The Popular Army militia was designed to augment the armed forces and also to provide internal security. The problem was that, since it was part-time, workers were absent from their jobs when performing these national duties. Employers received compensation for these absences, but that did not improve production levels and merely drained government revenue. Pensioners were recalled to fill the gap, and women took up more of the vacancies. The government also announced that any Arab could hold dual citizenship in Iraq and therefore become part of the workforce. The move was designed to appeal to Egyptian migrant workers, but Iraqis were rather ambivalent about these men who did not serve in the armed forces yet took the jobs.

Despite these efforts, the Iraqi economy was still struggling to meet the burden of war. Food production was affected by a severe drought in 1984 that reduced the national crop by two-thirds. This increased domestic prices. The price of oil had fallen, as had the value of the dollar, which reduced the purchasing power of the state and led to new restrictions. The reduction of imports and periodic power cuts in the capital (due to under-investment in energy generation) reminded the public of the hardships of war, but also caused a slowing of industrial production that depended on electricity. The state restriction on the money supply helped to curtail inflation, which had been rising steadily since the outbreak of war, and hoarding of goods became more common as people sought to survive or to exploit the prices and shortages for personal profit. The state media stations encouraged citizens to write in and complain and these were broadcast as a 'safety valve', providing a useful guide to the people's grievances; the public were evidently angry about rising prices, power cuts, bribes and unresponsive bureaucracy.

Saddam continued to benefit from the military victories of his armed forces and he used this persona to his advantage in domestic politics. He cultivated his image with great diligence and he was able to project himself as the leader who was able to thwart Iranian offensives and safeguard the Iraqi people. He had himself filmed praying at Shia mosques and shrines whenever an Iranian offensive was imminent, as in October 1984 and in March 1985. In Ramadan that year (May–June), he ordered Ba'ath Party officials to hold banquets at the end of each day's fast, cultivating the idea that this secularist organisation was still, at its heart, a Muslim movement.

The Second Popular Islamic Conference was held in April 1985 in Baghdad and once again condemned the Iranians as aggressors and oppressors. For three months the selected ulema toured Iraq to broadcast the conference resolutions, namely to cut Iran off from all diplomatic, cultural and economic ties with the Muslim world. There was no mention of Syria's support for Iran, of course, which rather undermined any idea of Muslim world unity on the issue. Moreover, Saddam's fundamental insincerity was brought out when he ordered the closure of eighty-six religious colleges and institutions and the execution or exile of their leaders. These were the 'unapproved' centres that Saddam feared could form the nucleus of anti-government resistance. The Ministry of Waqfs and Religious Affairs established its own Islamic Higher Institute to train 'approved' ulema and religious students. The Al Daawa organisation was naturally a prime target for the regime. Executions of suspects and of suspects' families were carried out from time to time to deter active resistance. Even for the rest of society, there were restrictions, particularly on the ability to travel overseas. Only men over 50 or immediate relatives of the war dead were permitted to go on the haj – thus projecting the right image abroad and preventing deserters from the army using the pilgrimage as an escape route.

Saddam consolidated his personal power at every opportunity and there were usually changes when the president felt the fortunes of war might be swinging against him. When the Iraqi army was enduring a series of hammer blows in the south, Saddam dismissed Barzan Tikriti, his chief security officer, and replaced him with his own son, Uday. Saddam was aware that Tikriti had close links with Abu Nidal, the notorious terrorist, which might deter foreign donors, and that his plans for closer surveillance of senior army officers were deeply unpopular within the Iraqi army. Removing Tikriti would ensure greater army loyalty, without jeopardising the security apparatus. Barzan loyalists were purged, but the rank and file, those who watched on street corners, in cafés, and in workplaces, were unaffected.

The situation was different in Iran. The regime's Guardian Council simply ignored or vetoed the decisions and complaints of the Majlis (the Iranian parliament) where it did not suit their own agenda. Legislation that had been passed in parliament was blocked by the supreme authority of the country. Where the Majlis wanted to impose state regulation of external trade and most internal commerce, the Guardian Council refused to accept the measures. Khomeini tried to clarify the position by saying that the state should prioritise military and strategic goods and simply supervise the rest, but there was a requirement to ensure than some consumer goods got through in order to safeguard public morale for the war effort. Khomeini merely stated that his approach adhered to Islamic principles. Indeed, Islam was now the regulatory system for all public and private life, and even banking was Islamicised in March 1984. There could be no room for opposition to the regime in Khomeini's mind as this would be an opposition to the government of God. Yet he was worldly enough to acknowledge that bazaar traders were fed up with being labelled 'economic terrorists' and knew they were influential on the public mood; in other words, he was quite prepared to make concessions in order to sustain the war effort and therefore the survival of the regime in the longer term. Rhetorically, he took the strongest and most unrelenting line on the war as the vehicle to mobilise the people behind the revolution, and the character of his message was always one of Islamic demands and requirements.

The Guardian Council's grip on power was now unchallenged. Hojatalislam Ali Khamenei, who was already the president, defeated other selected candidates in elections. Ironically, the other candidates were already in the government. However, in 1984, there was a reduced popular vote of 88 per cent, down from the previous 95 per cent. The government attributed the fall in voter turnout and the slight downturn in the popular vote for Khamenei as a result of necessary but unpopular war measures. In fact, despite the appearance of victory and unity, the Islamic Republican Party was torn apart by factionalism. The 'conservatives' supported the president, while the 'radicals' backed the prime minister, Mir Hosain Musavi. Khomeini insisted that the two factions work together in order not to divide the revolutionary movement. The division was no mere party-political problem as it reflected the factional nature of Iranian society, but it was Iraq that would suffer even more from this particular problem.

Kurdish insurgency

The long-standing issue of Kurdish resistance to Saddam's regime grew in importance during the Iran–Iraq War. Saddam had begun secret negotiations with Jalal Talabani, the leader of the Patriotic Union of Kurdistan (PUK) in October 1984 in order to try and neutralise growing resistance, but Talabani learned that Tariq Aziz, the foreign minister, had just visited Ankara to renew a secret deal that would enable Turkish troops to pursue Kurdish guerrillas up to 18 miles (29 km) into Iraqi territory. In May 1983, the Turks had already destroyed a base in Iraq where the KDP operated. Talabani, fearing that Saddam might be about to make a move against his organisation, broke off negotiations. Effectively, this brought all Kurdish groups together against Baghdad. They were supplied eagerly by Iran and also by Syria and Libya, so by mid-1985 they had stepped up their guerrilla campaign and controlled perhaps a third of the Kurdish north, namely Dohak, Arbil and Suleimaniya. The KDP, with 10,000 insurgents, were concentrated closest to the Turkish border. The PUK, with 40,000, operated in the southern area between Kirkuk and Qala Diza.

Iran did not support the KDP in direct military operations until 1985. It was concerned at the outbreak of war that the KDP might encourage Iranian Kurds to fight Tehran, but, anxious to fulfil its multiple-front war of attrition strategy, the KDP had been supported with arms and logistical support, including heavy weapons donated by the Libyans. Nevertheless, despite Tehran's appeals, the Kurds refused to mount conventional offensives. Instead, they avoided urban areas and fought as guerrillas in the countryside. In retaliation, the Iraqi armed forces carried out reprisals against Kurdish villages, which they suspected of harbouring insurgents. Bombing from the air and clearances became more frequent.

The support from Iran prompted the KDP to seize the opportunity to build a broad anti-Ba'athist coalition and, as a result, members of the Shia al Daawa were offered bases in Kurdistan. Al Daawa later claimed that 1,000 of its activists operated in the north. Moreover, deserters from the army, fearful of the capital punishment that awaited them, saw no option but to join either Al Daawa or the Kurdish guerrillas. Consequently, they formed entire units, equipped and armed by the Kurds. In June 1987, the Iranians were desperate to widen the northern front and they joined hands with these Kurdish and Iraqi insurgents to stage a major offensive.

The home fronts in 1986

The capture of the Fao peninsular in February 1986 was a cause for celebration in Tehran and the regime announced enthusiastically that this would be the 'Year of Victory'. This news, coupled with the anniversary of the revolution, was the opportunity for Khomeini to call for more volunteers, the mobilisation of all able-bodied men and the pursuit of victory, which would now be defined by the fall of Saddam Hussein. It was announced that 1.6 million public sector workers would be given military training and a fifth should expect to be on the front line at any one time. The progress towards the raising of 500 battalions was confirmed and it was decreed that the Basiji would be open to women, a measure designed to shame more men into service. The newly formed Supreme Council for War Support established ninety mobilisation centres and gave them quotas to fulfil. This was to be a people's war, with the entire nation in arms. The Revolutionary Guards led the mobilisation effort with a combination of threat and encouragement.

For Iraq, the loss of Fao came just as the economy was beginning to recover. The failure of its counter-offensive was also a bitter blow. To strike back at Iran, Saddam turned again to air power. In March and May, the Iraqi air force hit refineries outside Isfahan and Tehran, where two-thirds of Iran's output was processed. Then came the Iraqi Mehran counter-offensive. The failure of this attack was explained away as the result of an international conspiracy that was targeting the Ba'ath Party and its leadership, but Saddam gave no specific details. By September 1986, it was estimated that Iraq had suffered 100,000 war dead and the threat of manpower shortages led to the decision to call up 125,000 university staff and students. In addition, men could be drafted up to the age of fifty, and women could volunteer for military training. Iran's reaction was to organise a march-past of Iranian female volunteers in Tehran, as if to underline that it was already ahead of Iraq in this respect.

However, the Iranian war economy was suffering by 1986. Falling oil revenues, the result of the lower price of crude that year, meant that Iran struggled to pay for its imports of arms, ammunition and food, and there were drastic cuts. Foreign reserves, estimated at $7.4 billion, were halved in order to make the most vital payments. Local communities were ordered to clothe and feed their own Basiji militia who were serving at the front. All new development projects were halted. Unable to draw on foreign loans, the Iranian Central Bank was ordered to increase the money supply by printing more bank notes, leading to a steady rise in inflation. Khomeini authorised the raising of higher taxation, above the religious taxes of *zakat* and *khums*. A degree of criticism of the situation was permitted by the regime to prevent opposition developing underground, but it was all closely monitored and Iranians were careful not to make their complaints political.

Iraq, too, was finding the costs of war increasingly difficult to bear by the end of 1986. In the spring, Iraq had defaulted on loan repayments, and had had to reschedule agreements with West Germany, France, Japan and Turkey. It owed Jordan $525 million for the provision of food and consumer goods. In total, its debts in terms of loans reached $10 billion. Yet it had to carve 40 per cent off its imports and draw on its reserves of currency to sustain the war. Both Iran and Iraq were fortunate that oil resources could be used to offset a war that neither could otherwise have paid for. Saddam used the idea that, after the war, as long as he was maintained in power, lucrative reconstruction contracts would go to his generous donors. He was confident that, when peace returned, Iraq would expand its oil production and pay for the damage. Iraq had already opened up new pipelines to Saudi Arabia and was able to maintain an output of 1.7 million bpd. At street level though, corruption flourished amid the scarcity. The shortage of foreign currencies led to more black-market activity, and the regime attempted to suppress this by a high profile execution of six businessmen in August 1986. Capital punishment was also authorised for criticism of the government or the president, or attempting to mobilise opposition.

In Baghdad the mood of financial austerity and the desire to create the right mental attitude towards the war effort led the Iraqi government to enforce fasting during Ramadan in 1986, the closure of all nightclubs and the deportation of South-East Asian barmaids who had been brought in at the outbreak of the war to entertain soldiers. These measures did not impress the more extreme Islamist factions in the country, particularly the Supreme Assembly of the Islamic Revolution in Iraq, an Iranian-backed organisation committed to the overthrow of Saddam and the imposition of strict Islamic rule throughout Iraq. Tehran was nevertheless more pragmatic about the chances of exporting the revolution after several years of war. In contrast to the enthusiasm of 1982, Tehran was more focused on deposing Saddam first and was prepared to work with Kurds and Iraqi secular opposition groups to achieve that aim. It could leave the creation of an Islamic state until after the removal of Saddam.

Saddam responded to these war aims by again urging the Iranian people to revolt against their own government. On 21 January 1987 he issued a 'Letter to the Iranian People' denigrating Khomeini's claim of legitimacy through divine authority. He argued that the failure of the Iranian army to defeat Iraq was evidence of Allah's disfavour. Khomeini replied to this accusation on 11 February by stating that the Iranian war effort was 'a divine cause' and not dependent on a single final offensive, ignoring the promises that had been made before. Saddam had nevertheless failed to achieve any purchase among the Iranian people because, at the same time as his letter was issued, he had authorised the next phase of the 'war of the cities' bombing campaign. The Soviets tried to mediate in this air campaign, offering to supply Iraq with new MiG 27 and MiG 28 fighters if the air attacks on Iranian urban centres were halted. For two weeks the air campaign was indeed suspended, but in the previous weeks 3,000 Iranians had been killed and scores wounded. The Iranian retaliatory rocket attacks on Baghdad and artillery fire on Basra had left 300 Iraqis dead. It is worth noting that neither side had achieved any strategic outcome as a result of the bombardments of urban areas, nor made any appreciable impact on the loyalties of either public.

The home fronts in 1987

The development of air operations against shipping in the Gulf in 1987 (see Chapter 9), namely the 'reflagging' of Kuwaiti tankers, Iranian mining operations and the Americans' retaliation against Iranian offshore rigs, did not apparently cause any change in strategic direction of the war by Tehran. Khomeini was particularly defiant in public, threatening to step up the ground offensives against Iraq and initiate 'another Karbala' offensive. In fact, the Iranians were exhausting their options rapidly. There was a feint operation outside Basra and much shelling, but no major attack materialised. Tehran's strategic move was to make small gunboat raids on three tankers carrying Saudi oil on 16 November. Attacks on Kuwaiti vessels were conspicuous by their absence, indicating the desire to avoid further American action.

The oil industry was limping to some recovery – the modest increase in the price of a barrel of oil, some $16 in the spring of 1987, had doubled Iran's revenue from this commodity compared with 1986. Its production was fairly constant, despite air attacks, at 2.4 million bpd. At the end of 1987, bans on the purchase of Iranian oil by the United States and France severely affected sales and therefore revenue. Tehran took emergency measures by cutting purchases of industrial raw materials. This had an almost instantaneous effect of causing some firms to close and lay off their workforces. Unemployment had reached 14 per cent at the end of the previous year, so this was an unwelcome development. The cuts also had the effect of increasing the budget deficit still further, a phenomenon that had already caused a hike in inflation. While the official figure for inflation was a rate of 20 per cent, most insiders believed it was twice that and certainly the Iranian public were squeezed the hardest.

The flow of complaints increased dramatically and forced the regime to address the public's concerns. The Islamic Republican Party, which had become progressively more redundant once Khomeini was in power and new institutions were built, was abolished. Factionalism, however, did not disappear. The regime leaders announced that there would be 'a planned economy' where, in the language of the revolution, 'the rich would not be allowed to influence the Islamic state'. Price controls were introduced to cover a range of goods and services. A 'financial jihad' was launched in November 1987 whereby those unable to fight had to sponsor a soldier at the front for three months, which would cost them $2,800. The measure was directed at 'the rich', but the ambiguity of the measure suited the regime's purposes of creating unity and making the poor feel that the rich were being made to pay their way.

New efforts were placed on autarchy in arms manufacturing. In 1987 there was a new, unmanned aerial vehicle for reconnaissance, a new variant fighter plane, and trials of a new hybrid tank (made of Russian and American parts). There was also work on its own Iranian-manufactured combat helicopter to add to the arsenal of anti-tank weapons and 120mm artillery. The Iranians were attempting to modify and develop their own rocket based on the Chinese Type 83 and Soviet Scud-B. Tehran also claimed to be building its own variant of the Chinese Silkworm missile, some of which it claimed to have seized from Iraqi sites during the Fao offensive. Mortars and home-made ammunition, including up to six million artillery shells, could be manufactured annually. Half of all Iranian heavy industrial sites were engaged directly in arms production and an estimated 12,000 workshops provided components. The majority of universities and colleges were focused on military research and development. To ensure the smooth implementation of the new measures, no one could question the government's policies without risk of severe penalty. On 1 January 1988, when President Khamanei stated that the government would exercise its authority in accordance with the Sharia, Khomeini announced that the government had a 'God-given absolute mandate', which had authority over all other commandments, including the pillars of Islam. To break the impasse between the reform-minded ministers and the conservative Guardian Council, which had been blocking legislation, Khomeini appointed a Council for the Expediency of Islamic Order that drew personnel from both institutions. The revolutionary zealots saw this as a signal that the conservatives were out of favour and pushed for more reforms, but reactionary elements fought back with their own campaign, necessitating another intervention by Khomeini. Soon after, Rafsanjani was made acting commander-in-chief and unified the command structure of revolutionary and regular forces.

Iraq, meanwhile, had become fully militarised. In terms of regular troop numbers, Iraq had built up an army of 955,000 while Iran could field 655,000. However, the Iranians could add the Revolutionary Guards of 620,000 who, by the end of the war, were as well equipped as the regular forces. The Revolutionary Guards were more than a match for the Iraqi Popular Army which numbered 650,000, but which tended to be limited to an internal security role. Nevertheless, the Iraqis had 1.6 million men and women in arms out of a population in which only 2.8 million were men aged eighteen to forty-five. The Iranians had mobilised and armed 1.2 million men out of a similar age cohort numbering 9 million. Intensive research was being carried out in Iraqi institutions to make improvements to existing equipment and weaponry, including guided munitions, just as it was in Iran. The Iraqis commissioned the Egyptians to produce longer range surface to surface missiles, to exceed the range of the existing Scud-B. In August 1987, the Iraqis had test-fired such a missile that could fire out to 380 miles (612 km). However, the Iraqis still possessed the edge in terms of technology and in numbers of weapons. By the final year of the war, Iraq had 400 fighter aircraft against Iran's 70. Iraq could field 4,500 tanks along with 3,200 other armoured vehicles. Iran could manage 1,570 and 1,800 of each. Iraq had 2,800 medium and heavy guns against Iran's 1,750. Only in combat helicopters did Iran, temporarily, have the edge in numbers, for while Iraq had 193, Iran had 341.

The mobilisation of the Iraqi male population to fight was mirrored in a similar mobilisation of the industrial workforce. Layers of regulatory bureaucracy were removed to empower ministers and state company managers to direct production without intermediaries. It was forbidden to form trade unions. Fixed working hours and overtime payments were abolished. Saddam exhorted the people to work twelve hours a day, not eight. He even reined in the security services, ordering that under no circumstances were they to act in a way that interfered with production. Oil output was also boosted, creating a volume of 2.3 million bpd for export. This not only exceeded Iran's 1.8 million bpd in the same period, but gave Iraq $11.3 billion to spend on the domestic economy and war supplies.

Despite Saddam's popularity as a war leader, and his own efforts to consolidate his grip on power by appointing more relatives and loyalists into high-ranking appointments, there were still threats to his rule internally. Aside from the obvious Kurdish resistance, Al Daawa made an attempt to assassinate Saddam in a well-coordinated ambush outside Mosul on 9 April 1987. Six Al Daawa attackers were killed, but ten of Saddam's bodyguards also died in the shootout. Periodic bomb attacks were also made by Al Daawa in the capital. As always, the Iraqi intelligence services were relentless. They pursued Hojatalislam Mahdi Hakim – the man selected by Tehran to be the shadow-government foreign minister – to Sudan and murdered him there in January 1988, and they were just as ruthless with other suspected 'enemies of the state'.

Iran was also unable to match Iraq's diplomatic position. The Iraqis accepted UNSC Resolution 598, which called for an immediate ceasefire, without question. Iran had delayed. When Javier Pérez de Cuéllar, the UN secretary general, visited Tehran in the autumn of 1987, the Iranians demanded that Clause 6, the setting-up of a commission to establish responsibility for the conflict, be asserted before Clause 1, the imposition of an immediate ceasefire. They argued that such a panel would likely find Iraq to be the aggressor, but in return for the reordering of the Clauses by the UNSC, Tehran would offer a postponement of its demand for the deposing of Saddam Hussein and war reparations, which were intrinsic war aims. When de Cuéllar visited Baghdad, he found no acceptance of the Iranian proposal; the Iraqis wanted to proceed in accordance with the Clauses as the UNSC had determined.

Iran was bargaining without any real advantage. Moreover, the bargaining was insincere. Tehran had little interest in starting peace negotiations while it possessed what it regarded as the military advantage and might be on the verge of victory. De Cuéllar pressed ahead in secret with a peace plan that linked both Iranian and Iraqi demands, namely, that on a particular day UN observers would deploy to witness a mutual withdrawal by both belligerents to the international borders and that on that same day, or 'another day', a commission would 'commence enquiries into responsibility for the war'. The UNSC accepted the secretary general's plan. Effectively, this meant that embargoes of the belligerents, which would have made up part of the measures to implement the UN resolution, would be delayed.

Part IV

Breaking the Impasse

9

The Tanker War, the Arms Trade and International Intervention, 1985–87

On 18 February 1984, Iran and Iraq agreed to UN terms that there should not be attacks on urban population centres. Saddam, therefore, immediately ordered air attacks to be made against Iranian oil facilities, ships and ports. By 1 March, Iraq claimed to have hit seven Iranian vessels in the Gulf and announced that Kharg Island was 'under siege', which was a statement designed to deter foreign powers from purchasing Iranian oil. On 27 March, Iraq made use of French-made Exocet missiles to attack two small tankers south-west of the strategic island. In April, a tanker from Panama was struck; then a Saudi Arabian vessel carrying Iranian oil bound for France. The strategic aim was clear, to reduce Iranian revenue and isolate Tehran by waging an economic war in the Gulf. By these means, it was thought Iraq's air power would compel Iran to negotiate. The Iraqis may also have intended to internationalise the war, bringing the Gulf Co-operation Council (GCC), Europe and the United States into the conflict against Iran. Believing that any threat to the developed world's oil resources would elicit a rapid and belligerent response, Baghdad expected greater support at the very least, if not outright participation.

The Iranians could not retaliate against the flow of Iraqi oil because all of its product was carried in tankers owned by other states, particularly Kuwait and Saudi Arabia. Iran therefore felt compelled to expand the war across the Gulf. A Kuwaiti tanker was hit on 13 May just off Bahrain and this was soon followed by others. In total, ten foreign vessels were hit by the air forces of Iran and Iraq between April and May 1984. Surprisingly, the international oil market, which was notoriously volatile, remained steady, although insurance rates for vessels operating in the northern Gulf increased. Iran tried to offset this rise by offering a discount on the price of its oil. Nevertheless, investors and buyers looked elsewhere for their supplies, a trend initiated by the war and which continued throughout the 1990s.[1]

The UNSC, responding to the concerns of the GCC, announced a unanimous condemnation of attacks on tankers in the Gulf on 1 June 1984. There were reports of attacks on urban centres as the air forces on both sides struck against port facilities, and the UN was under increasing pressure to take more determined steps to end the conflict.

The risk of escalation was obvious, and was underscored when a Turkish tanker was struck and sank on 3 June and Saudi warplanes shot down an Iranian fighter over the Gulf. Both sides claimed the aircraft had been in their own national air space. However, neither side wanted to fight the other. Riyadh signalled its non-belligerent intentions and Tehran, too, announced that it did not wish to fight the GCC states but only on condition they did not involve themselves in the war.[2] The announcement was insincere as the Iranians had every intention of destroying Saudi and Kuwaiti ships carrying Iraqi supplies or oil. Their real objective was to force them to suspend shipping on behalf of Baghdad because of the increased risks. Consequently on 10 June, the Iranian air force attacked a Saudi super-tanker in the lower Gulf, well outside the war zone in the northern waters.

The increased air activity in the Gulf was matched by retaliatory attacks on civilian populations with the result that the casualty toll among non-combatants rose inexorably. On 11 June, the UN got both sides to accept that they would restore the agreement that population centres were to be excluded from targeting. UN observers were to be stationed in the capital cities to report on breaches in the agreement. On 15 June, Iran proposed that shipping in the Gulf might also be excluded, not least because production in Kharg was being increased. Yet insurance companies were offering high rates for losses of ships, which could therefore earn companies greater profits than sale for scrap, and some seamen were attracted by the high rates of pay for these dangerous missions. As a result, the volume of shipping in the Gulf had not diminished at all, with Kharg a favourite destination because the highest rates of return could be earned there. Instead of limiting traffic, the GCC states agreed to provide better security for the vessels in their waters. The Saudis purchased 400 stinger SAMs and a super-AWAC aircraft. Eight US warships accompanied tankers in the upper Gulf and Washington and Riyadh announced jointly the establishment of an Air Defence Interception Zone, known colloquially as the Fahd Line, inside which hostile aircraft would be engaged and destroyed.

The Iraqis stepped up their air attacks on Kharg Island, the terminals of which accounted for almost 85 per cent of Iranian oil exports. The Iranians bolstered their air defences, but in fact benefited from the fact that most pipelines were buried or lay below the sea. The more exposed port facilities were hit by Iraqi missiles and bombs. While Iranian revenue was depressed, the Iraqis never quite managed to cause such an acute economic crisis that the revolutionary regime was in jeopardy. Moreover, the Iranian retaliation, while teetering on the brink of conflict with other powers, did not cause an immediate military or naval response from the Western powers and GCC as expected.

Inside Iran, the war had the effect of driving the people closer to the revolutionary government and of permitting the revolutionaries to call for greater sacrifices and sterner measures against domestic enemies of the state. In the elections for the Majlis in 1984, the revolutionaries were the overwhelming majority. That said, this was due in part, to the weakness of the opposition. The Freedom Party boycotted the elections and other opposition groups had been crushed or suppressed. Consequently, the revolutionary delegates shared the conviction that, with Khomeini, the Iranian people were prepared to endure heavy casualties and a long war to achieve victory. Conviction, they believed, would compensate for the lack of military hardware and training, or a solid economic base.

Iran, the GCC and Iraq's diplomacy in 1984–85

The Gulf states each had more to lose by joining the war than maintaining the status quo. Even Iran did not want to risk conflict directly with Saudi Arabia while it was still fighting Iraq. When it lost a warplane, shot down over Saudi airspace on 5 June 1984, the Iranians held back from retaliation lest their southern Gulf installations became the targets of Saudi air strikes. Syria brokered the mediation between the two countries and for a while Iran ceased its attacks on Saudi-owned tankers. The Saudis, for their part, allowed an increase in the number of Iranian pilgrims on the haj. These developments prompted Tehran to use diplomacy to win over Arab states and perhaps isolate Iraq. In August 1984, Rafsanjani stated that exporting the revolution did not automatically mean a resort to arms and the revolution was really a message of support for the world's deprived and oppressed.[3] References were made to the Prophet's use of envoys, sent out to distant lands, to 'establish proper relations', to give the diplomatic campaign to Syria, Libya and Algeria some religious legitimacy.

While disapproving of the formation of the GCC Joint Rapid Deployment Force, the failure of Iranian land offensives meant that Tehran's diplomatic effort had to be intensified. The Gulf states themselves felt more confident when Iraq checked the Iranian offensives that year and they were equally reassured that the war, which had lasted four years, had not resulted in the closure of the Strait of Hormuz. However, negotiations between the Saudis and the Iranians in 1985 revealed that while Tehran still hoped to see Saddam deposed, Riyadh wanted to initiate a peace process without 'regime change'. Iran kept up the pressure, the vice-foreign minister touring Bahrain, Qatar and UAE ahead of the GCC summit in November that year. The summit accordingly pledged to end the war in a manner that respected the legitimate rights and interests of both belligerents, which was a far cry from the condemnation of Iran that Iraq was looking for.

Saudi Arabia and Kuwait continued to support Iraq financially and through the sale of oil on its behalf. Moreover, the failure of the Iranians to accept even the basis of a peace plan meant that the Gulf states remained unsympathetic to Tehran's diplomatic entreaties. Saudi Arabia and Kuwait accepted Iraq's notion that the Iranians would only negotiate if their economy was ruined. The Kuwaitis were particularly eager to support Iraq's attacks on Iranian installations because of air raids on its tanker fleet. UAE, by contrast, felt that an escalation of fighting in the Gulf imperilled its offshore oil terminals and drilling rigs. UAE was also making record profits from its trade with Iran and wanted to avoid attacks on the Iranian economy. Meanwhile, Syria interpreted a summit in Baghdad on 16 March 1985, involving Saddam Hussein, President Mubarak of Egypt and King Hussein of Jordan, as the reinvigoration of an anti-Syrian pact. Three days later, Damascus hosted the foreign ministers of Iran, Libya, Algeria and South Yemen to demonstrate its own strategic alignment. Libya took the opportunity to secure the sale of Scud missiles to Iran, while Syria agreed to continue its threatening air demonstrations along the Iraqi border to tie down some of Saddam's formidable air force. In return, Iran granted increased oil sales to Syria at a discounted price, adding to an existing ten-year economic pact. Each of Iran's partners also boycotted the Arab League summit in Morocco that year, but the states that did attend reaffirmed their support for Baghdad. Iraq, now the recipient of generous financial and material support from Egypt, urged the other Arab League representatives to readmit Cairo.

When President Reagan returned to office in November 1984, it was clear that the United States had moved closer to Iraq. The administration condemned Iranian attacks on neutral tankers, but declared the

Iraqi attacks on registered Iranian vessels were legitimate targets, which was, strictly speaking, correct, but hardly conducive to the idea that America occupied a position of complete neutrality. Saddam did not draw attention to the significant increase in the economic links between the two countries, nor that he had received a guarantee that America would finance an Iraqi oil pipeline through Jordan to Aqaba. However, he did announce that Iraq was in receipt of American air intelligence. The AWACs early-warning system gave Iraq notice when Iranian aircraft were taking off and then heading over the Gulf. In addition, assessments on Iranian ground activity every twelve hours could be relayed.

The Reagan administration tightened up Operation Staunch, initiated in 1983, and brought legal cases using the FBI against companies and individuals attempting to supply Iran. Washington also put pressure on London to restrict the activities of Iranian front companies that were handling arms supplies in Europe. The Americans were also aware that the complete isolation of Iran merely offered an opportunity for the Soviets to make diplomatic inroads in the future. To prevent this, contacts were to be cultivated with moderate elements inside Iran. The concern was that, following Khomeini's death, Iran might collapse in faction fighting that Moscow would exploit. In fact, despite rumours of arms sales from the Soviets, there was increasing tension between Tehran and Moscow over Afghanistan. Trade was in decline between the two countries and when Iraqi pilots made air raids on the projects on which Soviet advisers were working, Moscow withdrew them, despite Iranian protests.

The likelihood of American intervention in the Gulf meant that Tehran was not prepared to let go of the Soviets entirely. A new diplomatic effort commenced in April 1985, which resulted in the Soviets agreeing that they would not stand by if the Americans took military action against Iran. The Soviets also slowed their flow of arms and war materiel to Iraq, urging other Warsaw Pact states to do the same. In return, the Soviets were rewarded with Iranian oil. The Iraqis were critical but could not risk alienating their largest donor. When Tariq Aziz visited Moscow at the height of the Iranian offensive of March 1985, he obtained more spare parts, missiles (including SS-12s) and ammunition by airlift. Moscow was again rewarded with agreements that would enable it to develop Iraqi oilfields. Saddam himself visited Moscow to reassure the Soviets that, despite the assistance from the United States, Iraq remained closer to Moscow. He was able to secure yet more weapons, but not, interestingly Scud-Bs, which had been used against Iranian cities. For its part, Iran continued to obtain support from China, despite repeated denials from Beijing.

France continued to increase its support for Iraq, including a range of weapons and missiles, but the SNPE company, which was owned by the state, had allegedly already agreed to supply 500,000 artillery shells to Iran via South America, Greece, Yugoslavia, Pakistan or Thailand. Swedish companies also continued to supply explosives until they were discovered by customs officials in March 1985. Some Western European firms maintained sales to Iraq in more or less covert forms.

Not everyone was content with the economic climate in the mid-1980s. The Iraqis were dissatisfied that at the OPEC conference in October 1985 Iran was awarded a larger quota, so Saddam authorised his country simply to increase its production. Saudi Arabia was not content to allow its lion's share of the quota system to be reduced and it, too, increased production. The result was a sudden fall in the price of crude from $27 a barrel to $15. The Saudis hoped the pressure on non-OPEC producers would be sufficient to force them to comply with OPEC demands, but they also hoped to damage the Iranian economy sufficiently that Tehran would agree to a ceasefire. The Iranian response was to step up attacks in the south, launch air strikes on Iraqi oil installations and target Iraqi fields in the Kurdish north so as to damage their production levels. Fearing that Iranian attacks would soon be intensified in the Gulf, Kuwait and Saudi Arabia renewed their support for Baghdad. When the Iranians took the Fao peninsular in 1986, the Kuwaitis took Iranian warnings about retaliation very seriously. The Rapid Deployment Force was dispatched to the Kuwaiti border and urgent diplomatic traffic to Iran via Syria urged the Iranians not to attack Kuwait. When the Iraqis made raids on Iranian tankers to shift the strategic centre of gravity, the Iranians struck at four tankers. There was also a raid by Iranian-sponsored saboteurs on the Kuwaiti Mina Ahmadi oil installation in June 1986. By August, Kuwait, which was dependent on its tanker fleet, was looking to Moscow and Washington for protection.

The Saudis tried different tactics: opening dialogue with Iranian officials they offered sale of refined oil to help Iran at a time of depressed prices. By August 1986, the Saudis abandoned the strategy of lowering the price of oil. Its efforts to coerce the British and Norwegians into cooperation with OPEC had failed. Other OPEC countries were suffering and there was no evidence that Iran had been deterred from war by the pricing plan. Indeed, Saudi Arabia and Kuwait had probably actually increased the risk of Iranian retaliation. The Saudis therefore agreed a price of oil with Tehran, fixed at $18 per barrel, in order to improve relations.

Operations in the Gulf, 1985–86

There were twenty-three Iraqi and five Iranian attacks on tankers between September 1980 and February 1984, but the intensity of attacks was stepped up significantly during 1984 with thirty-seven Iraqi and seventeen Iranian attacks in the following months. The so-called 'tanker war' was Saddam's initiative and was designed to draw in foreign support. By shifting from attacks on Iranian civilian and military shipping to include foreign vessels, Iraq hoped to provoke a stronger Iranian reaction, particularly the closure of the Gulf at the Strait of Hormuz. Iranian ulema had already threatened such an extreme reaction if, and only if, their own shipping was halted. The first US task force of three ships and 2,000 Marines had deployed to the Indian Ocean on 13 October 1983 to enforce the international demand, led by the United States, to keep the Gulf open for all shipping. Ironically, it was Iraq that imposed an exclusion zone on part of the Gulf. In November 1983, Iraq had warned all vessels to avoid the war zone of the northern Gulf, and on 29 January 1984 extended this zone to include Kharg Island. Iraqi attacks on the island and its shipping averaged about four a month from that point.

Iran was eager to avoid being trapped by the Iraqi strategy. It declared that it did not intend to close the Strait of Hormuz because of the detrimental effects on its own economy, and tried to deny responsibility for attacks on Gulf shipping. More importantly, Iran simply lacked the capability to do more. It had only a limited number of aircraft (between sixty-three and ninety) and too few ships. Many of its vessels had been damaged by the Iraqis and the regular navy had also suffered from purges of its personnel. Shortages of spares meant that Iranian ships lacked basic electronic facilities, such radar for fire control. Iran designed a strategy to best fit its capabilities. It was reliant on fast boats and missiles strikes to make unexpected raids at night on unescorted tankers. It deployed a variety of vessels and some helicopters to lay mines. Its policy, while always denying its responsibility, was to harass civilian shipping, particularly Kuwaiti and Saudi tankers, to the point where these powers would abandon their support for Iraq and that the international community would demand action against Iraq.

Iraq's superiority in quality and quantity of aircraft, if not in the daring of its pilots, was evident by 1985. In the air operations against tankers, it struck thirty vessels between January and March 1985, whereas the Iranians had only enough aircraft to launch sorties against seven. In the year from April 1984 to April 1985, the total Iraqi strikes were sixty-five, and Iran's twenty-five. There were also more Iraqi attacks on Kharg Island, but the limits of their air power were gradually becoming apparent. It proved impossible to completely halt production there without heavier munitions, more accurate bombing or joint air-naval operations. Iraq had managed to reduce production by half, but the Iranians began to organise a more dispersed network of outlets, with floating jetties and fixed terminals further south along the mainland coast. Furthermore, the Iranian air force was ordered to strike back at Iraqi oilfields in the north of the country, while in the Gulf itself the Iranian revolutionary guards took to boarding freighters to check for arms and war materiel that seemed destined for Iraq. By November 1985, they had 'inspected' 300 vessels in this manner. To enforce their presence, a helicopter base was constructed at Rashadat just 75 miles (121 km) from the Qatari coast in the lower Gulf.

The Iranian Fao offensive had not been checked or defeated in early 1986 and so Saddam chose to make air strikes in the Gulf in the hope of damaging Iran's economy so comprehensively it would have to break off its campaign. By August 1986, the Iraqi air force had damaged five of the eleven-strong Iranian tanker fleet that operated out of Kharg. At Sirri Island – a storage facility that enabled foreign shipping to avoid the war zone – the Iraqis fired Exocets and destroyed three more tankers. Given the range from Iraqi bases it was clear that either the Iraqis had refuelled in mid-air en route or they had been provided with airbase facilities by one of the Gulf states. The Iranians reacted by moving their oil operations north-east of Sirri, closer to their shore-based air defences. New facilities were opened at Larak Island, too. Tankers and ships were coated with a less reflective paint to weaken their radar signature and reflectors were fitted at bow and stern to confuse incoming missiles. Aluminium chaff projectors were also fitted to screen ships from Exocets. Electronic jammers were used to prevent aircraft getting a missile 'lock', while small tugs were deployed along the coast to rescue stricken vessels.

Once again Iran chose to retaliate against Iraqi oil installations in Kirkuk and elsewhere, but while aiming a Scud-B rocket at a refinery outside Baghdad it hit a residential area. Artillery barrages against Basra were more deliberate attempts to damage the civilian infrastructure. Nevertheless, they had more success destroying Iraqi radars on disused oil terminals in the Gulf, although these were unlikely to cause much more than minor disruption. By contrast, new Iraqi air raids over Kharg and Larak caused a severe drop in production and in September the remaining storage tankers were hit and shut down. Iranian exports were halved.

Petrol rationing had to be introduced domestically and even then Iran had to import one third of its refined oil to meet demand.

Although the Iranians enjoyed some successes on the northern front in Iraqi Kurdistan in the spring and summer of 1987, the situation remained more problematic in the Gulf. To punish and deter Kuwaiti assistance to Iraq, particularly in the shipping of Baghdad's oil, the Iranians had been hitting Kuwaiti tankers with greater regularity over the course of the year, but they failed to prevent Kuwait's support from continuing entirely.

Gulf operations, 1987

A greater frequency of Iraqi attacks on Iranian oil installations in the spring of 1987 pushed Iran to step up its harassing attacks, but the higher tempo merely drew other powers into the Gulf to protect their interests. The USSR sent a frigate to escort its own ships to Iraq, and the USA increased its strength to a full carrier group in the Indian Ocean (with one carrier and eleven escort ships). The British Armilla squadron increased its presence, too, now spending 50 per cent of its time in the Gulf. It was generally felt that the advantage of a 'naval' strategy was that it could offer protection and project a policy without breaking one's neutrality or requiring any breach of another state's territorial integrity.

Security and protection need to be enforceable, and clearly not all states in the Gulf felt secure. On 13 January, Kuwait requested permission to 'reflag' its tankers as American vessels (by transferring half its fleet to the Chesapeake Shipping Incorporated, and sent a similar request to the Soviet Union). Was a positive American response to the request necessary? There were between 168 and 196 tankers moving through the Gulf every month and only small numbers were as yet affected by the Iranian threat, and of the 70–80 Kuwaiti ships a month, few had been threatened. Only 7 out of 284 ships attacked since the commencement of the war were Kuwaiti. However, the request was the result of a clear change of policy in Iran. From early 1987, the Iranians threatened to increase their attacks on Kuwait, and there had been episodes of sabotage around the country. Kuwaiti Shi'ites began agitating for change in high-profile and noisy demonstrations, with some inspiration from Tehran. The American decision to accede to Kuwaiti requests was prompted by an increased threat to American and Western interests rather than a desire to assist Kuwait per se. In late February 1987, the United States detected that the Iranians had test-fired a Silkworm missile in the Strait of Hormuz. This heavier calibre, Chinese-made weapon, with its 1,100lb

(499 kg) warhead meant that Iran could potentially sink vessels and not just inflict damage, and, more importantly, Iran could now extend its range to hit ports and ships of the southern Gulf states. The United States accepted the reflagging policy because the USSR had already agreed, and there was also a desire to find new, willing partners who could assist the United States to reassert its regional influence. It was assumed that the Iranians would be reluctant to attack a ship of the USA or USSR for fear of retaliation.[4]

The reflagging policy undoubtedly had the result of blunting the effectiveness of the Iranian policy, but the Iranians were capable of inflicting losses, so placing the American ships in the line of fire like this was a risk. It also further compromised American neutrality and had the potential to draw the United States into the war against Iran. The decision to reflag was taken by Reagan's administration without 'due policy process': the US navy was not consulted. European partners acknowledged that the American decision referred to 'Out of Area Operations' for a NATO ally, but expressed doubts and preferred a more general declaration for the freedom of navigation of Gulf waters.[5] To complicate matters further, Kuwait signed the reflagging agreement, but initially did not want to go public with the arrangements. One of the risks which did not seem to have been considered was that Iran might move closer to the Soviet Union over the issue. Certainly the Iranians would be determined to defend their own territory. In the short term, they showed themselves to be defiant and willing to step up the unconventional nature of their attacks, but they also made preparations to reinforce their existing strategy. By April, Iran had twelve Silkworm launchers at Hormuz and twenty missiles available. On the 20th of that month, it completed construction of a new missile site on the Fao peninsular where it would be able to strike Kuwait city and its port.

Many of the Iranian ships lacked the latest equipment, but they had four British-built frigates equipped with sea killer anti-ship missiles, and four patrol boats with 40mm and 76mm cannon and harpoon missiles. In addition, there were a variety of small fast boats and dinghies with six-man crews. These were difficult to detect by radar among the quantities of craft in the Gulf, and they were staffed by elements of the dedicated 20,000 strong naval element of the Revolutionary Guard. They had light aircraft, trained frogmen and a specialist suicide-bombing unit. Moreover, the Iranians used any vessels they had, including 'civilian' ones, to lay mines. Most importantly, the naval Revolutionary Guards controlled the Silkworm missiles. The islands were fortified and garrisoned by about 1,000 men each, as were disused oil platforms out in the Gulf. The intention was to wage a guerrilla war at sea and to focus on sabotage-like attacks. However, such a strategy revealed fundamental weaknesses. Their small garrisons were not mutually supporting. They lacked air power or the means to gather intelligence. This meant they had to approach tankers at night in small boats and identify them before they could make an attack. For all their armaments, they lacked the means to 'deny' the Gulf waters entirely and they were significantly outnumbered and outgunned. Above all, a strategy of direct confrontation with the West could only lead to defeat at sea, and quite possibly on land as well.

Both Iran and Iraq claimed different areas as the war zone or their own exclusion zones. The Iraqis pointed to the northern Gulf, close to the Iranian coast as the primary zone of operations, but the Iranian exclusion zone encompassed the eastern half of the Gulf for the whole area above the Strait of Hormuz. Their zone of operations, close to the Strait along the coast of UAE and Oman, forced tankers to follow a predictable route close to the western portion of the Gulf which could easily be mined. Operations therefore followed a pattern. On 2 May 1987 Iranian Revolutionary Guards boarded fourteen vessels, and attacked three tankers from bases on Farsi Island and an oil platform. They came up alongside under cover of darkness and identified the vessel, then returned some hours later to shoot and fire rockets at the bridge or crew quarters. The tactics were clearly designed to terrorise the international personnel manning the ships, but were motivated by a desire to retaliate against Iraqi attacks. These tactics were regarded at the time as a defiant escalation of the interests of the international community. Time was running out for Iran.

The importance of the oil economy meant that exports were always going to be a target for both sides. Iraq sought to prevent Iran from getting its oil out by air strikes against the tanker shuttles in the southern Gulf, but ultimately it could only force reductions in the volume of oil and was unable to prevent sales altogether. It lacked airbases in the southern Gulf states to strike at Iranian facilities in the south, and had to concentrate on the installations on Kharg Island and in the central Gulf. However, in this 'tanker war', Iraq's greater air power gave it a distinct advantage over Iran. Two academic experts, Elizabeth Gamlen and Paul Rogers, argued that Iraq also intended to use attacks on the tankers as a means to involve the Western powers in the conflict.[6] Can we say the Iraqi strategy was a success? It is interesting to note that Iraq was in breach of international law, but the West tended to focus on Iranian retaliation, despite the fact that the number of Iranian attacks, until the Kuwaiti request for reflagging of its tankers, were very small: in the region of 1 per cent of all Gulf shipping.[7] Gamlen and Rogers concluded that the

Iraqis and the Kuwaitis sought to internationalise the dispute for their own interests, but the United States chose to support their case with a naval presence in order to fulfil their own agenda of excluding Soviet influence and building American support in the Gulf region.

The Iranians were far more reactive in the 'tanker war', although, in the absence of Iraqi tankers to attack, they targeted all Gulf shipping that was transporting Iraqi, Kuwaiti and Saudi Arabia oil, and this included Western vessels trading with those countries. Iran did not possess enough air and naval power to close the Strait of Hormuz permanently against Western and particularly American capability. It had too few fighters for air strikes, and what air assets it had were prioritised to support the land campaign further north. The Iranians were therefore compelled to use unconventional tactics to harass Gulf shipping. Despite a supply of Chinese aircraft and missiles, attacks with small-arms fire and light rockets from fast small boats, and the periodic mining of sea lanes, were all it could manage. These tactics had a negative impact on world opinion and were important in alienating potential supporters. Iran's strategic objective was to coerce Kuwait and other Arab states to end their support of Iraq, and to persuade Western powers to avoid the risk of combat operations. However, Iran's decision to invade Iraq in 1982 and its capture of Fao in 1986, which brought them closer to Kuwait and gave them a significant edge over Iraq, made Kuwait, Saudi Arabia and many Western countries all the more determined to back Iraq, albeit still indirectly.

10

The Failure of Strategy: Iranian Offensives and Iraqi Counter-offensives, 1987–88

Saddam ordered renewed efforts to retake the Fao Peninsular in April 1986 when the landscape had begun to dry out, but the army still could not dislodge the Iranian troops. There were attacks on Iranian refineries at Tehran and Isfahan that spring which interrupted two-thirds of Iranian output and gave Saddam a propaganda victory. However, what the Iraqis wanted was a decisive victory in the land war. On 17 May 1986, four Iraqi divisions made an assault on the central front and took Mehran, a town in Iran. The Iranian garrison, numbering no more than 5,000, fought as best they could but suffered heavy casualties. The achievement was exaggerated for the purposes of propaganda. Saddam announced the attack represented a new strategy of 'dynamic defence' and a 'daring expression of the Iraqi leadership's political decision to force the Iranian leaders to yield, [thus] preparing the way for peace'.[1] The Iranian leaders appeared to be in no mood to negotiate after the loss of Mehran. Instead, the old suspicions about the army resurfaced and the Revolutionary Guards were the favoured focus of a new recruitment drive. Targets of an extra 300,000 recruits were established, to be distributed across all branches of the armed forces and the Basiji militia.

In fact, Saddam offered to exchange Mehran for Fao, but Tehran was unwilling even to open the dialogue. The Iraqi forces around Mehran tried, unsuccessfully, to push up into the hills, but had to consolidate on lower slopes. The Iranians used the cover of the higher ground to build up a sizeable force and in the early hours of 1 July 1986 they made a counter-attack, known as Karbala-I. By the end of 3 July Mehran had been retaken and Saddam had lost his bargaining counter. To deflect attention from the setback, Saddam reshuffled the leadership of the Ba'ath and Regional Command and hinted that Iraq was plagued by a conspiracy of foreign forces and internal enemies. Foreign powers were at that moment significantly assisting Iraq's strategic position. Saudi Arabia's decision to increase oil exports had lowered the price to $27 a barrel in December 1985 and Iran's revenue was being reduced throughout the spring of 1986. By April, the price was down to just $10 a barrel. Iraqi air strikes were making the Iranian production and revenue shrink even further, from $1,250 million in 1985 to $500 million in 1986.

Nevertheless, Saddam actually appealed to Tehran not to make a 'final offensive' in August 1986. He was no doubt concerned that the increased Iranian manpower might just overwhelm the Iraqi army at a number of points and cause the sort of losses in ground and lives that they had experienced at Fao. However, on 1 September, the Iranians attacked in a new operation, Karbala-II, in the north, near Hajj Umran. It succeeded in driving some depth into Iraqi Kurdish territory. In Karbala-III, just two days later, the Iranians struck again in the south. A second pontoon bridge was thrown across the Shatt al Arab to facilitate a further advance in Fao, but the attack bogged down and failed. On 10 October, Iranian Special Forces made a raid deep inside Iraq, near Kirkuk, the intention being to attack an oil pipeline. Aided by Kurdish irregulars, this operation was a success. Iraq responded with a new air raid on 25 November using long-range aircraft that reached as far as Larak Island, deep in the Gulf, and fired laser-guided bombs. There were 163 sorties that day, many of them on oil installations, but there were greater losses in Iraqi aircraft as the Iranians strengthened their air defences.

Saddam also authorised a significant increase in the number of men under arms. The Iraqis simply had to build a larger army to be able to reinforce every threatened sector. The Presidential Guard was expanded from 6 to 17 mechanised brigades totalling 25,000 troops. The 7 army corps were expanded to create forces of 100,000 men each. New defences were erected on each front – earth banks, barbed-wire obstacles, larger minefields, more dug-in tanks and guns. Troops manning the trenches were given one weeks' leave after every three weeks in the field and better welfare arrangements were put in place.

The Iranians also stepped up the pressure. On 23 December, they launched Karbala-IV with four divisions of regulars, Basiji and Pasdaran, pushing north-west towards Basra from a line between Abu Khasib and the Shatt al Arab. This was supposed to be a repeat of the Fao success. Instead, the Iranians withered beneath Iraqi firepower, delivered from bunkers, heavy artillery and combat aircraft. Iraqi intelligence on the Iranian build-up was in stark contrast to the Fao operations, and the Iranians failed to gain any parity in the air or in terms of artillery support.

One Iranian division was tasked with the retaking of Umm Rassas Island and three smaller islands lying to the south. The attacks were cut down and halted abruptly. Two days after the opening of the attack, Iranian troops were falling back to their start lines, leaving an estimated 8,000 dead in the reeds and waterways.

If there were any doubt remaining about the strength of Iraqi defences, especially around Basra, one need only consider the extent of Iraqi engineering to create new barriers against Iranian infantry attacks. In April 1981, the Iraqis had excavated a water-filled moat 12 ft (4 m) deep, 18 miles (29 km) long and almost 1 mile (1.6 km) wide. It was replenished with pumped water from the Shatt al Arab and proved to be a major obstacle. Channelled to its north and south, the Iranian troops were trapped in pre-prepared killing zones. In 1983, the Iraqis had enlarged the moat still further, making its width up to 6 miles (10 km) on the south-eastern side, whereupon it was renamed the Fish Lake. Two new channels were dug to the north and south-east, each over a mile wide. The task had required the excavation of 1,200 million cubic feet (33,960 cubic metres) of sand, soil and clay. To prevent the Iranians from draining this new feature, giant earth barriers were built. Any attacking force would thus have to surmount two waterways, the Shatt al Arab and the Fish Lake, while all the time subjected to intense artillery fire from batteries dug in behind the obstacles.

Land operations, 1987

Karbala V was supposed to be a short operation at the beginning of 1987 that would finally enable the Iranians to seize Basra, but the water barriers constructed after 1981 seemed impregnable.[2] Nevertheless on 6 January 1987, four Iranian divisions began their characteristic night-time infiltration of Iraqi lines south of the Fish Lake, and overran the town of Duaiji. A second axis was opened along the northern edge of the lake, and the Iranians managed to break through two of the four lines of defence. The main effort was made towards Shalamche on the Shatt al Arab, and within hours their overwhelming numbers had taken the town. Thirty-five thousand men were then poured into the gap between the southern edge of the Fish Lake and the town of Shalamche.

The Iraqis mounted counter-attacks led by infantrymen, with close air support and artillery fire. The more experienced Iranian units knew how to occupy the most advantageous terrain to survive the bombardment and from which they could inflict losses on the Iraqis. Anti-tank missiles helped to break up the Iraqi attacks, and surface-to-air rockets (Hawk missiles, Chinese HQ2 SAMs, and Swedish laser-guided RBS-70 SAMs) brought down some fifty aircraft by the end of the operation. Iraqi artillery rounds, which fell into the soft soil of the marshes, were also considerably less effective than usual. The Iranians tried to push the Iraqis back again, and to overwhelm the defences, but the Iraqis were simply too well entrenched for this. Alerted to the weight and axes of the Iranian thrusts, the Iraqis could easily contain the subsequent onslaughts. A week after the offensive began, the Iranians had captured a small space of 20 square miles (52 sq km), although they were within artillery range of Basra.

On 13 January, in an effort to maintain the momentum, the Iranians launched Karbala-VI on the central front near Qasr-e Shirin. This succeeded in taking some ground from the Iraqis. Then, on the 19th, there was a new thrust in the south, and another after a further week of intense fighting. This brought the Iranians only 3 miles (5 km) closer to Basra, and some civilians were evacuated from the city. The Iraqi Seventh Corps and elements of the Presidential Guard were brought in to stiffen the sector, but the net effect of all the offensives was that Iraqi reserves were dwindling. If a succession of new attacks were launched at different points along the border, it was possible that the Iraqis would have reached the limit of their reinforcement capability. The Iranians, however, were running out of options in terms of axes and fronts. Saddam ordered that air raids of Iranian cities and missile attacks were to be stepped up to persuade the revolutionary regime that its offensives would have grave consequences. Qom, Isfahan and Tehran were all hit by Iraqi air attacks; 1,800 Iranians, both civilian and military, were killed during January and 6,000 were wounded. The Iranians retaliated with missile strikes against Baghdad and artillery bombardments of Basra. The Iranians hoped that the flight of civilians from Basra, Iraq's second city, might impose an unbearable economic strain on Saddam's war effort. Instead of fighting through the empty city, the Iranians considered bypassing it altogether. They would concentrate on severing the line of communication to Baghdad, and cut off the capital from the north and south.

On 22 February, a new phase of Karbala V got underway as a two-pronged attack from Shalamche towards the Jasim canal that fed the Fish Lake. The idea was to overrun the Iraqi defences lining the waterway, but the results were again disappointing. For four days the Iranians tried in vain to exploit their toehold, but the Iraqis were too well entrenched to be dislodged, and their weight of fire was too great. The attack came to an end on 26 February.

Saddam used the ending of the Iranian offensive to launch his own attack on 1 March. With armour leading and covered by the air force, the Iraqis tried to throw the Iranians out of the positions they had taken in January. The tanks were channelled, as in Fao, into narrow axes and largely confined to dry causeways and roads. It proved difficult to coordinate the close air support in the marshy terrain as features were hard to distinguish. Once again, artillery fire was less effective than it might have been, with rounds often plunging into swampy ground and merely churning up the mud.

The close-quarter nature of the fighting and the intensity of the firepower deployed resulted in extremely heavy losses. This battle was among the bloodiest of the war, with an estimated 20,000 Pasdaran killed and a similar number wounded. A significant number of these were experienced soldiers, which impaired the performance of the Revolutionary Guards in subsequent operations. Iraqi losses were in the region of 10,000 and, given their experience and training, equally difficult to replace. Of particular concern was the loss of aircraft and pilots in the close-support role, and some thought was given to the relative merits of continuing such cooperation when losses had been so high.

Iraq had mobilised one million personnel and had neutralised the Iranian strategy of victory through attrition. Saddam used the repulse of Karbala-V and VI to stage a 'victory' demonstration in the capital. The idea was to highlight the emptiness of the Iranian claims that they had been certain of the final conquest of Iraq. The Iranians responded by making preparations for another offensive in the north of Iraq. As early as 4 March, the Iranians mounted Karbala-VII near Hajj Umran, using Revolutionary Guards to scale mountains to get inside Iraqi positions before assaulting them at close quarters. Iraqi counter-attacks had the disadvantage of always having to assault uphill to retake any positions that were lost. In effect, they failed to preserve their lines.

To keep the Iraqis off-balance and maintain the deployment of reserves, the Iranians started to engineer new drainage in the south that would draw water from the Iraqi defences. The Iraqis were then confronted by a new offensive, Karbala-VIII, on 3 April in the Basra area. The offensive secured no breakthrough, but it achieved its strategic objective of preventing two Iraqi corps from reinforcing the north.

Soon after, all Iraqi Kurdish groups agreed to cooperate against Saddam's regime and fought alongside the Iranians in Karbala-IX, which began on 13 April. The hills above Suleimaniya were captured. Fearing

that the Kurds would now engulf the Iraqi forces, on 15 April the decision was taken to use chemical weapons against twenty Kurdish villages
in the area, with devastating results.[3]

The Iranians kept up the tempo of their offensives. The Karbala-X
operation involved two thrusts from Iran's Sardasht towards Marwet
and Qala Diza. More territory was overrun and the entire northern front
looked decidedly fragile for Iraq. Saddam called an emergency meeting
with his commanders in May to discuss the issue. At the end of May, the
Iranians and their Kurdish allies launched another attack, entitled Nasr
(Victory), and captured Mawet in June, bringing them to within striking
distance of the dam on the Darbandi Khan Lake, Suleimaniya, Khurmal
and Arabit.[4]

The Iranian strategy at this point in the war was revealed in an
interview given by Rafsanjani with the Iranian newspaper *Ettela'at* on
23 July 1987. Rafsanjani explained that Iran intended incrementally
to obtain swathes of Iraqi territory in order to destabilise the Saddam
regime and cause its overthrow. He noted that there was a war of attrition taking place, but he was concerned that the Iraqis could use time
to their advantage – effectively bleeding Iran white. He felt that the
direct involvement of another power in the conflict was 'unlikely', but
he warned that such an eventuality would necessitate further mobilisation of manpower and resources, and then offensives, that would result
'inevitably' in the severing of Basra from Baghdad. He claimed that in
addition to the 500 battalions raised, Iran could find 2,000 more, and that
it would be able to fund all the logistical support these new troops would
need. To date the war had cost $3 billion, but the question of providing
more, despite an economic downturn, was, to him, merely 'a political choice'. However, he was prepared to acknowledge that the Iranian
people, the *mustazafin* (the oppressed), might be reluctant to support
the effort.

Dilip Hiro described Rafsanjani as 'extraordinarily honest and frank'
in this announcement, and that he 'had taken the Iranian public into his
confidence'.[5] However, a different interpretation could be offered. If the
intended audience was foreign, then it was a warning to Iraq that, should
it seek to internationalise the conflict, the Iranians would redouble their
efforts to wrest Basra from Iraq's grasp. Saddam was already aware that
Khomeini intended to remove him from power so the restatement of this
sentiment was not unexpected. If, on the other hand, the target of the
announcement was the Iranian public, then it could be seen as a warning
that, should others join Iraq, more would necessarily be asked of the
Iranian people in terms of manpower and financial sacrifice. Rafsanjani

admitted that: 'I asked myself if it was opportune to ask the people to tighten their belts further.'

Reading the article in search of a deeper analysis, one might suggest it reflected a growing Iranian realisation that, facing defeat, Iraq would try to involve other powers in the war, such as the Gulf states and per-haps even America. It had already attempted to turn the Arab states' and Iran's attention to the 'Israeli threat' over Lebanon and, in its desperate defensive battles, it had used chemical weapons freely. What else could Iraq do if the Iranians began to overrun it, except involve others in its defence? Moreover, Rafsanjani's statement seems to indicate that Iran's resources were being exhausted and this was an appeal to draw more from the Iranian people. In this sense, it marks the beginning of the end of the Iranian strategy. When the war was finally brought to an abrupt end in 1988, the Iranians had already passed what Clausewitz would have termed the 'culminating point'. Their capacity for large-scale offensives was declining and the effectiveness of their attacks was pro-gressively being reduced. Indeed, from 1987 the Iranians were back on the defensive. The attrition strategy had failed because Iraq had matched Iranian mobilisation, and Rafsanjani was prepared to admit that 'a war of attrition can be dangerous as our enemies can use time against us'.

In the Gulf, Iranian missiles and aircraft were attacking Iraqi and Kuwaiti tankers, including those that had been 'reflagged' by the United States, prompting an American warning that if Tehran continued attacks there would be a response. To avoid American retaliation, the Iranians used Silkworm missiles against unflagged vessels and Kuwaiti shore installations. The Americans attacked the mine-laying vessel *Iran Ajr*, which prompted an immediate revision of the Gulf strategy. In fact, Iraqi air raids were taking their toll and Iran knew that any military response would evoke more retaliation from the Americans. In Tehran, there was certainly some confusion: Rafsanjani explained to the *Teheran Times* on 30 August that Iran could either continue the war of attrition or make multiple all-out offensives into Iraq, but he continued to warn the Iranian people that more sacrifices, financial and otherwise, were likely. Inexplicably, there was no mention of the Iranian strategy for the Gulf.

In Iraq, Saddam intended to maintain the defence of the border areas so as to exhaust the Iranians, while continuing his air attacks against economic targets, urban areas and in the Gulf. His aim was still to break the economy of the revolutionary regime and turn the people against their government. However, Iraq also continued to spend well beyond its means, relying wherever possible on technology and fire-power. The growing tension between Iran and the Americans in the Gulf was welcomed in Baghdad and, to maintain his international image as a peace-broker, Saddam accepted the UNSC Resolution 598 (20 July 1987) without reservations. Iran delayed its response, once again hinting that Tehran was unsure of its strategy from this point.

Ultimately, Iran decided to strike again on land at Iraq's vulnerable northern sector. In June, Kurdish rebels made a series of attacks in Suleimaniya, under the broad title Operation Fatah (Victory), using Iranian weaponry and support. The offensive was the prelude to an announcement by various Kurdish factions that they shared a common objective of greater autonomy 'in confederation with a democratic Iraq'.[6] In October, the Kurdish groups made another broad attack prior to the Arab League Summit in early November, designed to remind that congress of the Kurdish question in any discussions about the war. Interestingly, Tehran had disapproved of any discussion about full Kurdish independence since it feared this would encourage a similar demand from its own Kurdish Iranian population.

For its part, Iran announced in November 1987 that it intended to launch another series of Karbala-style offensives to give the Iraqis 'no respite'. At first there were only small-scale attacks on the central front and some intensified shelling of Basra, which had suffered extensive damage already. In December, there were further probing attacks designed to keep the Iraqis off-balance and conceal the site of the main effort. The area north of Basra was the particular focus of these operations. But no major offensive came. Iraqi intelligence indicated the Iranians had not assembled the same giant concentrations of force even in the south. The revolutionary regime had simply not met its manpower targets, was still suffering acute financial problems and consequently delays and shortcomings in technology and equipment. Despite Rafsanjani's promise that Iran would provide all the manpower and material it needed to win the war, it was simply unable to do so. Conscription terms were changed from twenty-four months to twenty-eight months to sustain the armed forces' numbers, but it was far harder to find the munitions, logistics and equipment to keep them in the field. Iraqi air attacks on bridges, installations and assembly areas had also taken its toll. The rejection of the UNSC Resolution would prompt a stricter arms embargo and make this difficult situation worse. In this way, the war now dictated Iranian strategy. It was unable to complete an all-out offensive on every front and would have to sustain a war of attrition instead. In January, the Iranians launched a limited offensive called Bait al Muqqaddas-II, near Mawet in the Kurdish north. Other than that, there was a lull in land operations.

Iraq was frustrated that, at this critical juncture of the war, the attention of the UN was distracted by a Palestinian uprising against Israel and there seemed to be no progress towards enforcing the UNSC Resolution. To highlight Iraq's plight, Baghdad calculated that if it could provoke an Iranian offensive, which it could contain, Iran would be seen to be the aggressor and international action would follow. The 'war of the cities' resumed with Iraqi missile strikes on Iranian settlements, and these were met by Scud launches against Baghdad. The Iraqis returned fire with upgraded Scud-Bs against Tehran, 340 miles (547 km) from the international border. A total of 200 such missiles were fired, resulting in an estimated 2,000 dead and there was a steady flight of civilians from Tehran.[7]

Operations on land and at sea, 1988

At last, Iran did resume its land offensives, with the Zafar-VII operation near Khurmal and the Bait al Muqaddas-III near Suleimaniya, followed by a larger joint Kurdish and Iranian offensive, Wal al Fajr-X, which captured Halabja. Saddam authorised retaliation with cyanide and nerve gas bombs that killed 4,000 people, mostly civilians.[8] The international media was eager to condemn the outrage and less concerned with the Iraqi narrative about guerrilla warfare, ambushes, assassinations and raids. Nor were many interested in the suggestion that Iranian artillery had also fired chemical agents into the town.[9] Iran made certain the world witnessed the consequences of the attack, which had indeed been directed as much at the Iraqi Kurdish population, who were thought to harbour the guerrillas, as it had the Iranian forces. There was a palpable sense of fear that Saddam would use the Scud-Bs to mount similar gas attacks against Iranian cities. Tehran radio broadcast measures citizens could take to ameliorate the effects of gas, but morale sank as people speculated that it was only a matter of time before such an attack was made and many thousands died. The Iranians developed their own chemical arsenal, but Khomeini allegedly held back from using it, fearing it would offer just the pretext Iraq sought to attack Iranian urban areas.

Iranian offensives in Kurdish areas, the one area where Iran could achieve the greatest strategic effect with the least effort, resumed in February and March 1988. More land, including the eastern edge of the Darbandi Lake, had been taken, bringing the total area under occupation to 540 square miles (1,400 sq km). The Kurdish guerrillas were also active, claiming control of a large area. The Iraqi response to this war by proxy was to deploy the National Liberation Army (NLA). Set up in June of the previous year as a military wing of the Mujahideen-e Khalq and based in Baghdad, the Iranian personnel of the irregular force took up their place in the Iraqi lines in the south and then made an attack towards Dezful. Although they were checked in their advance, it was a clear signal that both states now had armed militias from each others' country which could be used to legitimise their cause.

On 10 April, the Iranians put further pressure on Iraq by expanding their attacks in the Kurdish north. Operation Bait al Muqqadas-V was widely expected to break through in the Panjwin area and force Baghdad to deploy its reserves from the centre and south to the threatened northern front. In fact, Saddam and his officers had a plan of their own to retake the Fao Peninsular as a prelude for taking the war back to the Iranians and the south, thereby forcing Tehran to abandon its northern operations.

At that moment, the mine strike by the American USS *Samuel B Roberts*, despite Washington's warnings to Tehran about mine-laying, forced the Iranians to withdraw their air forces deeper into the interior lest the United States retaliate.[10] New plans were drawn up to manage the expected American attack. The Iraqis realised the significance of the move, and commenced their counter-offensive on 16 April 1988. It was to be their largest offensive since 1980.[11]

An artillery barrage opened the attack, with high-explosive and nerve-gas shells detonating among the Iranian positions. Simultaneously, Iraqi commandos landed on the southern shoreline in boats and helicopters. They were unopposed there and they advanced rapidly. Meanwhile, the main Iranian perimeter line had collapsed under the weight of the Iraqi bombardment. The Iranians poured back across the Shatt al Arab in retreat. By the early hours of 18 April, the Fao Peninsular was entirely in Iraqi hands.[12] Fao had been held by just 5,000 men, which stood in contrast to the offensive strength with which they had taken the peninsular. There was undoubtedly some complacency in the Iranian high command about the situation. The Iraqis could muster up to 40,000 men in the sector, but there was an assumption that they would simply remain on the defensive. The Iraqi offensive had come as a complete surprise. However, for Saddam the outcome was a welcome relief. Iraqis were delighted and he could claim that the success was a result of the correct course pursued by the national leadership. Hoping also to bring missile strikes on Iraqi cities to an end, Saddam suspended further attacks on the Iranian urban centres.

Iran was fully occupied in preparing for the American attack, which they felt must be inevitable. On 21 May, the Iranians deployed fifty warships and support vessels with air, land and amphibious units in a combined arms exercise called Zulficar-III. The Iraqi success in Fao made it apparent that Baghdad would attempt to recover all its lost territory and the Iranians had to prepare forces in reserve that could counter-attack the moment the Iraqis began to lose momentum. However, many units were still under-strength and inadequately supplied.

On 23 May the Iraqis attacked in the northern and central fronts, and then with greater force in the south two days later. The target of the southern front was the Shalamche salient, and this was pounded with high-explosive and nerve agent, as well as with new surface-to-surface missiles that detonated 200 bomblets from their warhead after a flight of 35 miles (56 km). The cyanide gas they released incapacitated the defence and compelled the Iranians to withdraw.[13] The Iraqi ground forces found it relatively easy to mop up the surviving pockets of resistance. The Iraqi offensive was spearheaded by the Presidential Guard and commandos, while heavy-weapons support was provided by the battle-hardened Third Corps. As the elite units punched through the Iranian lines, Third Corps' armour poured through the gaps and drove into depth. Heavy mustard-gas concentrations were used in the rear areas to slow down Iranian counter-attacks, while the volatile nerve agents used on the front lines soon dissipated as the Iraqi lead elements approached. The Iraqi lines were pushed 25 miles (40 km) out from Basra, reaching the international border. Despite strong resistance at first, five Iranian divisions retreated, many abandoning their artillery and equipment en route. Trenches were overrun with weapons and unused ammunition, including anti-tank munitions. In ten hours of fighting with relatively light losses, the Iraqis had taken an area that had cost the Iranians 50,000 casualties to secure over a period of several weeks. Iran had lost ten per cent of its combat equipment. Recruitment statistics went into steep decline.[14]

Khomeini was still defiant, repeating that the war must be decided on the battlefield and not by negotiations. He tasked Rafsanjani to bring together all internal security, Revolutionary Guards and volunteers in a single chain of command. Interestingly, Rafsanjani decided that the regular armed forces should remain outside of the revolutionary structure and he was only prepared to merge the supply and procurement chain.

To restore some equilibrium on the battlefield, Rafsanjani ordered an Iranian counter-offensive to retake Shalamche. The attack went in on

13 June. While claiming to have inflicted 18,000 casualties (almost certainly a gross exaggeration) and driven 7 miles (11 km) into depth, the Iranians nevertheless pulled back to their start lines. The Iranian high command hoped the attack had perhaps succeeded in its real intent: to restore some credibility with its own forces and public opinion, and to disrupt Iraqi plans for another thrust. But on 19 June the Iraqis struck again. They used the same formula of artillery firing gas and high explosive and once again drove deep into the depleted Iranian lines. Mehran fell. However, this time the Iraqis handed over control of the town and the surrounding area to the National Liberation Army (NLA), the anti-Khomeini Iranian exiles who had been trained and equipped by the Iraqis. The experiment was not a great success. After three days the NLA had given up its positions.

On 25 June, the Iraqis made an attack on the heavily fortified Majnoon Islands. The gas and high-explosive mix of a 600-gun artillery concentration suppressed the Iranian defenders sufficiently to allow Iraqi troops to encircle the area and advance into the positions from the rear. Meanwhile, Iraqi paratroopers dropped to the east of the islands to erect a defensive cordon. Iraqi infantry made use of the extensive network of causeways, waterways and embankments to infiltrate the Iranian lines. The Iraqi's main attack involved 2,000 tanks, and elements of Third Corps and Sixth Corps, as well as the Presidential Guard. This vast concentration of force hammered the Iranians so effectively that the whole position was overrun in just one day. Iran tried to blame the outcome on an 'unholy alliance of Iraq, the United States and the Soviet Union', but its call for more volunteers failed to move much of the population which was alarmed by reports of Iraqi chemical warfare. The fact is that Iran was now losing the land war.

Stephen Pelletiere, an American analyst of the war, offered a major reinterpretation of the closing stages of the Iran–Iraq War and challenged the received wisdom of the time. He demonstrated that the war was not a standoff in which Iraq finally won a grinding war of attrition through luck, persistence, and the use of poison gas. Instead, he argued, Iraq 'planned the last campaign almost two years prior to its unfolding. [The Iraqis] trained intensively and expended enormous sums of money to make it succeed. What won for them was their superior fighting prowess and greater commitment. Gas – if it was used at all – played only a minor part in the victory'.[15] American military assessments of the Iraqi army just before the Gulf War in 1990–91 reached similar conclusions. While these planners may have been forgiven for looking only for the threats that Iraq might pose, since they were about to engage them in combat, the idea that there were 'no victors' in the Iran–Iraq War does not appear to be the case. A Western focus on the closing stages of the war in the Gulf, where its own forces were deployed, is understandable, but this has tended to overshadow the much more significant land operations. It was the land war that was the most important to Iraq and to Iran. For Baghdad and Tehran, this was the centre of gravity.

11

Fuelling the Flames: Gulf Operations, 1987–88

Both Iran and Iraq relied on oil revenue to fuel the war, and both had suffered when oil prices fell from $28 a barrel to $11 a barrel in late 1985. The costs of the war were such that even though OPEC cut production to restore the price rose to $18 barrel a year later, both Iraq and Iran were finding the economic costs crippling.[1] The critical importance of oil and the stalemate on the battlefield made attacks on enemy oil exports a tempting strategic option. The risk, however, was of alienating foreign support that was just as vital for the continued flow of arms. This strategic dilemma was not easily resolved. Foreign intervention made a significant difference to the protagonists' ability and willingness to attack tankers and oil installations. Indeed, these attacks on the oil supply of the world made Western intervention inevitable, and it is interesting to see how both sides attempted to manage the strategic problems they faced.

Iran had achieved a strategic surprise at the commencement of the war by destroying Iraqi facilities in the Gulf, thereby preventing exports. When Syria aligned itself to Iran in 1981, Iraq also lost its land pipeline to Turkey. Nevertheless, Iraq soon rebuilt its exports, with links through Turkey to the terminal at Ceyhan, with new pipelines to Saudi Arabia, with the cooperation of Kuwait and Saudi Arabia (which sold oil for Iraq as 'war relief' on the understanding it would be repaid or replaced after the conflict), and by moving 70,000bpd via Jordan in trucks. Moreover, Iranian installations were as vulnerable as Iraq's. Iraqi air attacks meant that Iran could not reach full production scales and had to import refined oil at some points in the conflict. Its main northern Gulf facility, Kharg Island, was not closed completely, but Iraqi air attacks kept damaging it and suppressed its potential full volume of production. Iran's tanker shuttle to the lower Gulf was more secure as it was out of range of most

Iraqi aircraft, but several vessels were crippled or sunk, and facilities at Sirri, Larak and Lavan were damaged. Iran aimed to build new ports and pipelines, but these were still potentially vulnerable to air attacks and time-consuming to build. They also cost a great deal, which added further strain to the war economy. Iran even had to pay Syria for its continued support, although, even then, its backing was uncertain and its provision of arms declined during the conflict.

International responses to US–Iranian clashes and the Iraqi attack on the USS *Stark*

The American response to the increased level of attacks in the spring and early summer of 1987 was threefold: first, to engage the UN to end the conflict by calling for a ceasefire in order to re-establish the *status quo ante-bellum*; second, to limit Soviet influence; and third, to put direct pressure on Iran itself. In response to Iraqi air strikes on refineries at Isfahan and Tabriz, the Iranians had continued to escalate their attacks in the Gulf, but the prospect of greater Soviet involvement had redoubled American interest. The Iranians had machine-gunned and made rocket attacks on the Soviet freighter *Ivan Korotoyev* on 8 May 1987 and they mined a reflagged Kuwaiti-Soviet tanker.

American involvement was almost certainly promoted by the attack on the USS *Stark*. On 17 May 1987, at 21.12hrs, an Iraqi Mirage fighter fired two Exocet missiles and hit the ship; thirty-seven US sailors died. Various issues had led to the catastrophe, including the blinding of the air defences and human failure to prepare for a combat environment rather than peace-time routine, but the attack sparked a furious debate in the United States about the role and the risks of the American forces in the Gulf. The question has often been posed: did the Iraqis intend it to look like an Iranian attack so as to embroil the United States further in the war on Iraq's side? The Iraqi pilot claimed the ship was barely outside the Iranian exclusion zone, but he made no attempt to identify the target and maintained radio silence until the last moment. He returned precisely on course after the attack, which suggests he knew exactly where he was, ruling out a navigational error. In light of the attack on the USS *Stark*, Iraq refrained from attacks on tankers for a month, concentrating on Iranian oil installations and verified Iranian tankers instead. In the United States, the attack led to discussions of a possible American withdrawal from the Gulf, and analogies were drawn with the suicide attack in Lebanon in 1983. These discussions undoubtedly encouraged the Iranians to defy international interests with more confidence. In short, Iran felt it could compel a change in American policy by further unconventional warfare.

While the UN, on American prompting, reiterated its calls for the implementation of Resolution 582, the call for a ceasefire, Iran rejected them all and threatened the United States. It staged high-profile naval exercises, while Hasan Ali, commander of the Revolutionary Guards' naval element, warned that the Americans would get a 'bitter and unforgettable lesson' if it challenged the Iranians in the Gulf.[2] Iran began laying mines in the northern Gulf and some drifted to the Kuwaiti shore. Both Iran and Iraq then attacked several tankers, including foreign ones, which meant that in the first half of 1987 53 vessels had been damaged and 226 seamen had been killed. Insurance claims stood at $1.5 billion.

Consequently, UN Resolution 598 calling for immediate ceasefire was passed on 20 July 1987. If honoured, this would have favoured Iraq as it endorsed the restitution of the *status quo ante-bellum*, ensured Saddam stayed in power, and compelled the Iranians to give up on their territorial gains. The only aspect that appealed to Iran was that it would have returned the Shatt al Arab border to that agreed in the 1975 Algiers Accord, namely the *thalweg* principle. Iran rejected the UN demand and focused on trying to get more international support for its cause. The UN therefore became part of the war strategy for both Iraq and Iran – they realised that international backing could win or lose them everything in the war. But in diplomacy Iraq gained the upper hand because it was willing to deal with everyone; it had an experienced cadre of diplomats and represented the international order, rather than revolutionary politics. However, Western efforts were not without their problems. The United States could not get other UNSC members to agree on an arms embargo, and the USA and USSR disagreed over the nature of the sanctions that could be imposed against Iran.

Furthermore, the situation was changing all the time, and the Western powers found themselves drawn further into the conflict by the reflagging policy and the mining of the supertanker *Bridgetown*. Operation Earnest Will, the name given to American reflagging, began in July 1987. To ensure security for the reflagged vessels, it was decided that a convoy would be established: to accompany two tankers, there would be three escorts per tanker plus air protection, as well as a number of other patrolling ships in the region. It was reasoned that convoys reduced the security commitment and the chances of Iranians making small attacks unseen, and the plan was to make journeys every two weeks. There were, however, a variety of problems to deal with. There was a lack of suitable bases inside the Gulf and it was difficult to maintain mutual support of ships outside the convoy, especially if faced by a saturation attack by many small craft. Above all, the first convoy lacked adequate mine warfare defences. There were simply not enough American minesweepers or AWM (Anti Mine Warfare) helicopters on station, and there was not enough coordination with Western allies who possessed these assets. The Iranians had a wide range of mines available, and they had a large area in which mines could be laid, or over which Iran could attack, and the narrow strait of Hormuz could be covered by a variety of older or more sophisticated weapon systems. To make matters worse, the Western media tended to expose American vulnerabilities, and this information went straight to Iran. Sailing times were known, so that all movements could be predicted and plotted. It is therefore not surprising that the *Bridgetown* struck a mine on 24 July. The Iranians had laid three minefields and approximately sixty mines covertly. One had damaged the tanker (flooding four of the thirty-one bulkheads), which had slowed the convoy. In what seemed like an anachronism of modern naval warfare, American sailors had to man the bows with riflemen and machine-gunners to shoot at mines in the Gulf. Characteristically, the Iranians denied the attack, but they did not conceal the fact that they were delighted with the results.

The day after the *Bridgetown* had been holed, more mines were located. The US Navy struggled to get anti-mine warfare assets into position, and it was evident that a lack of shore bases for American Special Forces and air assets was problematic and slowed down operations. Fortunately, Kuwait permitted a small flight to work from its shores, but Saudi Arabia and Bahrain were trying to keep a low profile. The United States obtained Kuwait's permission to station two barges in Kuwaiti waters as heli-pads. The first was established just 20 miles (32 km) from Farsi Island to watch over that Iranian base. Four Saudi minesweepers were deployed and Bahrain eventually agreed to lease some old oil platforms as 'bases for the US'. In response, Iran agitated its 70,000 'pilgrims' in Mecca in staged demonstrations designed to inflame the Arab world and to cause a change of policy in Saudi Arabia, Kuwait and Bahrain. Iran, though, was more vulnerable than ever: it could not risk an overt struggle with the United States, an embargo on its oil, or on its arms imports. If Iran provided the Americans with a pretext for retaliation, its apparent strength would quickly be exposed.

International reaction was sharply divided by the convoy and the *Bridgetown* incident. The USSR capitalised on it by condemning

American 'aggression' and provided more weapons for Iraq to win favour in Baghdad. The Western Europeans were more alienated by Iranian tactics. The issue increased American resolve to confront Iran, particularly when Iran carried more attacks. In August, Iran staged another overt naval exercise, entitled Operation Martyrdom. On the 8 August, an American aircraft released a missile to engage a threatening Iranian fighter at maximum range, but it was evaded. The US Marine Corps deployed TOWs (Tube-launched, Optically-tracked, Wire data link missiles), stinger missiles, and more helicopters; the US Navy brought in SEALs (US Navy Special Forces) patrol boats (armed with 20mm and 40mm cannons), and built up its force towards a total of 31 ships and 25,000 personnel in the region. Clearly the prospects of a direct clash between the United States and Iran had increased.

Another tanker hit a mine shortly afterwards, but the fact that more mines had been discovered in the assembly area that lay to the south of the strait gave the impression that Iran was deliberately raising the stakes. Again, Iran denied they were theirs, even accusing the Americans of laying them themselves, but it was clear that these North Korean versions of Soviet mines had indeed been laid by the Iranians. The incident prompted the UK to swing its weight behind the United States, sending four minesweepers and two more frigates, while France also announced it would send three more minesweepers with other ships. Iran intended to continue its low-cost strikes, knowing that even if its small units were destroyed it need not fear a major American retaliation. It was calculating on American reluctance to become involved in the war. It believed that the risk of even light casualties on the American side, would lead Congress to enforce its will and limit the president's actions.[3] Consequently it still felt confident enough to use two fast patrol boats to attack a Liberian tanker, *Osco Sierra*, south of Hormuz, outside the Gulf, which appeared to the West to be another escalation. Meanwhile, Iraq continued attacking Iranian oil installations at Kharg. The problem for the Iraqi air force was that the Iranians had hardened facilities and sufficient anti-aircraft defences, against Iraq's limited numbers of planes. It was difficult for the Iraqis to sustain an air offensive and to curtail Iranian land offensives at the same time, but the cost of its losses threatened to outweigh the costs of damage it could inflict, too.[4]

September 1987 was the most intense period of mutual attacks on tankers, with twenty ships hit in seven days. It is hardly a testament to the effectiveness of the UN that Iraq had calculated there was no chance of a ceasefire in the immediate future and had intensified its operations accordingly. Iran responded for the same reasons. The ineffectiveness of the UN effort was illustrated by the decision of the Italian government, in light of an Iranian attack on an Italian tanker with speedboats, to send eight warships to the Gulf and to change its UN 'peace-force' status. However, the difficulty in reaching a consensus was highlighted in the same period. On 3 September, Iran fired a Silkworm at Kuwait from the Fao peninsular. It had landed 2 miles (3 km) from an oil loading point, on an empty beach, prompting speculation whether it had malfunctioned or had been deliberately aimed off. The Iranians issued the usual denials, but then fired two more on the 4th and 5th. Kuwait expelled Iranian diplomatic staff to register its anger, but Iran called for the Americans to leave the Gulf, claiming Kuwait only protested because the United States had compelled it to do so. Nevertheless, the Europeans could not agree on joint action, although they did offer more assets to accompany the tankers. The Netherlands sent two minesweepers and obtained British air protection for them. Belgium followed with an offer of two minesweepers of its own (although one, of Second-World-War vintage, broke down in the Mediterranean). The United Kingdom already had its Armilla Patrol, consisting of the frigate *Andromeda*, the Type 42 destroyer *Edinburgh*, and *Brazen*, a Type 22 frigate. The British also provided a minesweeper command ship and three minesweepers, and three stores and support ships. The United States had eleven ships in the Gulf, with their associated helicopters and missile systems, with a further thirty-five ships in the area. West Germany agreed to send three ships to the Mediterranean to release other allied vessels for service in the Gulf. There were other developments, too, for the Europeans: when Iran attacked a British reflagged vessel, killing one crewman and starting fires on board, the UK government expelled the Iranian Logistical Support Centre in London and took a much more belligerent stance in Gulf operations. Any doubts that had existed over the reflagging were swept away and the Americans could count on European backing.[5]

Despite Western assumptions that the Iranians were deliberately pursuing a new, more aggressive foreign policy, they simply seemed to be reacting more aggressively to Iraqi air attacks on their oil installations which had intensified that autumn. There seemed to be some ambiguity in the Iranian escalation. If the focus of its strategic effort was Iraq, what purpose could be served by intensifying its harassment operations in the Gulf? The Iranians appeared to be oblivious to the risk that they were confronting a much more powerful international coalition and that they were inviting a clash, desspite their clandestine tactics.

The *Iran Ajr* attack, the destruction of the Rustam platform, and international reactions

The United States warned that it would pursue any Iranian vessel found to be laying mines and brought US Special Forces to track and, if necessary, neutralise this threat. Consequently, when an Iranian landing support vessel, the *Iran Ajr*, was caught in the act of laying mines, and US helicopter crews with night-vision equipment had identified and confirmed this activity, they engaged it with machine-gun and rocket fire. Five Iranian crewmen were killed and the ship disabled. The US Navy SEALs then boarded the vessel and took twenty-six prisoners. The ship was sunk the following day. Perhaps most importantly the Americans captured charts and Soviet-made mines so that Iranian attempts to disown the ship were shown to be lies. Khomeini was particularly exposed by his denials which led to speculation that the American administration had made the move to shame Iranian moderates into action. There is no evidence that the operation was calculated to have this effect. More crucially, the incident demonstrated that the Americans had the ability and the willingness to strike back. The Iranian unconventional warfare strategy now looked dangerously risky. Moreover, it showed to an international audience that the Guards were not acting alone as a rogue element, as the *Iran Ajr* and its crew were regular Iranian navy with orders from the highest echelons of government. Only the Soviet Union, predictably, objected to the American action.

The Iranians now appeared to court combat with the Western powers. In October 1987, an Iranian ship put a missile lock onto the USS *Kidd*. The Iranians were warned three times to desist, but only when the Americans threatened to fire did the Iranians break off. The Iranians also attacked ships close to Western escorts, including some Japanese tankers. But on 8 October, an Iranian corvette and three speedboats opened fire on US helicopters 8 miles (13 km) outside of the Iranian exclusion zone – the Americans returned fire and sank one patrol boat. Eight personnel aboard were killed and six taken prisoner, and the SEALs discovered a US Stinger missile on board that had been taken from Afghanistan (Iran claimed that it had six of them). On 15 October 1987, the Revolutionary Guards fired a Silkworm missile at Kuwait, but hit an American-owned tanker under a Liberian flag. The United States did not retaliate because it did not want to jeopardise the UN peace process then underway or give the impression it was committed to the defence of Kuwait. However, the next day Iran fired another Silkworm missile and hit a US-flagged Kuwaiti tanker, *Sea Island City*, near Sea Island. The attack wounded nineteen, some seriously. French minesweepers detected four Iranian mines on the same day.

The United States felt it now had to respond with force.[6] It was decided to select targets carefully. The mainland of Iran was ruled out lest it looked like America was joining the war, but also because Silkworm sites were set up at night, fired before dawn, and then the launchers were dispersed. US aircraft would have had to run the gauntlet of Iranian anti-aircraft missiles to locate these uncertain targets. Instead, the decision was taken to make attacks on the Rustam oil platform where the Iranians had set up small bases from which they had fired on a helicopter. The US Navy warned the Iranians so that they could evacuate and the platform was destroyed along with its surveillance equipment. The American government felt the United States had made its point, although the navy would have preferred to have inflicted more damage so as to deter Iranian attacks. The navy suggested an Iranian ship would have made a better target. Britain, France and West Germany sent messages of support to the United States, but Belgium, the Netherlands and Italy, no doubt concerned about potential escalation, were silent. The smaller Gulf states and Saudi Arabia expressed their satisfaction, although the Saudis would have preferred to see the destruction of the Silkworm launchers.[7] The USSR called for restraint and condemned American 'military adventurism', but ironically increased its sales of weapons to both sides. Iran protested that it had lost oil production (although, in fact, Rustam did not produce anything), but thanks to the Soviet condemnation of America, it cut its criticisms of the USSR from its public announcements. The United States still had to ensure that it did not derail the UN peace efforts and that it did not drive Iran into the arms of the Soviet Union, but, at the same time, it had to maintain the protection of international shipping and work in concert with its allies.

The Iranians still tried to maintain their strategy. On 22 October, Iran fired another Silkworm at Kuwait's Sea Island, hitting an oil pipeline in a loading area, which led to the closure of the island's facilities for a month. The United States arranged to set up another defensive barge from which to stage helicopters, reconnaissance teams, SEALs, and surveillance equipment. It also set up decoys which diverted at least one silkworm missile. The attack unnerved the UAE, which put in requests to the Americans for more anti-aircraft missiles, including Stingers. Iran did its best to alter American policy short of military or naval action: it made threatening statements in its communiqués, a bomb was detonated at the Pan Am office in Kuwait, and new pictures of the US hostages were broadcast. The Iraqis used the opportunity to bring more international pressure on Iran. They were keen to prevent any ceasefire just in the Gulf; they wanted a settlement for the entire war. More Iraqi air attacks followed and Iran retaliated by firing Scuds into Iraqi cities. In early November, the Iranians made an attack against another American-flagged tanker, *Grand Wisdom*, using small fast boats armed with machine-guns and rocket-propelled grenades. The attack took place in close proximity to the USS *Rentz*, but the navy chose not pursue. There was a similar attack on a Japanese tanker near a French warship on escort duty. On 16 November, more fast boats attacked two more US-flagged vessels, including *Esso Freeport*, a tanker owned by Exxon. More mines were discovered, some of which were old and some undoubtedly new deployments. Frustratingly, although the convoys continued, the number of attacks was causing delays.

The options for the United States were, first, to continue as before offering protection where it could; second, it could request the UNSC to implement more sanctions against Iran; third, it could build a coalition of states willing to implement American-led sanctions; or, fourth, it could increase its military and naval presence to the point where Iran was deterred from any further attacks, and make a direct threat to the Iranians. Interestingly, although the decision taken is not yet available for public scrutiny, it is worth noting that Iran focused on Kuwait and Saudi Arabia in seventy-three out of eighty of its missile strikes. Although, in late December, the Iranians crippled three tankers bound for Kuwait and made them unusable, they refrained from further attacks for the rest of the winter. This can be attributed in part to the practical difficulties of attacking vessels close to American warships. Captains of other nations deliberately joined onto the rear of US convoys. However, it is more likely that a direct threat from the United States was the real reason for the cooling of Iranian naval ardour at this time.

As a result of the lull, everyone was able to enjoy the benefits. Kuwaiti oil production increased from 997,000bpd to 1.2 million, Lloyd's insurance premiums fell from 0.75 per cent to 0.45 per cent and there was a greater sense of security for tankers and their crews throughout the Gulf.[8] Better mine warfare capabilities from the Western powers also reduced Iranian effectiveness, no less than eighty sea mines had been neutralised through 1987. There were constant alarms about Iraqi fighters flying near and almost engaging US ships. Nevertheless, the reduction in the Iranian threat was sufficient to permit several ships to be withdrawn and convoys were completed without incident through to the spring 1988.[9] The only bleak news for the West was that Iran seemed to have acquired new Chinese versions of the Soviet Styx anti-ship missile, giving it enhanced capability to destroy a warship. As a result, the United States extended its Rules of Engagement, formalising an understanding that already existed, to defend any NATO ship from attack.

A brief review of Iranian strategy in 1987, namely its pin-prick attacks on international shipping and its sabre-rattling against the United States, could not conceal its lack of capability to inflict really significant damage on the United States or other powers. The best that Iran could hope for was a change in American policy induced by some striking unconventional attack. But Iranian strategy had failed; the United States had created stability in the Gulf and achieved its objectives. The Soviet Union had been unable to extend its influence in any meaningful way. Iran's attacks had isolated it in international relations, but American restraint, protection and partnerships had built up the number of its allies and supporters. Iran's isolation made it more difficult for Tehran to procure arms, and the supply of weapons in the war was still tilted towards its enemy. This evident failure of Iranian strategy in the Gulf in 1987 may itself have been the cause of a more radical and aggressive approach in 1988, but it was a policy that ultimately caused the Iranians to be defeated.

International reactions to the Iran–US clashes of 1988

On 13 April 1988, the USS *Samuel B. Roberts* struck a mine. The blast lifted the stern, blew a 22ft (7 m) gash in the hull, and wounded ten sailors. The explosion also broke the keel, such that it had to be lashed together with wire. Major fires broke out but were soon brought under control. The stricken vessel was found to be surrounded by mines which made extraction more hazardous, but some of them were recovered and bore date stamps and Iranian markings. It appeared that, in preceding days, the Iranian Revolutionary Guard had laid a new minefield in the northern Gulf using its small craft. In response, the American plan was to strike at three Iranian oil platforms in order to show how vulnerable Iran's oil exports were, but, for reasons outlined earlier, to avoid direct involvement in the conflict.[10] The president briefed Congress leaders on 18 April, coincidentally as the Iraqis retook the Fao peninsular in a combined land and amphibious operation of their own.

In the American operation, an air screen was established and the Iranian troops on the Saasan platform were warned of the impending attack. They evacuated and the platform was destroyed. A second platform was warned, but here the Iranians fired on the US ships as they approached. Several shells were fired and the Iranians fled. As the US navy proceeded to its third and final objective, the Iranian ship *Joshan* approached to within 10 miles (16 km) of the American vessels. It was warned to keep clear, but *Joshan* fired a Seacat missile, whereupon the USS *Wainwright* used chaff to screen itself, before responding with four missiles; the *Joshan* was hit and sunk. Two inbound Iranian aircraft then fired on *Wainwright*, which once again defended itself. One Iranian aircraft was damaged. Nearby, three Iranian speedboats fired on a US helicopter, but without effect. At this point, the decision was taken not to attack the third platform, as it may have been regarded as an unnecessary escalation.

Elsewhere in the Gulf, the Iranians fired on a US support vessel, a UK tanker, and a US oil platform off Abu Dhabi. In the latter case, the order was given to engage and one Iranian patrol boat was sunk and another crippled, the third escaped.

On the same afternoon afternoon, the Iranian frigate *Shahand* closed on the US forces south of Qeshm Island. Radio intercepts had given warning of its approach and intent. Once it was within range, it fired on US aircraft and on US ships. The US Navy returned fire with a harpoon missile, while an American aircraft fired two Sea Skipper 2 bombs. The Iranian ship was hit, caught fire and sank. The Iranian frigate *Sabalan* also opened fire on US ships and at American aircraft. A US fighter attacked the *Sabalan* and damaged it. The US permitted it to be dragged back into harbour at Bandar Abbas by tugs rather than finishing it off. The only American loss in these engagements was one helicopter, which was the result of an accident, not enemy fire. Intelligence analysts suggested there had been, surprisingly, no Silkworm missiles fired. However, there seemed to be some uncertainty about this. Eyewitnesses reported seeing five fired, although there were no hits by these unidentified missiles because of ECM (Electronic Counter Measures) and 'chaff' deployments.

Any assessment of Iranian strategy must conclude that it was once again, a failure. Its mine-laying effort was designed to reinvigorate a naval strategy of harassment, especially as it was losing in the fighting around the Fao peninsula. However, its attempts to attack US ships were clumsy and probably mounted as a hasty response to the attacks on the oil platforms. The Iraqi use of poison gas, the quietening of the Kurdish front, and the fruitless attempts to stem Iraqi air attacks in the 'war of the cities' may have added to the Iranian frustration and the need for an aggressive response. Hardliners were certainly in the ascendant in the Iranian *majlis* (parliament). The result of their actions was the loss of a significant proportion of their naval strength in the Persian Gulf. Had they expected the developing world to express sympathy, and to draw the USSR closer, when the Americans inevitably defeated the Iranians at sea? Was it a desperate last gasp of their war effort? If they had expected international condemnation of the United States' policy, then they were bitterly disappointed. Congress supported Reagan's stance wholeheartedly. Although British and French-escorted convoys had been temporarily halted by the fighting, the UK and other Western European nations also affirmed their support for a firm line and they returned their minesweepers to operations in the Gulf.[11] Predictably, the USSR and China disapproved, but probably on grounds of ideological principle, not the merits of the case. The Gulf states were also supportive, but still hoped for more overt American protection. The United States announced it would indeed offer protection to any vessel of any nationality that was attacked, and respond at the time and place of its own choosing.[12] This put Iran on notice that it could no longer attack shipping with impunity.

Defeats in the land war promoted new naval attacks by the Iranian Revolutionary Guards. On 2 July 1988, their gunboats fired on a Danish freighter, but the attack stopped as soon as USS *Montgomery* fired a warning shot.[13] The next day, in the early hours, a pack of thirteen Iranian gunboats in three groups were observed challenging merchant ships and there were reports of gunfire. As USS *Vincennes* and *Montgomery* approached, so the Iranian gunboats started to close in on them. A surface fire-fight broke out, but, at this point, an Iranian commercial airliner, Flight 655, was on a bearing that appeared to approach the *Vincennes*. The flight was 27 minutes behind schedule so, in the heat of the action, its identity as a civilian airliner was ruled out.[14] The *Vincennes* assumed it was a hostile aircraft and issued warnings on two international frequencies. When it was at a range of 8 miles (13 km), it was felt that the risks were too high not to open fire. A missile was launched: 280 civilians died instantly in the resulting explosion. Enquiries confirmed that understandable judgements, assumptions and errors had coincided to cause the mistake. The USS *Wainwright* also engaged an unidentified aircraft that did not respond to warnings, and damaged an Iranian fighter that was inbound on an attack path.

Iran initially hoped it would revive support for its side, but it did not. President Reagan apologised immediately, and the Iranians remained as diplomatically isolated as ever. More crucially, the cost of the war simply could not be sustained any longer. According to an Iranian source, Iran's war costs had reached $1,000 billion, but its estimated oil income over eighty years (the longevity of its industry from first discovery to the outbreak of war) was $260 billion. In essence, Iran had spent four times its actual oil income and, like Iraq, was mortgaging its future.[15] Iran was also losing the military campaign in the southern theatre. It had too few armoured vehicles left, was losing ground rapidly, and there were signs that the military personnel had reached their limit. On 14 July, the Iranians withdrew from the last piece of occupied territory, and three days later, on 17 July, Iran requested a ceasefire.

Part V

Consequences and Conclusions

12

The Iran–Iraq War in Retrospect

On the outbreak of the Iranian Revolution in 1979, Saddam Hussein convinced the Western powers, particularly those of the UNSC, that Iraq was a bulwark against Islamic extremism in the Middle East. His precipitate, if limited invasion exposed him to an Iranian counter-offensive, but this reinforced Western fears that Iran was the greater threat to the international order in this strategically sensitive region of the world. Both belligerents were to a large extent reliant on external sources of arms and munitions, especially aircraft, but Iraq was the favoured recipient for aid. The prospect of revolutionary Iran acting as a magnet for radical Islamist groups, and supporting those groups in the export of terror, meant that, surprisingly, both the USA and USSR supported Baghdad. France had important financial reasons to back Iraq, while Egypt, Brazil, Spain and Britain saw commercial opportunities in the region. However, Iran was not without its own backers. Libya, Syria and North Korea sided with Iran because, in part, they believed they too lay outside of the international system. Other countries sold arms, including China, Taiwan, Argentina, South Africa, Pakistan and Switzerland, with the most surprising contributions from Israel.

Checked on the battlefield and in the air war, Iraq made attacks on Kharg Island and other oil installations on which Iran was dependent. Unable to defend these vital economic facilities properly, Iran launched an unconventional campaign, attacking or mining ships in the Strait of Hormuz and the upper Gulf, and stepped up the scale of its ground offensives against Iraq. Anxious about losses to their tanker fleet, there were strenuous efforts by the Gulf states to seek Western backing. They were more determined on a peaceful solution to the conflict following the Iraqi defeats in the Fao offensives (1985–86) because an Iranian victory seemed a very real possibility. However, despite indirect Western support for Iraq, Saddam's calculations about the involvement of the West were not entirely realised because the Western powers were determined to remain outside of the conflict while protecting their national interests. The Iraqi attacks on Gulf shipping and use of chemical warfare – and the possibility that agents would be used against Iranian cities – also deterred full Western backing.

Operations Badr and Fao (1986) marked the high-water mark of Iranian successes, and Iran found it had no strategic answer to the Iraqi bombing of its cities and the attacks on its oil industry or tanker fleet, except to step up its harassing policy against almost all international shipping in the Persian Gulf. This and the United States' pursuit of a more vigorous Gulf policy in 1987–88 also marked a turning point in UNSC attitudes towards Iran, not least with the introduction of Resolution 598. Western European powers, particularly Britain, took a more determined line against Iran when their interests in the Gulf were threatened directly.

In the end, the combined effect of these factors, a crippled economy, decisive US navy operations in the Gulf, and the fact that Iraq regained ascendancy on the battlefield in 1988, compelled the Iranians to seek a peaceful resolution to the conflict. This chapter highlights the international perspective that was so crucial to ending the war, and reflects on how the actions of the United States, the UNSC and Western Europe were dependent on the political resolve and national interests of the individual member states.

The significance of foreign intervention in the Iran–Iraq War

Foreign influences played a significant role in the conduct and outcome of the Iran–Iraq War. At the very least, foreign supplies of weapons and munitions to Iraq, the favoured recipient of external support, helped to blunt the power of Iranian land offensives. Iran, by contrast, experienced a slow decline in the quantity and quality of its arsenal. But the supply of weaponry and its uneven distribution also shaped the nature of the war, with Iraq relying on armour and airpower as force multipliers, while Iran was compelled to rely on the moral power of its manpower and the offensive. Foreign intervention, particularly that of the US navy, made the tilt of the United States towards Iraq in the late 1980s more than a diplomatic gesture, and may even have been a key factor in the outcome of the war. Less positively, the unwillingness of the world's states to condemn Iraqi use of chemical warfare, or to take steps against Iraq, led Saddam Hussein to believe that the use of such weapons systems were entirely legitimate and may even have fostered his overwhelming sense that the world would respect his massive armed forces and his role as regional power broker.

Until 1971, the United States had been content to see Britain as the guarantor of Western interest in the Gulf region, but the departure of British garrisons gave rise to the 'surrogate strategy' whereby Saudi Arabia, smaller Gulf states and Iran acted as buffers to Soviet influence and as the 'representatives' of Western interests.[1] The United States bolstered this support with more than $20-billion-worth of weapons and military equipment to Iran.[2] In 1979, the fall of the Shah, Mohammad Reza Pahlavi, and the revolutionary politics of Ayatollah Ruholla Khomeini, who replaced him, overthrew this balance of power. Iran could not be replaced as a major military ally by Saudi Arabia, which was far weaker despite a rapid infusion of American weaponry. The surrogate strategy was, self-evidently, no longer viable. As a consequence, in January 1980, President Carter spoke of 'vital interests' that required a *direct* presence, and that an attack on the region would be 'repelled by any means necessary, including military force'.[3]

The 'vital interests' which Carter alluded to were, ultimately, the oil reserves of the region. Such was the West's dependence on oil that it was imperative to protect the flow of oil onto the world's markets, and with 65 per cent of the world's oil being produced in the Persian Gulf and its littorals, this region was of considerable importance to the West.[4] It was not, of course, necessary to physically possess the oil, although owning a proportion of it assisted a sense of security, but rather it was essential to keep others from trying to control it or restrict it. The energy crisis of 1973, when a restriction of production had caused economic hardship across the Western world and created years of 'stagflation', had reminded everyone that the West's first priority, beyond the protection of its sovereign territory, was energy security. This fundamental point, that national interests always came first, was often at odds with more altruistic policies involving the collective interests of the United Nations or European allies, but the events in the Persian Gulf revealed that certain factors *had* to be considered by national governments: the relative power position of each state, the strategic value of the region (its geostrategic location, economic importance *and* military value), the value of its resources (particularly the need for stability and predictability in the prices of oil), and the destabilising revolutionary influence of radical Islam.[5] The relationships of power in the region meant that it was inevitable that there would be challenges to Western interests by other states, especially the USSR, China, Saddam's Iraq, and Revolutionary Iran. However, the United Nations found itself relatively weak in the face of these national interests, and had to follow the lead of the United States to reach a solution. Indeed, the UN Resolution that brought the war to an end was prompted by the United States and supported by its allies.

American security concerns at the outbreak of the war were that there could be a regional arms race between Iran and Iraq; that the conflict would open the possibility of Soviet penetration, especially of revolutionary Iran; that there would be a polarisation of Sunni and Shia Muslims that might lead to more instability; or that there could be an oil crisis like that of 1973. Despite the glut of oil production and falling prices from mid-1985, there were concerns that this situation might be reversed sharply, or that there could be a decade-long rise in prices after the war in the 1990s. For the West, the Persian Gulf was the centre of gravity: its aim was to ensure that the oil continued to flow out to the world's markets. The United States was seen as the only power that could ensure security during, and indeed after the war, but there was a concern, which the war had highlighted, that the West's dependence on the oil reserves of the Persian Gulf was itself a security risk.

There were three strategic implications of the war for the West, namely: what would be the future governments and policies of Iran or Iraq and would these be favourably disposed towards the West? Would the 'buffer states', which checked Soviet interests, continue to be viable? What would be the availability and hence price of oil exports in the future?

As far as future governments and their policies were concerned, the Western powers clearly favoured Iraq as a bulwark to Islamic militancy, but there were no illusions within the United States of Iraq becoming an ally in the future or a replacement for the position that Iran had once occupied. Allegedly, Secretary of State Henry Kissinger remarked, with a hint of irony, that it would be in the West's interests for neither side to win. The official line for all Western powers was one of strict neutrality. However, efforts were made to attract Iranian moderates, to support Iraq indirectly and to tacitly generate a willingness to cooperate with the West in the future. At the same time, the United States wanted Iran and Iraq to be strong and independent, to act as buffers against the USSR, so as to prevent the Soviets getting access to the world's largest oil reserves on which the West depended. A collapse or defeat of one side or the other could provide an opening for Soviet intervention as had occurred in Afghanistan in 1979. Indeed, there was some concern when the Soviet Union carried out an invasion exercise of Iran, based on its operations of 1941. President Carter's statements in 1980 about protecting 'vital interests' in the Gulf 'with all means' were clearly intended primarily, not for the Iranians, but for the Soviets.

The impact of the war on oil exports was a concern throughout the conflict, but there was not a significant adverse effect on oil flow because of lower prices from mid-1985 and from the greater volume of production by other states. The fact that 25 per cent of the world's reserves were located in Saudi Arabia, with another 10 per cent in the smaller states of the Gulf, gave greater importance to the fact that Iran and Iraq had the ability to threaten the oil installations of Gulf states and therefore restrict world production. A sudden price rise could have had a seriously disruptive effect on the world economy, so the key objective of the Western powers was to ensure that the price was kept stable and that any rise of prices was carefully managed or gradual. Announcements by the Iranians that they might close the Strait of Hormuz (thus severing Iraqi and Kuwaiti production as well as their own) were empty threats. Iran depended on the export of oil for its domestic revenue and one of the key factors in persuading the Iranians to bring the war to a close was the rapidly rising costs of the war. All the Gulf states, including Iran, needed to sell oil and so any restriction, let alone severance, would be unsustainable for their economies. However, from a strategic point of view, the fundamental problem for the West did not change as a result of the war. The glut in oil and low prices meant that there was little investment in alternative sources of supply or systems, despite the fact that oil production fell in the USA for the first time in 1986. The West was still dependent on Persian Gulf oil supplies for maintaining affordable energy.

The land war, the 'tanker war', and the arms trade

After the failure of the Iraqi invasion in 1980–81, and the Iranian counter-offensive into Iraq which culminated with the capture of the Fao peninsula, the two sides had reached a stalemate by 1986. Neither side possessed a decisive edge over their adversary. However, the stasis in the land campaign pushed the belligerents to seek advantages in other ways. Strategically, Iran could apply pressure anywhere along an extended Iraqi front, and the Iraqis did not have the strategic depth to be able to fall back and counter-attack for fear of losing its key cities, although Saddam Hussein prevented manoeuvre warfare. Iran also had the advantage in a war of attrition, given the greater size of its population, and was making steady if small progress in taking bites of territory.[6] This increased the moral and manpower costs to Iraq.

Iraq maintained itself against this onslaught with arms imports, and used its greater technological capability to limit Iranian successes, which included the liberal use of chemical weapons. However, Iraq had no obvious strategic advantage in land warfare as there were no vulnerable points on the Iranian side within striking distance of its ground forces. Saddam therefore turned to air strikes against Iranian cities in the hope of causing a collapse of morale and a greater willingness to negotiate a settlement favourable to Iraq. In fact, sustaining morale in Iraq was even more precarious for Saddam. Many Iraqis viewed Saddam's government as a Tikriti elite and not a national government. The genuine popularity of Saddam in his early years in office had been based on the country's substantial oil wealth post 1973, but this was squandered in the war. Moreover, the conflict was seen as 'Saddam's war' and the miseries it inflicted as his responsibility. Saddam's promise of liberation for southern Sunni Iranians in the province of Khuzestan, a declared war aim, was not appealing. Few in the south-west of Iran wanted to exchange the revolution, for all its faults, for an Iraqi police state. Nevertheless, with foreign aid and the expenditure of oil revenue, Saddam sustained the economic strain on the country until 1985. After the fall of oil prices it became far harder to conceal or ameliorate the effects of war on the economy. Iraq spent 25 per cent of its GDP on arms at the beginning of the war, but this increased to 50 per cent by the war's end and arms and ammunition represented 45 per cent of all imports. By 1988, both sides were being crippled by the costs of the conflict. Throughout the war, Saddam hoped for a negotiated settlement as an alternative to his strategic weakness, but time and again Iran rejected it.

The sheer strategic value of the oil economy meant that pipelines, shipping and exports were a target for both sides. Iraq used air strikes against the tanker shuttles in the southern Gulf and air raids on the key installations in the upper Gulf. These raids had a cumulative effect, but generally Baghdad could only force reductions in the volume of oil and reduce Iranian revenue. Yet, by the end of the war, it had caused significant disruption and hardship for the Iranian public. The Iranians were far more reactive in the 'tanker war', and, in the absence of Iraqi tankers to attack, they had to interdict Gulf shipping that was transporting Iraqi, Kuwaiti and Saudi Arabia oil, and this included Western vessels trading with those countries. Iran did not possess enough mines, aircraft, missiles or ships to close the Strait of Hormuz permanently against Western capabilities. What air assets it had were prioritised to support the land campaign further north and the Iranians were forced to use unconventional tactics to harass Gulf shipping, namely boarding, machine-gun attacks from fast patrol boats and mine warfare in the primary transit lanes.

Throughout the conflict, Iraq enjoyed superiority in the quantity and quality of armour and other weapons technology. It received $17.6-billion-worth of military aid between 1979 and 1983, while Iran obtained only $5.4-billion-worth ($2 billion of that figure was received before the revolution). Even what it possessed was not always operative. There was some sabotage by ex-Shah officers just after the revolution and prior to the outbreak of the war, especially in aircraft and communications, and it was always short of parts. When the United States cut its military supplies, Iran found it hard to maintain its American-made equipment, and there were problems of interoperability with replacement Chinese and other foreign material. Iraq got 55 per cent of its arms from the USSR as the Soviets tried to prevent the country moving into the American orbit. Between 1986 and 1988, the Soviets delivered to Iraq arms valued at roughly $8.8 to $9.2 billion, comprising more than 2,000 tanks (including 800 T-72s), 300 fighter aircraft, almost 300 surface-to-air missiles (mostly Scud Bs) and thousands of pieces of heavy artillery and armoured personnel vehicles.[7] The 2,000 tanks proved critical in the final offensive of the war. From a strategic point of view, the USSR had initially been 'strictly neutral', like the USA, and wanted to be able to influence Iran, but its overtures were rejected and it increasingly moved to a pro-Iraq tilt, especially as Iran was at that time backing the Shia Mujahideen in Afghanistan against the Soviet Union. France, a long-term investor in Iraq, provided 25 per cent of the military aid and the other 41 countries (or dealers from those countries), such as Brazil, Argentina, Vietnam, Italy and Sweden, supplied approximately 20 per cent of the arms and parts, bridging equipment, vehicles, patrol boats, anti-aircraft missiles, and explosives.[8] Britain observed the UN ban on arms sales, but allegedly sold components and machine tools that could facilitate weapons manufacturing.[9] Egypt also sent emergency supplies after the Iraqi setback at Fao in 1986. Despite the abundance of materiel, Iraqi procurement throughout the war was haphazard and there were gaps in certain key components which tended to limit air operations in the Gulf.

Officially, the policy of the United States was not to support either of the belligerents, and the intention was to stop others from supplying them, too. However, it was almost impossible to prevent Iran receiving equipment from North Korea and China. Although 70 per cent of its foreign war materiel was obtained from these two countries, neither was entirely enthusiastic about the arrangement because of Iran's persecution of communists. From Iran's side, its personnel needed extensive retraining to make use of the equipment. It needed new maintenance chains, too, but it could not always get a full set of spares to make a system operable.

Desperate for more equipment, Iran made efforts to contact every supplier in the West, both legal and illegal ones, and, as a result, got caught out in several scams. Iran opened a London 'Logistics' office in the United Kingdom as a conduit for European materials. Despite official denials, France made some illegal sales to Iran, selling artillery ammunition and missiles. The UK sold dual-use technology, including air-defence radars, tankers and logistical ships, but the bulk of British sales went to its traditional clients, the smaller Gulf states, which had the effect of strengthening confidence in Britain.[10] The Iranian London office obtained new engine parts for its fleet of chieftains, but was duped over a consignment of TOW missiles.

Indeed, Iran got caught in a calculated American sting operation on 19 April 1986, nick-named the Demavand project. Demavand was the cover name for arms dealers trying to sell material to Iran via France, Turkey and various European banks, but the deal was blown by American and Israeli intelligence when they set up a mock attempt to get captured Iraqi tanks in return for new aircraft, tanks and helicopters.[11] Seventeen people were arrested in the case. Nevertheless, Israel allegedly supplied genuine arms to ensure a more compliant Iranian foreign policy and to open a second front against the Arab states, especially Iraq.[12] Cooperation with Iran offered the prospect that it could influence Syria, its ally, or limit the aggressive activities of militant Shia groups operating against Israel in south Lebanon. Their aim was also to secure the rights of Iranian Jews, to obtain foreign currency, and to gain intelligence through the trade of a few captured Soviet vehicles, although this latter deal with Iran failed.

However, there were also covert American supplies to Iran which were not stings but part of a deliberate attempt to undermine the regime, free American hostages or to finance covert operations in Latin America. Selling arms to Iran offered a way to raise revenue outside of the United States in order to finance a covert war against Nicaragua without the supervision of Congress and Senate. Lieutenant-Colonel Oliver North, United States Marine Corps, was a key figure in the attempts to sell anti-tank and anti-aircraft missiles, and it is alleged he made five consignments of $30–87-million-worth of arms between August 1985 and November 1986. The allegation was investigated in the affair known as Irangate and Colonel North was made to appear before a Congressional hearing, but his conviction was overturned in 1991 on legal grounds.[13]

The interests of the Western European states in the Iran–Iraq War

The disunity of Europeans was exposed by the Iran–Iraq War. Until the very last stages of the conflict, it was impossible to speak of a collective policy even though they shared an interest in the continued free flow of oil onto the world's markets and for their own domestic consumption.[14] While the Western European states adopted a policy of neutrality towards the two belligerents, France was more overt in its support for Iraq. The country owed France some 15 billion Francs through its sale of military technologies in the 1970s and its assistance with the construction of Iraq's nuclear facilities at Osirak. France also had a general policy of opposition to Islamic militant movements in North Africa, which it felt also applied to Iran. Yet there is no doubt that France had specific national commercial interests of the future in mind when it supported Iraq. The Iraqi Foreign Minister, Tariq Aziz, noted in 1983 that Iraq would favour any country after the conflict that had shown support to Baghdad.[15] Italy also had commercial interests at stake, but was prepared to take a more principled stand on neutrality. Although it was contracted to supply Iraq with eleven warships before the war, its neutrality meant that the vessels were never delivered. Iraq consequently refused to pay its $2 billion debt. However, Italy managed to retain its contracts for the construction of oil pipelines with both countries.

West Germany assumed a very low profile in the conflict, but played an important diplomatic role. The foreign minister, Hans Dietrich Genscher, visited Iran in 1984 and obtained the release of a West German hostage held in Beirut, before travelling to Baghdad to arrange for the rescheduling of Iraqi debts. Genscher was critical of the general Western policy of isolating Iran and consistently advocated that both Iran and Iraq should work towards a ceasefire.[16] However, his criticisms of Iraqi chemical warfare were devalued when accusations were made in the media that it was West German companies that had supplied the chemical weapons in the first place.[17]

Smaller European states were typically in favour of a UN-led peace process or a collective policy, but the major European states pursued their own agendas of national self-interest. In fact, it was difficult to achieve consensus on a common European policy even when it concerned terrorism, reactions to hostage-taking, or Iraqi use of chemical weapons. Britain, for example, took a tough line on hostage-takers and refused to negotiate. France, on the other hand, saw negotiation as essential, a fact which angered the British and other nations and led to accusations that the French were undermining the West's credibility and perhaps even encouraging further kidnapping or terrorism. After years of domestic Irish terrorism, the British had taken a hard line on from the outset, and they had used the Special Air Service to break the siege of the Iranian Embassy by a pro-Iraqi group in 1980.[18] In 1987 they arrested the Iranian vice-consul for theft and relations were soured when Iran deliberately arrested the British head of chancery in retaliation. The nadir of diplomacy with Iran came just after the war when the Iranian regime issued a fatwa calling for the killing of the satirical novelist Salman Rushdie in 1989.

The government of the United Kingdom, led by Prime Minister Margaret Thatcher, believed there was little chance that either Iran or Iraq could achieve a decisive victory, but, like the United States, it shared concerns about how the war might affect oil prices globally. Britain's North Sea oil reserves gave it greater flexibility in policy and there was interest in keeping open channels of communication with revolutionary Iran in order to benefit from the post-war commercial and diplomatic climate. For this reason it permitted the Iranian Embassy and the Iranian Logistical Centre to remain open in London. Nevertheless, Britain's historic legacy of interventions in both Iraq and Iran proved a handicap in maintaining a diplomatic discourse. Despite accusations by Iran that Britain was an ally of the United States still trying to play a 'Great Game' against Iranian interests, the British government knew it simply lacked the power to impose its interests on either of the belligerents. Unlike the United States, the British also felt that the Soviets would find it difficult to influence either Iran or Iraq. Iraq had executed twenty-one communists in 1978 and there was evidence of bad relations between Moscow and Baghdad. Initial Soviet support for the revolution in Iran did little to improve matters.[19]

While there was an awareness that the Soviets would try to push forward their cause, the British were less concerned about the likelihood of success in this than the United States. Moreover, the British were themselves very sceptical that force could change the situation in the Gulf and they were concerned that the Americans might take too hard a line in this respect. Britain opposed any idea that the NATO Rapid Deployment Force should be used in the Gulf, and the Americans also felt that it would be detrimental to draw forces from the European theatre. The British did establish the modestly sized Armilla Patrol in 1980 to escort UK merchant shipping in the Gulf, and perhaps to indicate that it had a presence in the region to the littoral states, but there was no question of it being used in an offensive combat role. When it was increased in size, this tended to be in a minesweeping capacity. That said, Iranian attacks on Gulf shipping and their deliberate mining programme prompted the British to take a more muscular line from 1987 and this brought the UK into closer alignment with the American position.

As one might expect, this view was contested in Iran. The Iranian viewpoint was largely that a divided Europe simply followed American policy.[20] When Iraq made use of chemical weapons, the Iranians were bitter that the Europeans were apparently silent. In fact, the Europeans were not silent but consistent in their call for a ceasefire. At the April 1985 Brussels Summit, for example, European governments called the cessation of the use of chemical weapons and for the war to be ended.

The role of Western intelligence

There are also suggestions that, from the outset, Iraq benefited from Western intelligence support. In a secret document assessing changes to the United States' policy of strict neutrality, dated October 1983, there is a clear reference to tactical intelligence having been made available following the Iranian invasion of Iraqi territory in 1982.[21] Tactical intelligence included AWACs early warnings, PHOTINT (Photographic Intelligence), SATINT (Satellite Intelligence), and naval intelligence systems from the Gulf. Efforts were stepped up in 1985 onwards because of the setbacks to Iraqi forces. France also supplied intelligence support of variable quality and Israel is thought to have made available selective information. Details on American intelligence support is still classified, but it likely to have included Iranian force strengths (although assessing the Iranian order of battle was difficult as there was little standardisation – formations were put together for specific offensives), warnings of attacks, unit tracking, concentrations of formations, and assistance to Iraqi targeting. There has been a suggestion that the United States offered some intelligence support to Iran, but this was more likely to have been either deliberate misinformation or, if genuine, part of the package to release the US hostages. For example, at a secret meeting in Frankfurt in 1986 the Iranians were alerted to the Soviet exercises on their border, and this information was probably used as a lever to pressure the Iranians to end the conflict. It is likely the Americans continued to provide covert support to anti-Khomeini elements and it is alleged that Colonel North provided intelligence to Iran that may have assisted it in its attack on Fao in 1986.[22] The value of that intelligence, even if it was provided, would have been extremely limited. The static nature of Iraqi positions made it relatively easy for the Iranians to locate and bypass them in their offensive. Moreover, there was a lot of cloud cover which obscured US satellites and therefore, rather exceptionally, the Iranian build-up was not detected. The American advice to the Iraqis had been for the Iraqis to maintain a reserve at Basra to meet any thrust near the city, which was sound under the circumstances. The Iranian success at Fao owed more to their numbers and infiltration tactics than any information provided by intelligence sources. Furthermore, the Iraqis intelligence systems let them down on several occasions. Iraq lacked some basic intelligence procedures and organisation, which made the situation worse. It possessed some SIGINT and electronic support measures, and some PHOTINT assets, but in the case of the latter it had no means to distribute them efficiently. Worst of all, Iraqi intelligence was subject to political interference.

The United Nations and the war

On the outbreak of war, the United Nations referred to the situation as one likely to endanger international peace and security, under Article 34 of the UN Charter, and authorised the UNSC to take the appropriate action, under Article 37.[23] No reference was made to Iraqi aggression or occupation (Articles 39 and 40) and the belligerents were simply encouraged to resolve the dispute through peaceful means. In effect, a ceasefire in the first few months of the war would have left Iraq in possession of Iranian territory, and, perhaps unsurprisingly therefore, Iran rejected peace overtures. When Iran counter-attacked into Iraqi territory, the UN felt no obligation to penalise Iraq as the aggressor. Indeed, Iraq appealed for a ceasefire on several occasions and therefore appeared to be acting within the parameters laid down by the charter. By contrast, Iran's revolutionary and belligerent rhetoric merely alienated members of the UNSC. Nevertheless, the Iranians felt that the UN favoured the Iraqi cause and had failed to recognise the fact of Iraqi aggression.[24] The ratification of Resolution 598 (1987) reiterated the demand for a ceasefire and in paragraph 6 noted that the UN secretary general should enquire through an impartial body the causes of the war. Clearly the UN believed that the causes of the conflict did not begin with the Iraqi invasion, but with a catalogue of unresolved border disputes dating back to 1975 and earlier.

Iran informed the UN that Iraq had used chemical weapons against its forces on 28 October 1983, and following verification of the use, the president of the UNSC issued a statement calling for the belligerents to honour the 1925 Geneva Protocol, which banned the weapons, while listing incidents where Iraqis had made attacks.[25] The UN called on all states not to supply either party with the materials for such weapons. Once again, the Iranians felt that the UNSC had not taken sufficient notice of the Iraqi use of the weapons against Iran. However, doubts remain as to the extent to which Iranians retaliated with the same weapon systems.[26] The United States condemned publicly the Iraqi use of chemical weapons and banned the exports of all precursors as early as 5 March 1984.[27] The UN secretary general authorised nine investigations into alleged war crimes during the conflict, all but one of which were related to the use of chemical weapons. The Iranians also drew the UN's attention to Iraqi attacks on cities as civilian targets, which was acknowledged from 1983, but the Iranians were dissatisfied that no action was taken against Iraq. Less persuasive were Iranian complaints that the Iraqis had attacked their oil installations thus threatening the marine environment, not least because the Iranians had themselves made similar attacks and caused extensive damage to Iraqi well heads. Moreover, Iran and Iraq were both in breach of the Paris declaration of 1856 and the Second Geneva Convention (1949), which banned violations of the free navigation of international waters.

The new Security Council membership in January 1987, alongside the permanent members, included Germany, Italy and Japan, and the UNSC convened in light of the Iranian seizure of the Fao peninsula to discuss the escalation of the conflict and to insist on a ceasefire. The draft Resolution was accepted immediately by Iraq which had called for a ceasefire for some time and, after further negotiations, Iran, too, accepted that the resolution must ultimately be binding on it. However, Iran refused to accept the full Resolution for a year, believing that it had a military victory within its grasp.[28] In September 1987, President Reagan had informed the Iranians that if they did not accept the Resolution, the UNSC would be forced to take 'special measures'. However, Chinese and Soviet opposition prevented any such enforcement and the Iranian delay continued. As a result, UNSC members began to implement measures of their own. France banned the purchase of Iranian oil, Britain shut down the Iranian office for the procurement of military equipment, and the United States banned the import of Iranian goods and restricted military-related exports. More importantly, naval actions in the Persian Gulf compelled the Iranian regime to accept the UN Resolution and conclude the conflict.

A new perspective

When, in 1979, Iran seemed poised to launch an Islamic fundamentalist jihad across the Muslim world and thereby damage the international order, Iraq's pre-emptive strike was backed by powers that were eager to see Iran contained and its revolution neutralised. Iraq mobilised a diverse population without significant internal opposition, eventually reaching a total of one million men. During the course of the war, Iraq strengthened and increased the capability of this force so that, in the land operations in 1988, it was able to defeat the Iranians in the field. Moreover, its diplomatic efforts ensured a Western coalition neutralised Iran's power at sea.

Yet, for much of this long conflict, Iran had had the upper hand. Despite the difficulties in finding sufficient resources to wage the war, the Iranians had come close to victory in 1986. Their light infantry forces had exhibited fanatical courage despite severe losses and their alliance with Kurdish guerrillas threatened Iraq strategically and with great significance. On both sides, there had been inept leadership, rivalry between the ruling political party and the regular armed forces, and determined internal opposition. Iraq made extensive use of chemical weapons, conducted missile and air bombardments of Iranian cities and deliberately targeted economic and political installations. Iran responded with an escalation of the war, including air strikes against Iraqi cities and attacks on shipping of neutral countries in the Gulf.

Iran's revolutionary and Jihadist ethos meant that it tended to reject conventional military thinking and there was a general reluctance to negotiate with countries it fully expected to defeat at some stage. However, Iran's lack of vital military resources meant that it turned to the physical courage of its young men and sheer weight of numbers for the first four years of the war, making vast human wave assaults against Iraqi defences, using infiltration tactics and maximising the use of broken terrain or concealment at night. The loss of Iranian oil installations, its relative isolation, defeat on the battlefield and signs of growing unrest at home, forced the Khomeini regime to finally agree to a peace settlement.

This was an extremely costly conflict. In the Iraqi counter-offensive at Fao in February 1986, for example, some 10,000 Iraqis and some 20,000 Iranians were killed in action. The two-week battle was marked by an unprecedented use of chemical weapons. Gas was used extensively during the war, including against the Kurdish insurgents of northern Iraq between 1986 and 1988. The war eventually took the lives of

200,000 Iraqis, with a further 400,000 wounded and 70,000 taken prisoner. Iranian losses are estimated at half a million. Yet this was also
a war waged against elements of their domestic populations. The Iraqi
regime executed thousands of its ideological opponents while the Iranian
revolutionaries were just as capable of killing or torturing their own
adversaries.

In financial terms, the conflict cost approximately $350 billion and
plunged Saddam Hussein's regime into debt, spurring him on to further military action in the Gulf, while Iran was forced to abandon its
ambitions for a regional Islamic revolution and had to focus on the reconstruction of urban areas, some of which were very badly damaged in
the conflict. The war produced few benefits: there were no changes in
the borders, political systems remained intact, and the heads of state
remained unchanged. Neither side achieved their strategic aims as envisaged at the outbreak of the war. On the basis of his forces' battlefield
success in the final months of the war, Saddam claimed a 'historic victory' and Khomeini was forced to accept defeat, but peace negotiations
failed and the Iraqi dictator could produce no peace dividend for his
people.

The effect on the psychology of the political elites and the broad mass
of the population was far-reaching. Iraqis were persuaded that they had
won the conflict, while Iranians reached for the consolation of sacrifice –
a concept, incidentally, the war enhanced within the psyche of the nation.
Given that both regimes tried to rewrite the history of the war from their
own, more positive perspectives (even one year after the war, the Iraqi
authorities were already offering a revisionist view of the Karbala operations which omitted the setbacks and errors), a reappraisal of that war,
twenty years on, offers a new perspective.

The recent conflicts of the Middle East, including Iraq's invasion of
Kuwait, the Gulf War of 1990–91, the Iraq War of 2003 and confrontation between the UN and Iran over the nuclear issue, can be traced to the
Iran–Iraq War and its ideological foundations. Iran's desire to assert its
regional influence, its anxiety about internal security, its sense of being
encircled by hostile states, the fear of foreign intelligence operatives,
its desire for an independent programme of nuclear enrichment and its
deeply embedded aggressive, revolutionary ethos are all linked to the
conflict. On the Iraqi side, Saddam Hussein found himself embroiled in
a war that was so costly that he was indebted to his Arab neighbours, he
could not demobilise his armed forces for fear of plunging the country
into economic chaos and he faced the prospect of economic and political
collapse. His attempt to intimidate Kuwait led directly to the First Gulf

War in 1990–91. His sheer determination to retain power, and concerns that any further weakening would provide an opening for the Iranians, reinforced his defiant stance towards the West in the 1990s. With the defeat of Saddam's regime in 2003, and the American-led coalition's difficulties in trying to quell the insurgency in Iraq, Iran believed it had a much better opportunity to establish its influence in the first decade of the twenty-first century. That said, Tehran was deeply concerned by the contamination of Western, liberal-democratic ideas, and anxious about domestic unrest, inspired perhaps by external forces. The Iran–Iraq War is therefore particularly important if we are to understand Iran's fundamental desire to develop its own nuclear programme to enhance its national security.

Notes

1 Introduction

1. Anthony Cordesman, *Iraq's Insurgency and the Road to Civil Conflict* (Westport, CT: Praeger Security International, 2008), vol. I, p. 51.
2. John Ballard, *Fighting for Fallujah: A New Dawn for Iraq* (Santa Barbara, CA: Greenwood Publishing, 2006), pp. 3–5.
3. Anthony Cordesman and Abraham R. Wagner, *Lessons of Modern War, II, The Iran-Iraq War* (Boulder, CO: Westview, 1991 edn).
4. Anthony Cordesman, *The Iran-Iraq War and Western Security, 1984–87* (London: Jane's, Royal United Services Institute, 1987), p. 3.
5. Ibid., p. 3.
6. Ibid., p. 15.
7. Contemporary statistics bore little relation to the actual costs of total war. Cordesman, *Iran-Iraq War and Western Security*, pp. 4–5.
8. Joe Stork, 'Iraq and the War in the Gulf', MERIP Reports, 97, Iraq (June 1981), p. 3.
9. Fritz Fischer, *War of Illusions* (London: Chatto and Windus, 1975).
10. Dilip Hiro, *The Longest War* (London: Paladin Grafton Books, 1990), p. xxii.
11. Cordesman, *Iran-Iraq War and Western Security*, p. 6.
12. Ibid., p. 39.

2 Iran's Revolution and Iraq's Ambitions

1. Efraim Karsh, *The Iran-Iraq War* (Oxford: Osprey, 2002), p. 64.
2. Vali Nasr, *The Shia Revival* (New York: W.W. Norton, 2006), pp. 35–8.
3. Jasim M. Abdulghani, *Iran and Iraq: The Years of Crisis* (Baltimore, MD: John Hopkins Press, 1984), p. 3.
4. H.R. Roehmer, 'The Safavid Period', *Cambridge History of Iran*, vol. 6 (Cambridge: Cambridge University Press, 1986), pp. 189–350.
5. Nukki R. Keddie, *Modern Iran: Roots and Results of Revolution* (New Haven and London: Yale University Press, 2003), pp. 24 and 36.

6. John Gleason, *The Genesis of Russophobia* (Harvard Historical Studies, 57: Octagon, 1971); G.J. Alder, 'The Key to India? Britain and the Herat Problem, 1830–63', *Middle East Studies*, 1974; 10, 306; Robert Johnson, *Spying for Empire: The Great Game in Central and South Asia, 1757–1947* (London: Greenhill, 2006); H.W.C. Davis, 'The Great Game in Asia', The Raleigh Lecture on History. *Proceedings of the British Academy* (1926).

7. Captain G.H. Hunt and George Townsend, *Outram and Havelock's Persian Campaign, to which is Prefixed a Summary of Persian History, and Account of the Various Differences between England and Persia and an Inquiry into the Origin of the Late War* (London: Routledge, 1858).

8. Keddie, *Modern Iran*, pp. 52–53.

9. Ibid., pp. 67–70.

10. Antony Wynn, *Persia in the Great Game* (London: John Murray, 2003), pp. 248ff.

11. Peter Sluggett, *Britain in Iraq, 1914–32* (London: Ithaca, 1976).

12. See David Fromkin, *A Peace to End All Peace: Creating the Modern Middle East, 1914–22* (New York: Henry Holt and Company, 1989); Georgina Howell, *Gertrude Bell: Queen of the Desert, Shaper of Nations* (London, Farrar Straus Giroux, reprtd., 2008).

13. Mohammad A. Tarbush, *The Role of the Military in Politics: A Case Study of Iraq to 1941* (London: Kegan Paul, 1982).

14. Daniel Silverfarb and Majid Khadduri, *Britain's Informal Empire in the Middle East: A Case Study of Iraq, 1929–41* (New York: Oxford University Press, 1986); Hiro, *Longest War*, p. 11; see also Daniel Silvberfarb, *The Twilight of British Ascendancy in the Middle East: A Case Study of Iraq, 1941–1950* (Basingstoke and New York: Palgrave, 1994).

15. G. Lenczowski, *Russia and the West in Iran, 1918–48* (London: Ithaca, 1949), p. 168.

16. Matthew Elliot, *Independent Iraq: British Influence 1941–58* (London: I B Tauris, 1996); Keddie, *Modern Iran*, p. 139.

17. Shahram Chubin and Sepehr Zubin, *The Foreign Relations of Iran: A Developing State in a Zone of Great Power Conflict* (Berkeley, CA: University of California Press, 1974), p. 183.

18. Edmund Ghareeb, *The Kurdish Question in Iraq* (Syracuse, NY: Syracuse University Press, 1981), p. 133.

19. Behcet Kemel Yesilbursa, *The Baghdad Pact: Anglo-American Defense Policies in the Middle East, 1950–59* (Abingdodn: Frank Cass, 2005), pp. 65–66.

20. The worst of the fighting was around the Konjam Dam in February and March 1974, but there were also clashes in the disputed parts of Mehran. Cordesman and Wagner, *Lessons of Modern War*, p. 19.

21. Christine Moss Helms, *Iraq: Eastern Flank of the Arab World* (Washington DC: Brookings Institute, 1984), p. 118.

22. Hiro, *Longest War*, p. 17.
23. Tariq Y. Ismail, *Iraq and Iran: Roots of Conflict* (Syracuse, NY: Syracuse University Press, 1982), p. 66.
24. NIO/Middle East, *The Implications of the Iran-Iraq Agreement*, May 1, 1975. Secret, CIA Report, released for publication in 2004, and accessible online at http://www.gwu.edu/~ nsarchiv/NSAEBB/NSAEBB167/01.pdf. Accessed January 2010.
25. Michel Aflaq, *Fi Sabil al Ba'ath* (Beirut: Dal al-Tali'ah, 1959); Kamel S. Abu Jaber, *The Arab-Ba'ath Socialist Party: History, Ideology and Organisation* (New York: Syracuse University Press, 1966).
26. Majid Khadduri, *Independent Iraq: A Study in Iraqi Politics from 1932–1958* (Oxford: Oxford University Press, 2nd edn, 1960).
27. Walter Lacquer, *Communism and Nationalism in the Middle East* (London: Routledge and Kegan Paul, 1956).
28. Majid Khadduri, *Socialist Iraq: A Study in Iraqi Politics since 1968* (Washington DC: The Middle East Institute, 1978), p. 65.
29. Nasr, *The Shia Revival*, pp. 60, 68–69, 74–75.
30. Dilip Hiro, *Inside the Middle East* (London: Routledge and Kegan Paul, 1982), p. 144.
31. Khomeini in an interview with *Der Spiegel*, 7 November 1978.
32. *The Times*, 8 July 1981.
33. *The Guardian*, 28 February 1979.
34. See Majid Khadduri, *The Gulf War: The Origins and Implications of the Iran-Iraq Conflict* (New York and Oxford: Oxford University Press, 1988).
35. Fuad Matar, *Saddam Hussein: The Man, The Cause, The Future* (London: Third World Centre for Research and Publishing, 1981).
36. Ofra Bengio, 'Shias and Politics in Baathi Iraq', *Middle Eastern Studies* (January 1985), pp. 6–7; Hiro, *Longest War*, p. 30, and note 27, p. 274.
37. *The Observer*, 24 June 1979.
38. S. Ruhollah Khomeini, *Hukumat-e Islami: Velavat-e faqih* (Teheran: Amir Bakir, 1978); Vasant Kaiwar and Sucheta Mazumdar, *Antimonies of Modernity: Essays on Race, Orient, Nation* (Duke, 2003), p. 221.
39. Gilles Kepel, *Jihad: The Trail of Political Islam* (London: I B Tauris, 2008), pp. 109–110.
40. *The Times*, 8 July 1981, p. 9.
41. Khomeini, *Hukumat-e Islami*, p. 75.
42. Speech to the Iranian people, 8 August 1979, cited at http://www.iran-heritage.org/interestgroups/government-article2.htm. Accessed December 2009.
43. Keddie, *Modern Iran*, pp. 148–169.
44. Ibid., pp. 234 and 238.
45. Ibid., p. 227; Kepel, *Jihad*, p. 110.
46. Robert Graham, *Iran: The Illusion of Power* (London: Croom Helm, 1979).

47. Daily Report. Middle East & North Africa, FBIS-MEA-79-203, 'Iraq', Foreign Broadcast Information Service, 17 October 1979 (published 18 October 1979), p. E1.

48. 'Developments Concerning Relations with Iraq', Daily Report. South Asia, FBIS-SAS-80-078 *on* 21 April 1980, Foreign Broadcast Information Service, p. I8; and the response can be found at: 'Ath-Thawrah criticises Iranian Regime', Daily Report, Middle East & Africa, FBIS-MEA-80-077, 'Iraq', Foreign Broadcast Information Service, 18 April 1980, E3; *Washington Post*, 18 April 1980.

49. Cited in Hiro, *Longest War*, note 40, p. 274.

50. The information about this plan and the invasion preparations was allegedly acquired by the communist Tudeh party and passed on by the General Secretary, Nurreddin Kianuri, to Khomeini. If true the Iranian regime failed to act on this intelligence. The Iraqi plan also envisaged the Iranian army turning on the revolutionaries in Teheran. Eric Rouleau, 'The War and the Struggle for the State', *MERIP Reports*, 98, 'Iran Two Years After' (July–August, 1981), pp. 3–4.

51. Cordesman, *Iran-Iraq War and Western Security*, p. 2.

52. Abdulghani, *Iran and Iraq: The Years of Crisis*; Tareq Y. Ismael, *Iran and Iraq: Roots of Conflict* (New York: Syracuse University Press, 1982); Judith Miller and Laurie Mylroie, *Saddam Hussein and the Crisis in the Gulf* (New York: Random House, 1990), p. 109.

3   The Iraqi Offensive of September 1980 and the Failure of Saddam's 'Limited War'

1. Broadcast on Baghdad Radio, 28 September 1980.

2. Interviewees with the author, anonymised, 15 October 2007 and 4 November 2008.

3. See Kenneth Katzman, *The Warriors of Islam: Iran's Revolutionary Guards* (Oxford: Oxford University Press, 1993).

4. Broadcast on Baghdad Radio, 18 October 1980.

5. Broadcast on Baghdad Radio, 4 November 1980.

6. Keith McLachlan and George Joffe, *The Gulf War: A Survey of Political Issues and Economic Consequences* (London: Economist Intelligence Unit Special Report, no. 176, 1984).

7. *New York Times*, 8 March 1981.

8. Anthony Cordesman and Abraham R. Wagner, *Lessons of Modern War, II, The Iran–Iraq War* (Boulder, CO: Westview, 1991 edn), p. 119.

9. *Baghdad Observer*, 18 December 1980.

10. Major Ronald E. Bergquist, *The Role of Air Power in the Iran-Iraq War* (Maxwell Air Force Base, Alabama, 1988), p. 51.

11. *Le Monde*, 30 July 1980.

12. *Sunday Times*, 24 May 1981; *International Herald Tribune*, 23 June 1981.
13. Tehran Radio, 21 June 1982.
14. Major Robert E. Sonnenberg, USMC, *The Iran-Iraq War: Strategy of Stalemate* (Quantico, Virginia: Marine Corps Command and Staff College, 1 April 1985). Available online at http://www.globalsecurity.org/military/library/report/1985/SRE.htm Accessed December 2009.
15. *Time Magazine*, 19 July 1982.

4   Human Waves: Iran's Counter-Offensives into Iraq

1. 'Unabated Gross Violations of Children's Rights in Iran', International Children Rights Monitor, Spring 1983, p.16; 'Iran Chronology of Childhood Lost', International Children Rights Monitor, Autumn 1983, p. 5.
2. *New York Times Magazine*, 12 February 1984, p. 21.
3. *Tehran Times*, 'Youth Future of the Islamic Republic-Khamenei', 23 February 1982, p. 1.
4. *Financial Times Magazine*, 'The Hero and the Heroin', 16 April 2005.
5. Cited in Baham Nirumand, *Krieg, Krieg, bis zum Sieg*, in Anja Malanowski und Marianne Stern, *Iran-Irak. Bis die Gottlosen vernichtet sind* (Reinbek: Rowohlt, 1987), pp. 95–96.
6. Cordesman and Wagner, *Lessons of Modern War*, p. 152.
7. Vali Nasr, *The Shia Revival* (New York: W. W. Norton, 2006), p. 120.
8. Dilip Hiro, *The Longest War* (London: Paladin Grafton Books, 1990), p. 92.
9. Cordesman and Wagner, *Lessons of Modern War*, pp. 154–155.
10. Ibid., p. 158.

5   Escalation: Operations Wa al Fajr and Khaibar, 1984

1. Cordesman and Wagner, *Lessons of Modern War*, p. 159.
2. Details of precisely what intelligence was passed on are still classified. However, it is clear that the Americans were able to give the Iraqis warnings of build-ups of Iranian formations. It is likely that this consisted of force strengths, tracking of movements, and perhaps even assistance with specific targeting. French and Israel intelligence product was considered unreliable by the Iraqis. Cordesman, *Iran-Iraq War and Western Security*, p. 36.
3. Cordesman and Wagner, *Lessons of Modern War*, p. 166.
4. Ibid., pp. 167–168.
5. The same missiles had just had a devastating effect against British warships in the South Atlantic. Ibid., pp. 170–174.
6. Ibid., p. 176.
7. Ibid., p. 180.

8. Ibid., p. 182.
9. J. Borak and F.R. Sidell, 'Agents of Chemical Warfare: Sulfur Mustard', Annals of Emergency Medicine, 1992; 21(3), 303–308.
10. CW Use in the Iran-Iraq War, http://www.fas.org/irp/gulf/cia/960702/72566_01.htm Accessed January 2010.
11. M. Balali, 'Clinical and Laboratory Findings in Iranian Fighters with Chemical Gas Poisoning', Archives Belges 1984; (suppl), 254–259.
12. Julian Perry Robinson and Jozef Goldblat, 'Chemical Warfare by Iraq in the Iran-Iraq War', SIPRI FACT SHEET, Chemical Weapons I (Stockholm International Peace Research Institute May 1984) and A. Heyndrick, N. Sookvanichsilp and M. Van Den Heede, 'Detection of Trichothecene Mycotoxins (Yellow Rain) in Blood, Urine, and Faeces of Iranian Soldiers Treated as Victims of a Gas Attack', Rivista di Tossicol Sperimentazione Clinica. 1989; 19 (1–3), 7–11; H. Kadivar and S.C. Adams, 'Treatment of Chemical and Biological Warfare Injuries: Insights Derived from the 1984 Iraqi Attack on Majnoon Island', Military Medicine 1991; 156(4), 171–177.
13. Broadcast on Baghdad Radio, 28 February 1984.
14. Newsweek, 19 March 1984.

6   Foreign Intervention, 1980–84

1. Dana Steinberg, Iran-Iraq War, Cold War International History Project, http://www.wilsoncenter.org/index.cfm?topic_id=1409&fuseaction=topics.item&news_id=90411. Accessed December 2009.
2. Kenneth Timmerman, The Death Lobby: How the West Armed Iraq (New York: Houghton Mifflin, 1991), p. 76.
3. See Zbigniew Brzezinski, Power and Principle: Memoirs of a National Security Advisor 1977–81 (New York: Farrar Strauss Girou, 1983).
4. Izvestia, 23 September 1980.
5. The Nation (United States), 8 August 1981, p. 97.
6. Kayhan, 11 November 1980.
7. Maxwell Orme Johnson, The Military as an Instrument of US Policy in Southwest Asia: The Rapid Deployment Joint Task Force, 1977–82 (Boulder, CO: Westview, 1983), p. 15.
8. The Daily Telegraph, 4 February 1981; Petroleum Economist, January 1982, pp. 23–24.
9. Iraq had been sponsoring guerrillas there in the past. See Miller and Mylroie, Saddam Hussein and the Crisis in the Gulf.
10. Broadcast on Baghdad Radio, 19 January 1981.
11. New York Times, 19 April 1982.
12. New York Times, 8 March 1982; Defence and Foreign Affairs Daily, 20 January 1983.

13. Haim Shaked and Daniel Dishon (eds), *Middle East Contemporary Survey, VI, 1981–82* (New York and London: Holmes and Meier, 1984), p. 610.

14. The JRDF was renamed the Peninsula Shield Force in 1984 and consisted of two brigades of approximately 10,000 men under Saudi command.

15. Telegram US Embassy Tel Aviv to Department of State, Washington, Secret, 12 December 1980, National Security Archive, 82, now accessible at http://www.gwu.edu/~nsarchiv/NSAEBB/NSAEBB82/#docs. Accessed December 2009.

16. Cordesman, *Iran-Iraq War and Western Security*, p. 6.

17. Richard M. Preece, *United States-Iraqi Relations* (Washington DC: Congressional Research Service, Library of Congress, Government Printing Office, July 1986), p. 12.

18. *Newsday*, 22 May 1984.

19. William Maley, *The Afghanistan Wars* (Basingstoke and New York: Palgrave, 2002).

20. National Security Archive, *The Chronology: The Documented Day-by-Day Account of the Secret Military Assistance to Iran and the Contras* (New York: Warner, 1987), p. 22.

21. Iraq received $27,444 million between 1981 and 1988. SIPRI http://armstrade.sipri.org/armstrade/html/export_values.php. Accessed January 2010.

22. SIPRI, http://armstrade.sipri.org/armstrade/html/export_values.php. Accessed January 2010.

7   Turning Point: Operations Badr and Fao, 1985–86

1. See Marion Farouk-Slugett and Peter Farouk-Slugett, *Iraq Since 1958: from Revolution to Dictatorship* (London: KPI, 1987).

2. Antony Cordesman and Wagner, *The Lessons of Modern War*, p. 219.

3. Ibid., pp. 223–224.

4. 'The Gulf: A Bridgehead to Fao', *Time Magazine*, 24 February 1986.

5. Cordesman and Wagner, *The Lessons of Modern War*, pp. 224–225.

6. *Washington Post*, 26 March 1986.

7. Cordesman, *Iran-Iraq War and Western Security*, p. 36.

8   War of the Cities, Home Fronts, Internal Security and Insurgency

1. Keith Lachlan and George Joffé, *The Gulf War: A Survey of the Political Issues and Economic Consequences* (London: The Economist Intelligence Unit, 1984), p. 71.

2. Keddie estimates that over 700 were executed in the revolution and, citing Amnesty International, about 2,500 in the last year of the war in Iran,

but figures are not available for the years 1981–88. Keddie, *Modern Iran*, p. 344, note 10; pp. 345–346, note 25.

3. Dilip Hiro, *Iran under the Ayatollahs* (London: Routledge and Kegan Paul, 1985, reprtd. 2000), p. 239.

4. Lachlan, Keith and George Joffé, *The Gulf War* (London: The Economist Intelligence Unit, 1984), pp. 71–72.

5. *The Sunday Times*, 7 April 1985.

6. *The Financial Times*, 15 June 1985.

9   The Tanker War, the Arms Trade and International Intervention, 1985–87

1. Barry Barton, Catherine Redgwell, Anita Ronne and Donald N. Zillman, *Energy Security: Managing Risk in a Dynamic Legal and Regulatory Environment* (Oxford: Oxford University Press, 2004), p. 5.

2. *Washington Post*, 9 June 1984.

3. Tehran Radio, 17 August 1984; Foreign Broadcast Information Service, 30 October 1984.

4. Anthony H. Cordesman and Abraham R. Wagner, *The Lessons of Modern War: Volume II, The Iran-Iraq War* (Boulder and San Francisco: Westview Press, 1990), p. 278.

5. *The Guardian*, 10 June and 4 August 1987; *New York Times*, 10 June 1987.

6. Elizabeth Gamlen and Paul Rogers, 'US Reflagging of Kuwaiti Tankers' in Farhang Rajaee (ed.), *The Iran-Iraq War: The Politics of Aggression* (Gainesville, University Press of Florida, 1993), p. 145.

7. Bahman Baktiari, 'International Law: Observations and Violations' in Rajaee (ed.), *The Iran-Iraq War*, pp. 153–154.

10   The Failure of Strategy: Iranian Offensives and Iraqi Counter-offensives, 1987–88

1. *Al Anaba*, 24 March 1986.

2. Stephen Pelletiere and Douglas V. Johnson III, *Lessons Learned: The Iran-Iraq War* (US Army War College: Strategic Studies Institute, 1991), Appendix A, pp. 83ff.

3. F. Barnaby, 'Iran-Iraq War: The Use of Chemical Weapons Against the Kurds', Ambio. 1988; 17(6), 407–408.

4. Iranian Republic News Agency, 'Iraqi Counter-Attack Smashed'; IRAN, 'Continuing Reportage on Operations Against Iraq', Daily Report. Near East & South Asia, FBIS-NES-87-121, 24 June 1987, Foreign Broadcast Information Service.

5. Hiro, *Longest War*, p. 88.

6. *The Financial Times*, 4 September 1987.
7. Cordesman and Wagner, *Lessons of Modern War*, pp. 363–367.
8. Ibid., pp. 37–31; Hiro, *Longest War*, p. 201; *Observer*, 27 March 1988.
9. Cordesman and Wagner, *Lessons of Modern War*, p. 371. The case remains controversial. Much of the civilian population had already fled because of a failed uprising against the Iraqi army in May 1987. There is also confusion over which chemical agents were used, with some suggesting only Mustard gas was used, while others point to evidence of air-delivery of phosgene, nerve agents and cyanide.
10. Cordesman and Wagner, *Lessons of Modern War*, pp. 375–376.
11. Ibid., p. 373.
12. Ibid., p. 373.
13. Ibid., p. 381.
14. Ibid., p. 383.
15. Pelletiere and Johnson, *Lessons Learned*.

11   Fuelling the Flames: Gulf Operations, 1987–88

1. Cordesman, *Iran-Iraq War and Western Security, 1984–87*, pp. 47–48.
2. *Washington Post*, 24, 25, 27 and 29 June 1987, cited in Cordesman and Wagner, *Lessons of Modern War*, p. 291.
3. Cordesman and Wagner, *Lessons of Modern War*, p. 306.
4. Moreover, Iraq's attacks on Iranian tankers were not as effective as they had hoped. Small arms and cannon fire could not penetrate their 22 mm of steel hulls, and although missiles could, they were often muffled by the sheer volume of crude stored within. There were 17 compartments and missiles might only damage one or two. Crude was, of course, not as flammable as petroleum, and even the relatively vulnerable liquid gas tankers had two hulls. The Iraqis therefore found it hard to knock out a tanker, and Iran only needed 10 tankers to get through to sustain its economic activity. A more lethal combination of munitions was needed, such as napalm, cluster bombs or incendiary weapons to disable or sink a tanker, but co-ordinating such an attack was beyond the capabilities of the Iraqi air force. Moreover Iraq had to avoid alienating potential world support which forced it to focus on Iranian land facilities, despite their stronger defences.
5. Japan also supported the United States indirectly, donating $10 million to UN peace building efforts and offering to finance US Navy research into technology that could locate mines more efficiently. *Washington Post*, 26 September 1987.
6. President Reagan, *Letter to the Speaker of the United States' House of Representatives*, 20 October 1987.
7. Cordesman and Wagner, *Lessons of Modern War*, p. 331.
8. *The Economist*, 30 January 1988, p. 32.
9. The American naval presence went from 39 to 25 ships of all types. The US Navy consolidated command of all shipping in Gulf area under a single

officer on the flagship of the ME Task Force, a decision which ended the division between naval operations and specific Gulf operations, and which offered a single chain of command through CENTCOM to the chairman of the Joint Chiefs of Staff in Washington.

10. Admiral Crowe, news briefing, Pentagon, 18 April 1988.
11. *Pentagon Current News*, 20 April 1988.
12. Pentagon Press Release, 29 April 1988.
13. *The Guardian*, 4 July 1988.
14. Gamlen and Rogers, 'US Reflagging of Kuwaiti Tankers', p. 142; *The Guardian*, 6 July 1988, p. 9.
15. Reza Ra'iss Tousi, 'Containment and Animosity: The United States and the War' in Farhand Rajaee (ed.), *Iranian Perspectives on the Iran-Iraq War* (Gainesville: University Press of Florida, 1997), p. 58.

12   The Iran–Iraq War in Retrospect

1. While the text of the National Security Decision Memorandum 92, which called for a greater US presence in the Gulf, was never made public, an unclassified summary can be found in the testimony of Deputy Assistant Secretary of Defense, James H. Noyes, in House Committee on Foreign Affairs, *New Perspectives on the Persian Gulf* (n.d.), p. 39. The plan was designed by Henry Kissinger and signed by President Nixon. See James H. Noyes, *The Clouded Lens* (Stanford, CA: Hoover Institution Press, 1979), pp. 53–54.
2. Michael T. Klare, *American Arms Supermarket* (Austin, TX: University of Texas Press, 1985), pp. 109–162.
3. President Carter, 'State of the Union Address', January 1980, cited in Jeff Macris, *The Politcs and Security of the Gulf: Anglo-American Hegemony and the Reshaping of a Region* (London and New York: Routledge, 2010), p. 210.
4. BP Amoco, *Statistical Review of World Energy* (London, 2000), pp. 4 and 7. The Persian Gulf states, including Saudi Arabia, produced an average of 21.3 million barrels of oil per diem in 1999, representing some 30 per cent of global production. Some 65 per cent of the world's reserves are thought to be located in the region.
5. John Chipman, 'Europe and the Iran-Iraq War' in Efraim Karsh (ed.), *The Iran-Iraq War: Impact and Implications* (London: Macmillan and Tel Aviv University), pp. 215–216.
6. In terms of manpower, the annual numbers reaching military age (21 years) in Iran was 2.7% of the population, and only 0.49% in Iraq. Iraq brought in foreign workers to release Iraqi men to fight, while Iran called up younger men early into its order of battle.
7. Mohiaddin Mesbahi, 'The USSR and the Iran–Iraq War: From Brezhnev to Gorbachev' in Farhang Rajaee (ed.), *The Iran–Iraq War: The*

Politics of Aggression (Gainesville, University Press of Florida, 1993), pp. 88–89.

8. Chipman, 'Europe and the Iran-Iraq War', p. 217.

9. Ahmad Naghibzadeh, 'Collectively or Singly: Western Europe and the War' in Farhand Rajaee (ed.), *Iranian Perspectives on the Iran-Iraq War* (Gainesville: University Press of Florida, 1997), p. 46.

10. The Wall St Journal ran the story on UK enterprises; see *Wall St Journal*, 30 January 1987, p. 1.

11. See *New York Times*, 2 February 1987.

12. Joseph Alpher, 'Israel and the Iran-Iraq War' in Karsh (ed.), *The Iran-Iraq War: Impact and Implications* (New York: St Martin's Press, 1999), pp. 154–155.

13. US Select Committee on Intelligence, Preliminary Report, 1987.

14. Naghibzadeh, 'Collectively or Singly', p. 40.

15. Chipman, 'Europe and the Iran-Iraq War', p. 218.

16. Ibid., p. 222.

17. Naghibzadeh, 'Collectively or Singly', p. 46.

18. Peter Harclerode, *Secret Soldiers: Special Forces in the War Against Terrorism* (London: Cassell, 2000), pp. 385–408.

19. Robert S. Litwak, 'The Soviet Union and the Iran-Iraq War', in Karsh (ed.), *The Iran-Iraq War: Impact and Implications* (New York: St Martin's Press, 1999), p. 202.

20. Naghibzadeh, 'Collectively or Singly', p. 41.

21. 'Iran-Iraq War: Analysis of possible US shift from position of Strict Neutrality', Memorandum, secret, Nicholas A. Veliotes to Mr Eagleberger, 7 October 1983. Declassified US Department of State, National Security Archive, electronic briefing book, 82, http://www.gwu.edu/~nsarchiv/NSAEBB/NSAEBB82/ Accessed December 2008.

22. Reagan denied any transfer of arms or intelligence. See Ronald Reagan, *An American Life* (New York: Simon and Schuster, 1990), pp. 520–21.

23. The Charter of the United Nations, http://www.un.org/en/documents/charter/chapter6.shtml. Accessed June 2010.

24. Bahram Mostaghimi and Masoud Taromsari, 'Double Standard: The Security Council and the Two Wars' in Farhand Rajaee (ed.), *Iranian Perspectives on the Iran-Iraq War* (Gainesville: University Press of Florida, 1997), p. 63.

25. *Note by the President of the Security Council*, S/17932, 21 March 1986.

26. Joost Hilterman criticises the views of Stephen Pelletiere on this issue. He notes that while Pelletiere acknowledges the extensive Iraqi use of chemical weapons, the American intelligence analyst sustained the argument that Iran too had used CW and perhaps even contributed to the attacks on the Kurds in northern Iraq in 1988. See Joost R. Hilterman, 'Outsiders as Enablers: Consequence and Lessons from International Silence on Iraq's use of Chemical Weapons during the Iran-Iraq War' in Lawrence G. Potter

and Gary G. Sick (eds), *Iran, Iraq and Legacies of War* (New York and London: Palgrave, 2004), p. 151. See also the original UN report, *Report of the Mission Despatched by the Secretary General to Investigate Allegations of the Use of Chemical Weapons in the Conflict between the Islamic Republic of Iran and Iraq*, S/18852, 26 May 1987, p. 2.

27. George P. Schultz, *Turmoil and Triumph: My Years as Secretary of State* (New York: Charles Scribners, 1993), p. 239.

28. Djamchid Momtaz, 'The Implementation of UN Resolution 598' in Farhand Rajaee (ed.), *Iranian Perspectives on the Iran-Iraq War* (Gainesville: University Press of Florida, 1997), pp. 123–125.

Select Bibliography

Abdulghani, Jasim, *Iraq and Iran: The Years of Crisis* (Baltimore, MD: John Hopkins Press, 1984).

Adib-Moghaddam, Arshin, 'Inventions of the Iran-Iraq War', *Critique: Critical Middle Eastern Studies*, vol. 16, no. 1 (2007).

Ali, Javed, 'Chemical Weapons and the Iran-Iraq War: A Case Study in Noncompliance', *The Non Proliferation Review*, vol. 8, no. 1 (Spring 2001).

Axelgand, Frederick, 'Iraq and the War with Iran', *Current History*, February (1987).

Bakhash, Shaul, *Reign of the Ayatollahs: Iran and the Islamic Revolution* (London: I.B. Tauris, 1985).

Behdad, Sohrab, *Iran after the Revolution: Crisis of an Islamic State* (London: I.B. Tauris and St Martin's Press, 1995).

Bergquist, R.E., *The Role of Air Power in the Iran-Iraq War* (Washington: Air University Press, 1988).

Brown, Ian, *Khomeini's Forgotten Sons: The Story of Iran's Boy Soldiers* (London: Grey Seal Books, 1990).

Brumberg, Daniel, *Reinventing Khomeini: The Struggle for Reform in Iran* (Chicago: University of Chicago Press, 2001).

Bullock, John, and Harvey Morris, *The Gulf War: Its Origins, History and Consequences* (London: Methuen, 1988).

Chubin, Shahram and Charles Tripp, *Iran and Iraq at War* (London: I.B. Tauris, 1988).

Chubin, Shahram and Sepehr Zubin, *The Foreign Relations of Iran: A Developing State in a Zone of Great Power Conflict* (Berkeley, CA: University of California Press, 1974).

Cordesman, Anthony H., *The Iran-Iraq War and Western Security, 1984–87: Strategic Implications and Policy Options* (London: Jane's, Royal United Services Institute, 1987).

————, *Iran's Military Forces in Transition* (Westport, CT: Praeger, 1999).

————, and Abraham R. Wagner, *The Lessons of Modern War, II, The Iran-Iraq War* (Boulder, CO and San Francisco, CA: Westview Press, 1990).

Farouk-Slugett, Marion and Peter Farouk-Slugett, *Iraq Since 1958: From Revolution to Dictatorship* (London: KPI, 1987).

Ghareeb, Edmund, *The Kurdish Question in Iraq* (Syracuse, NY: Syracuse University Press, 1981).

Helms, Christine Moss, *Iraq: Eastern Flank of the Arab World* (Washington DC: Brookings Institute, 1984).

Hiro, Dilip, *Inside the Middle East* (London: Routledge and Kegan Paul, 1982).

————, *Iran under the Ayatollahs* (London: Routledge and Kegan Paul, 1985, reprtd. 2000).

————, *The Longest War: The Iran-Iraq Military Conflict* (London: Grafton Books, 1989 (first edition)).

————, *Neighbours, Not Friends: Iran and Iraq after the Gulf Wars* (London and New York, 2001).

Hollis, Rosemary, *Gulf Security: No Consensus* (London: RUSI, 1993).

Ismail, Tariq Y., *Iraq and Iran: Roots of Conflict* (Syracuse, NY: Syracuse University Press, 1982).

Johnson, Maxwell Orme, *The Military as an Instrument of US Policy in Southwest Asia: The Rapid Deployment Joint Task Force, 1977–82* (Boulder, CO: Westview, 1983).

Joyner, Christopher, ed., *The Persian Gulf War: Lessons for Strategy, Law, and Diplomacy* (New York: Greenwood Press, 1990).

Karsh, Efraim, 'Escalation in the Iran-Iraq War', *Survival* (May/June 1989), pp. 241–255 (with Philip Sabin).

————, *The Iran-Iraq War: A Military Analysis* (London: The Adelphi Papers, International Institute for Strategic Studies, 1987).

————, ed., *The Iran-Iraq War: Impact and Implications* (Tel Aviv: Jafee Centre for Strategic Studies, 1987).

————, *The Iran-Iraq War* (Oxford: Osprey Essential Histories Series, 2002).

———— and Inari Rautsi, *Saddam Hussein: A Political Biography* (London: The Free Press, First Edition, 1991).

————, 'Survival at All Costs: Saddam Hussein as a Crisis Manager' in G. Barzilai, A. Klieman and G. Shidlo (eds), *The Gulf Crisis and its Global Aftermath* (London and New York: Routledge, 1993), pp. 51–67.

————, 'Why Saddam Hussein Invaded Kuwait', *Survival* (January/February 1991), pp. 18–30 (with Inari Rautsi).

Katzman, Kenneth, *The Warriors of Islam: Iran's Revolutionary Guards* (Oxford and Boulder, CO.: Westview Press, 1993).

King, Ralph, *The Iran-Iraq War: The Political Implications* (London: The Adelphi Papers, International Institute for Strategic Studies, 1987).

Lachlan, Keith and George Joffé, *The Gulf War: A Survey of the Political Issues and Economic Consequences* (London: The Economist Intelligence Unit, 1984).

Liesl, Graz, *The Turbulent Gulf: People, Politics and Power* (New York: I.B. Tauris, 1992).

Macris, Jeffrey R., *The Politics and the Security of the Gulf: Anglo-American Hegemony and the Shaping of a Region* (London and New York: Routledge, 2010).

Marr, Phebe, *Modern History of Iraq* (London: Longman, 1985).

McKnight, Sean, Neil Partrick and Francis Toase, eds., *Gulf Security: Opportunities and Challenges for the New Generation* (London: RUSI and RMAS, 2000).

McNaugher, Thomas, 'Ballistic Missiles and Chemical Weapons: The Legacy of the Iran-Iraq War', *International Security*, Fall (1990).

Mofid, Kamram, *The Economic Consequences of the Gulf War* (London: Routledge, 1990).

Moin, Baqer, *Khomeini: Life of the Ayatollah* (New York: St Martin's Press, 1999).

Naff, Thomas, ed., *Gulf Security and the Iran-Iraq War* (Washington DC: National Defense University Press, 1985).

O'Balance, Edgar, *The Gulf War* (London: Brassey's Defence Publishers, 1988).

Pelletiere, Stephen, *The Iran-Iraq War: Chaos in a Vacuum* (New York: Praeger, 1992).

Pelletiere, Stephen and Douglas V. Johnson III, *Lessons Learned: The Iran-Iraq War* (US Army War College: Strategic Studies Institute, 1991).

Potter, Lawrence G. and Gary G. Sick, ed., *Iran, Iraq and the Legacies of War* (New York: Palgrave, 2004).

————, *Security in the Persian Gulf: Origins, Obstacles and the Search for Consensus* (New York: Palgrave, 2002).

Rajee, Farhang, ed., *The Iran-Iraq War: The Politics of Aggression* (Gainsville: University of Florida, 1993).

————, ed., *Iranian Perspectives on the Iran-Iraq War* (Gainsville, University of Florida, 1997).

Rundle, Christopher, 'The Iran-Iraq Conflict', *Asian Affairs*, vol. 17, no. 2 (1986).

Segal, David, 'The Iran-Iraq War: A Military Analysis', *Foreign Affairs*, Summer (1988).

Sick, Gary, 'Trial by Fire: Reflections on the Iran-Iraq War', *Middle East Journal*, Spring (1989).

Staudenmaier, William, *A Strategic Analysis of the Gulf War* (London: Strategic Studies Institute, 1982).

United States Marine Corps, 1990 Strategic Studies Institute Report, *Lessons Learned: The Iran-Iraq War*, volume I. Accessible at http://www.fas.org/man/dod-101/ops/war/docs/3203/.

Zabih, Sepehr, *The Iranian Military in Revolution and War* (London: Routledge, 1988).

Index